Our First Glimpse of Japan

Prominent American Visitors to Japan in the 1870s

WILLIAM HENRY SEWARD
Introduction by Jeff Ludwig

CHARLES APPLETON LONGFELLOW
Introduction by Professor Julie Joy Nootbaar

ULYSSES S. GRANT
Introduction by Edwina S. Campbell

ANDREW CARNEGIE
Introduction by John Sagers

Compiled, Edited, and Introduced by Samuel Kidder

©2024 by Samuel Kidder
All Rights Reserved

Material from *Charles Appleton Longfellow: Twenty Months in Japan, 1871–1873,* edited by Christine Wallace Laidlaw, is copyright © 1998 by the Friends of Longfellow House. That material is reprinted in this book by permission of the Friends of Longfellow House–Washington's Headquarters, Inc. (www.friendsoflongfellowhouse.org), a nonprofit organization that supports work at the Longfellow House–Washington's Headquarters National Historic Site, located at 105 Brattle Street, Cambridge, Massachusetts 02138.

Published by Piscataqua Press
32 Daniel St.
Portsmouth, NH 03801

ISBN: 978-1-958669-24-2

Our First Glimpse of Japan

Prominent American Visitors to Japan in the 1870s

TABLE OF CONTENTS

PREFACE	1
INTRODUCTION: IT'S 1870	3
TIMELINE	15
WILLIAM HENRY SEWARD	19
CHARLES APPLETON LONGFELLOW	107
ULYSSES S. GRANT	159
ANDREW CARNEGIE	325
ADDITIONAL RESOURCES	363

PREFACE

This book presents personal accounts of visits to Japan in the 1870s by prominent Americans. Taken from contemporaneous published works or personal diaries or journals, the travelers are: William H. Seward, secretary of state during the Lincoln and Andrew Johnson administrations; Charles "Charley" Longfellow, son of poet Henry Wadsworth Longfellow; former President Ulysses S. Grant and his wife, Julia Dent Grant; and Andrew Carnegie, industry tycoon.

Introductions to each section have been provided by subject experts. Director of Education at the Seward House Museum in Auburn, New York, Jeffery Ludwig, PhD, introduces the book's first section, the Japan portion of William H. Seward's *Travels Around the World*, published in 1873. Professor Julie Nootbaar of Oita Prefectural University in Kyushu, Japan, opens the section on Charles Longfellow. "Charley" Longfellow spent twenty months in Japan in the early 1870s. Edwina Campbell, author of *Citizen of a Wider Commonwealth: Ulysses S. Grant's Postpresidential Diplomacy* sets the stage for the former president's two and a half month stay in Japan recounted in John Russell Young's *Around the World with General Grant*, published in 1879. Finally, Professor John Sagers, PhD, of Linfield University in Oregon, prefaces Andrew Carnegie's descriptions of his time in Japan in *Round the World*, first distributed to friends then published for the general public in 1884.

The published works of prominent American travelers helped set the tone for the reading public's understanding of Japan and its culture. The works included here and others noted in the bibliography at the end of this book, were products of an American elite. This elite was self-confident and often arrogant about the superiority of American political and social culture. While providing fascinating and perceptive insights into a very different society, they also contributed to distorting perceptions of the Japanese and the foreign "other." Some terms used by mid-nineteenth century writers may seem offensive to readers but are left in their original form to allow the reader to learn not just about Japan but also about the formation of American attitudes toward the Pacific and Asian

PREFACE

nations.

For those readers less familiar with Japan in the Meiji period and in America's earliest engagements with the Pacific and Japan, I hope the following few pages will be a useful introduction.

—Samuel Kidder

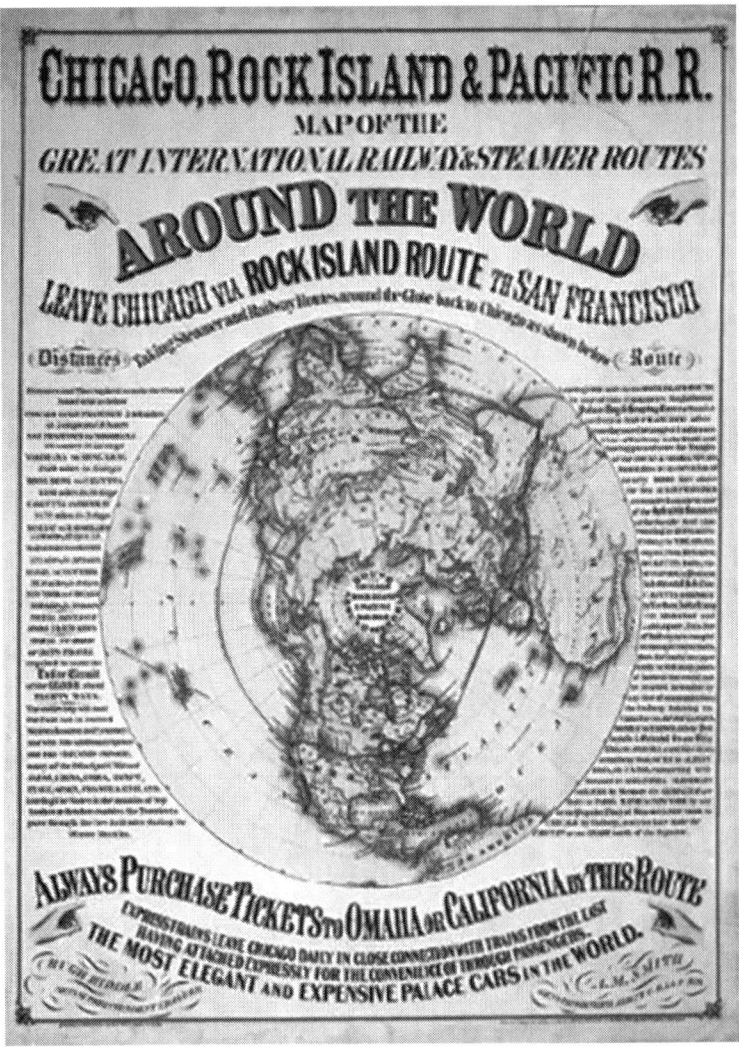

Poster, 1870

Chicago History Museum Collection; ICHi-031192

INTRODUCTION

Samuel Kidder

Samuel Kidder first arrived in East Asia as an undergraduate exchange student. After training and deployment in Korea as a U.S. Army linguist, he studied East Asian history at Harvard, the University of Washington and as a Fulbright scholar at Yonsei University. For several years, he worked with an Australian company, setting up their offices in Chicago and Seoul. He then entered the foreign service and was assigned tours in Seoul, Tokyo and New Delhi. The experience and knowledge gained over a quarter of a century as a diplomat were invaluable preparation for an eight-year term as executive director of the American Chamber of Commerce in Japan. Kidder's first book, Of One Blood All Nations, *examined the 12 years Ohio Congressman John Bingham spent as America's senior diplomat in Japan. A prominent but largely forgotten Reconstruction Era political leader, Bingham served four presidents and his tenure remains the longest of any American ambassador to Japan. The travelers in* Our First Glimpse of Japan *are more familiar figures. Kidder hopes that reading their impressions of Japan in their own words will make this seminal period in the relationship between Japan and the United States come alive.*

INTRODUCTION: IT'S 1870

It's 1870. A poster distributed by the Chicago, Rock Island & Pacific R.R. touts a trip around the world. The travel time is 80 days. The cost for the package of rail and ship tickets is $1600. For a few dollars more you can visit cities and sights along the way. To see the Great Buddha in Kamakura, Japan, or the Pyramids in Egypt, all you need is money and time.

Buy your ticket in Chicago and get on board the train for California. From San Francisco, a Pacific Mail and Steamship sidewheel steamer will take you to Yokohama. A stop in Japan is now on the itinerary of

INTRODUCTION

any self-respecting, globe-circling American traveler. Regular steamship service between Yokohama and San Francisco was inaugurated in 1867. In 1869, the Suez Canal opened and the transcontinental railroad began operation. Steam had encircled the globe.

The United States Reaches the Pacific

The Lewis and Clark Expedition first sighted the Pacific in 1805. By that time, whalers out of New England had already rounded Cape Horn and were hunting along the coast of Chile. By 1811, John Jacob Astor had established a fur trading outpost at the mouth of the Columbia River. By 1820, the first American Protestant missionaries, Hiram Bingham of Vermont and his wife, Sybil, arrived in Hawaii. You could hear tales of Pacific riches and adventures from seamen in the taverns of Provincetown, Rhode Island, or New Bedford, Massachusetts. You could read how the gospel was reaching across those distant waters in the new Protestant monthly, *Missionary Herald*, on the table in the narthex of your local church.

In 1834, Richard Henry Dana Jr. interrupted his studies at Harvard, signed on as a merchant seaman and sailed around South America to the Pacific. Dana was 19 years old and his eyesight had been weakened by a case of measles. It was hoped that fresh air from the voyage would help him recover his vision. When Dana's *Two Years Before the Mast* was published in 1840, it sold ten thousand copies that year. The American reading public now had a gripping, real-life account of adventure at sea and a description of life along the Pacific coast. It was a world of Hawaiian sailors, Spanish speaking Californians settled in mission outposts, and indigenous cultures at home on the coast for millennia. For the political class of the United States, the Pacific coast was mysterious and alluring.

Less commercially successful than Dana's book, Herman Melville's novel, *Moby Dick*, published in 1851, brought a vivid image of the wide Pacific into libraries and sitting rooms. Melville's fictional accounts of the Pacific and lands beyond were anchored in history and showed an awareness of Japan. He reported on Captain Coffin's 1819 visit to whaling grounds off Japan's coast, and described Captain Ahab of the

INTRODUCTION

Pequod pouring over nautical charts that showed the Japanese islands. The Coffins were a famous Nantucket whaling family and Ahab's charts referred to Niphon, an early spelling of Nippon, a common name in those years for Honshu, Japan's largest island and Shikoke, plainly Shikoku, the smallest of Japan's four main islands, then and now home of Japan's whaling industry.

Introducing the *Pequod*, Melville noted that the ship's masts were replaced with Japanese timber after being destroyed in a typhoon. Hobbled whaling ships did reach Japanese waters. But Melville also described Japan as "that double-bolted land." It was a characterization often borrowed since by westerners to describe Japan's self-imposed diplomatic isolation during the Tokugawa Era (1603-1868). But while Japan remained inaccessible, for Melville the Pacific was not remote. The following is his lyrical ode to the Pacific.

"To any meditative Magian rover, this serene Pacific, once beheld, must ever after be the sea of his adoption. It rolls the midmost waters of the world, the Indian ocean and Atlantic being but its arms. The same waves wash the moles [breakwaters] of the new-built Californian towns, but yesterday planted by the recentest race of men, and lave the faded but still gorgeous skirts of Asiatic lands, older than Abraham; while all between float milky-ways of coral isles, and low-lying, endless, unknown Archipelagoes, and impenetrable Japans. Thus this mysterious, divine Pacific zones the world's whole bulk about; makes all coasts one bay to it; seems the tide-beating heart of earth."

During the 1840s, domestic and international political developments began to broaden the way Americans viewed the Pacific. In 1846, the Oregon Treaty settled the United States' northern boundary dispute with Great Britain making what we now call the Pacific Northwest American territory. In 1848, the Treaty of Guadalupe Hidalgo ended the Mexican War. The territory which now includes California, Utah, Nevada, Colorado and most of New Mexico and Arizona was ceded by Mexico to the United States.

Then, in 1848, gold was discovered in California. When Dana had visited San Francisco in 1835 the only other vessel in port was a Russian brig wintering there from its arctic station in Russian America. A publication of the Museum of the City of San Francisco estimated the city's population at less than 500 settlers in 1847.(1) The same source

INTRODUCTION

said that at the end of 1849, just two years later, approximately 25,000 people lived there. A new generation began to imagine a Pacific destiny. California statehood in 1850 and Oregon's in 1859 provided the formal, legal punctuation. America was to have a Pacific identity. And that would mean engagement with Japan.

Daniel Webster, secretary of state to three presidents, was the early architect of America's Pacific policy. In 1842, President John Tyler, at the urging of Secretary of State Webster, announced American opposition to any European colonization of Hawaii, a policy applied more broadly to the Pacific and known as the Tyler Doctrine. In 1852, back in office as secretary of state, this time under President Millard Fillmore, Webster put in motion the mission to Japan led by Commodore Mathew C. Perry. First arriving in Tokyo Bay in 1853, then returning in 1854 to sign the Convention of Kanagawa, Perry's visits unlocked the double bolt Melville had written about. The United States soon began the process of establishing formal diplomatic relations with Japan. The European powers scrambled to follow.

Once Americans began to pass through the newly opened door, they began to get a more complete image of Japan. One source that circulated widely was the account of Perry's visit to Japan. This detailed narrative included an introduction to Japan's history, culture and geography and contained excellent illustrations. *Narrative of the Expedition of an American Squadron to the China Seas and Japan Under the Command of Commodore M.C. Perry, United States Navy* was first issued under congressional order in 1856. It was then published for wider commercial distribution by Appleton & Co., New York, in 1857.

Japan's treaties with the western countries set up foreign trading ports where foreigners were exempt from Japanese legal jurisdiction. Missionaries, still restricted from proselytizing beyond these foreign enclaves, settled in the treaty ports. Articles about Japan became regular features in publications such as the *Missionary Herald*, distributed to Protestant churches and homes throughout the country. One of the best known of these early missionaries, Presbyterian James Hepburn, M.D., arrived in Nagasaki in 1859 and soon relocated to Yokohama. Hepburn developed a system of romanization of written Japanese that bears his name and is still in standard use today. The editors of the *Missionary Herald* chronicled these achievements.

INTRODUCTION

Even before Perry's second visit, commercial interests had slipped through cracks in the still formally barred door. In 1854, the Walsh Brothers, Thomas and John, opened their trading company in Nagasaki. In 1859, joined by Francis Hall, Walsh, Hall & Company opened in Yokohama. The most prominent American business in Japan in those years, Thomas Walsh and Walsh, Hall & Company are mentioned often in the following sections of this book. In America, shoppers now discovered Japanese tea and silk.

The Civil War, Reconstruction and the Meiji Restoration

By the early 1860s, formal and informal contacts between Americans and Japanese were transforming the bilateral relationship. In 1860, a Tokugawa delegation sailed from Yokohama to San Francisco and on to Panama where they crossed by the newly built railroad to the Caribbean. From there, the Japanese sailed to Washington, D.C., where they met with President James Buchanan and exchanged ratifications of the Treaty of Amity and Commerce of 1858, often called the Harris Treaty. Townsend Harris, America's first permanent resident minister in Japan, had hammered out the details of the agreement with the Tokugawa government.

Media excitement created new American impressions of Japan that spilled over from the libraries and church parlors and into the street. The welcoming parade when the Japanese mission visited New York was spectacular. Thousands of soldiers marched in the parade. Windows of buildings along the bunting-decked route were rented out to sightseers. Shopkeepers waved Japanese and American flags.(2) Japan began to have a growing space in America's public consciousness.

The Civil War preoccupied Americans in the early 1860s, but developments involving Japan during those years continued to influence attitudes toward Japan. The whaling industry, in decline for decades as whale oil was replaced by refined coal oil or kerosene for lighting, largely disappeared. This disappearance was accelerated by the destruction of Union civilian shipping in the Pacific by the Confederate ship *Shenandoah*. Built in a British naval yard, the *Shenandoah* took as many as sixty prizes in Pacific waters, many of them whalers.

INTRODUCTION

In 1863, local forces of the Choshu domain in western Japan fought and lost to foreign forces from Britain, France, the Netherlands, and the United States. The confrontation took place near the Strait of Shimonoseki which separates Honshu, Japan's largest island, and Kyushu, the southernmost of Japan's four main islands. As a result, Japan was forced to pay significant compensation, called the Shimonoseki Indemnity. This financial burden was a major factor contributing to the weakening of the military-led Tokugawa government that had been in power for two and a half centuries.

Return of the American portion of the indemnity to Japan became a cause celeb among American politicians who argued the indemnity was unjust and the money should be returned to help Japan fund its modernization. Politicians who favored return of the indemnity were often supported by constituents who were readers of the missionary journals, a not uncommon American melding of proselytising and foreign policy.

In the latter half of the 1860s, the changes in government and society in Japan and the United States were monumental. The tottering Tokugawa regime fell, unable to meet the challenges posed by western incursion. The young Emperor Meiji ascended the Chrysanthemum Throne, and the Meiji Restoration was inaugurated. In the new political structure the emperor was placed in an elevated role as the symbolic focus of national political and military authority. Blessed with a cadre of young, talented leaders, rapid reforms tore down the rigid hierarchical social structure of the Tokugawa government which had been dominated by local lords and established effective administrative control by the central government.

During America's Reconstruction Era, following the northern victory in the Civil War, equally tectonic political and social changes were instituted. Slavery was abolished and the role and power of the federal government increased. The same year the Meiji government was promulgated, 1868, the 14th amendment to the United States Constitution was ratified. In both countries, change was not without unrest. But it was irreversible.

In 1869, a new guide to international travel, *Our New Way Round the World*, by popular journalist Charles Carleton Coffin, was published. Coffin's book not only provided observations about Japan but also gave practical traveling tips. Coffin, along with his wife, Sally Farmer Coffin,

INTRODUCTION

journeyed eastward around the world, leaving New York in the summer of 1866 and returning shortly before the transcontinental railroad was completed. Coffin was one of the foremost journalists of the Civil War and enjoyed close relationships with Union generals, including Ulysses S. Grant. The Coffins limited their time in Europe, which was more familiar to most Americans, in order to travel more extensively in Asia.

Coffin's fame introduced travel in Asia to a new segment of America's reading public. However, Coffin's visit to Japan coincided with a period of uncertainty in the transition between Tokugawa and Meiji rule. His descriptions of Nagasaki, Hyogo (the Kobe area) and the treaty port of Yokohama are detailed. And although his recounting of Japan's history to that period is well researched, he was unable to visit Tokyo. Due to security concerns, Tokyo, or as it was then called, Yedo, was off-limits to foreign travelers.

In the closing years of Tokugawa rule, people-to-people exchanges between America and Japan were well underway. Local daimyo hired American teachers or technical experts and sent students to study in the United States. American missionaries began arriving in the treaty ports, with numbers increasing after the end of the Civil War. Business representatives began operations in Nagasaki, Yokohama and Kobe. Still tiny, the number of Americans with experience in Japan was accelerating.

In 1860 Harvard professor and geologist, Raphael Pumpelly, was commissioned by the Tokugawa government to survey Japan's northern island, Hokkaido, a trip he began in 1861 and that also took him to China. Including accounts of his work and residence in Arizona, Pumpelly published *Across America and Asia: Notes of a Five Years Journey Around the World*, in 1870. Hardly a popular potboiler, Pumpelly's book does show that information about Japan in various fields, from art and religion to science and industry, was getting out to American readers.

As the decade of the 1870s got underway, a new genre of travel books, the adventures of globe-circling tourists, began. In 1872, Cleveland, Ohio journalist William Perry Fogg published *Round the World: Letters from Japan, China, India, and Egypt* bringing under one cover his world-circling adventures that had been serialized in the *Cleveland Leader*. Perhaps in a nod to the Ohioan, in Jules Verne's wildly popular

INTRODUCTION

bestseller *Around the World in 80 Days* published in 1873 and translated into English by George Towle, the French novelist named his lead character Phileas Fogg.

The numbers of these travelers were small. Even by the end of the decade only a handful of vessels were making the voyage across the Pacific, a trip that averaged about three weeks. Even the larger ships like the *City of Tokio* had space for only 120 passengers in first class, 260 in second and 1000 in steerage, the latter group made up almost entirely of Chinese laborers. Although new steamship companies did begin operating during the decade of the 1870s, there were at most several dozen passenger ships crossing each way per year. When travelers were as well-known to many Americans as were Seward, Grant and Carnegie, the impact of their published accounts was significant.

THE TRAVELERS

William H. Seward (1801-1872)
In Japan September 25 to October 14, 1870.

William Seward was appointed by President Abraham Lincoln to serve as secretary of state. He had been elected as New York's governor and then as senator from New York and is credited with having steered Great Britain away from support of the Confederacy during the Civil War. A target of assassination the evening Lincoln was shot, Seward, already bedridden as a result of a carriage accident, was seriously wounded and took months to recover. He remained in office under President Andrew Johnson and in 1868 finalized the purchase of Alaska, perhaps his most often noted achievement. The move to incorporate Alaska into United States territory was not an isolated whim but part of a consistent policy approach toward the Pacific that Seward had espoused since his days in the Senate. Historian Michael Green, always at the center of American policy discussions regarding Japan in the current generation, notes that Seward was America's last grand strategist for Asia for decades.(3)

Editor's Note: *The original text I used was provided by the Carnegie Library of Pittsburgh system and the scanning done by Ryan Tomazin, owner of Tomaz-*

INTRODUCTION

in Scanning Services of Bridgeville, Pennsylvania. I have a rather floppy 1873 edition of Travels Around the World *which a small library in Pennsylvania had in its collection until they decided my $50 would be more useful than the battered book. Several scanned reprints are also available.*

Charles Appleton Longfellow (1844-1893)
In Japan September 25, 1871 to March 13, 1873.

In 1998, Friends of the Longfellow House in Cambridge published *Charles Appleton Longfellow: Twenty Months in Japan, 1871-1873.* (4) The book was lovingly edited by Christine Wallace Laidlaw and is graced by extensive notes and annotations. Laidlaw writes of the many connections the Longfellow family had to others involved with Japan. Among these connections, a friend and a relative by marriage had been on the Perry expedition. Richard Henry Dana II was their backyard neighbor in Cambridge. Harvard geologist, Raphael Pumpelly, mentioned above, had been to Japan and had published a book which covered his experiences there.

And there were other connections. Poet Longfellow's close friend was Massachusetts Senator Charles Sumner, a vocal advocate on Capitol Hill for the Alaska purchase. Five years after his Japan sojourn, Charley's sister Edith married Richard Henry Dana III. Charley's uncle, Thomas Appleton, collected Japanese art and was an avid yacht sailor, a pursuit that Charley also loved. His trip to Japan was hardly Charley's first adventure and not his last; Charley made travel and adventure with his father's money his life's work.

Editor's Note: *The original documents that were the source material for* Twenty Months in Japan *were letters, primarily between Charles and his family and journals he kept of his activities and travels during his time in Japan. Archivist Kate Hanson-Plass of the Longfellow House-Washington's Headquarters National Historic Site in Cambridge was extremely helpful in providing access to these materials as well as the photographs contained herein. The source materials are handwritten and were not intended for publication. The journal sections, particularly, abbreviate and omit words and spelling and punctuation is often inconsistent. I provide a more extensive editor's note at the beginning of the section.*

INTRODUCTION

Ulysses S. Grant (1822-1885)
In Japan June 21 to September 3, 1879.

On May 17, 1877, former president Ulysses S. Grant, along with his wife, Julia Dent Grant, and a young reporter for the *New York Herald*, John Russell Young, left Philadelphia bound for Liverpool. The decision to continue on from his tour in Europe to go "East of Suez" to visit India, Siam, China and Japan was made in the final weeks of 1878. By that time, the party had been away from the United States for over a year and a half. On January 31, 1879, Grant sailed from Suez and continued his trip around the world, returning to San Francisco on September 20 of that year. Young's reports of Grant's visits in the *Herald*, and then in the two volume book, *Around the World with General Grant*, provided Americans with a thorough view of Asia and the challenges of American diplomacy in that part of the world. In Japan, Grant's stay stretched over two months and the former president had several meetings, some extended, with the young Meiji emperor. The visit was a high point of good feeling in the diplomatic relationship between Japan and the United States.

The Japan chapters of *Around the World with General Grant* are much more than a travelogue. Young's reporting on Grant's activities, observations of the political and diplomatic context of the time and Grant's discussions with key Japanese leaders make this account a remarkable primary historical source. Edwina Campbell's *Citizen of a Wider Commonwealth: Ulysses S. Grant's Postpresidential Diplomacy*(5) shows how important the whole trip was to America's emerging diplomatic role in the world. Japan's financing of its rapid industrialization, the growing poison in America's Asian diplomacy caused by anti-Asian immigration policies, and strains in Sino-Japan relations were just some of the issues in Grant's discussions with Japanese leaders.

Editor's Note: *As with Olive Risley's volume on Seward,* Travels Around the World, *the original text was provided by the Carnegie Library of Pittsburgh system and the scanning done by Ryan Tomazin, owner of Tomazin Scanning Services of Bridgeville, Pennsylvania. Other versions are available online and scanned and printed copies are available for purchase.*

INTRODUCTION

Andrew Carnegie (1835-1919)
In Japan November 16, 1878 to December 3, 1878.

Round the World opens in Pittsburgh. "What is this? A telegram? Belgic sails from San Francisco 24th instead of 28th. Can we make it?" He does, of course. In his early 40s, Carnegie was a man on the go. A Herbert Spencer fan and later friend, he was confident that his business ventures along Pittsburgh's rivers were "well calculated to survive the struggle for existence" including "that infant Hercules the Edgar Thompson Steel Rail Works."(6) He had the money and he chose to take the time. Heading west to Omaha, and San Francisco, his first overseas stop on his world tour was Japan.

As Carnegie heads west around the globe at a well-paced clip, Grant's party is making more measured progress heading east. In India, aware that Grant is scheduled to visit soon, on February 11, 1878, Carnegie writes that he hopes when Grant visits he will learn from England "the folly of conquest when conquest involves the government of an alien race." Nine years earlier, President Grant had initiated an effort to annex the Dominican Republic, an initiative Carnegie strongly opposed.

On February 12, Carnegie viewed the Taj Mahal in Agra. On February 28, Grant spoke at a dinner in Agra. He did not meet the tourist from Pittsburgh.

Editor's Note: *First printed to share with friends and associates,* Round the World *was originally issued shortly after Carnegie returned to America. In 1884 it was published for a larger readership. Reprints of the original text are available. But even in the Allegheny County Library network, an area that includes Pittsburgh and a number of towns where Carnegie had business interests, not every local library can claim an original edition of* Round the World. *I was fortunate to meet Anna Rittner, Senior Clerk at Carnegie Library of McKeesport, who shared with me their library's original edition of* Round the World. *If you have read this far, I hope you are and will be enjoying this book. More importantly, I hope it helps you discover the wealth of materials, online, in libraries or even bookstores, where history is not offered to you by historians but by its participants. Reading history by historians can be fun. But holding and reading original documents is a special pleasure.*

INTRODUCTION

Anna Rittner, Carnegie Library of McKeesport, Pennsylvania.
Check out your local library.
You will be surprised at what gems they have.

TIMELINE

1805: Lewis and Clark expedition reaches Pacific Ocean at mouth of Columbia River.

1811: Fort Astoria, first permanent American settlement in Pacific Northwest founded with financing by John Jacob Astor of New York.

1820: American Protestant missionary Hiram Bingham arrives in Hawaii.

1839-42: First Opium War.

1840: Richard Henry Dana, Longfellow family neighbor in Cambridge, Massachusetts, publishes *Two Years Before the Mast*, a recognized literary masterpiece that includes descriptions of his sailing journey around South America to the Pacific Ocean and his visit to the California coast.

1842: At the urging of Secretary of State Daniel Webster, President John Tyler announces American opposition to any European colonization of the Hawaiian islands. An important element of what became known as the Tyler Doctrine, the policy extended the Monroe Doctrine to the Pacific.

1842: Treaty of Nanking between the Qing Dynasty in China and Great Britain ends the First Opium War. Hong Kong ceded to the British. First of the Unequal Treaties between China and the West.

1845: Annexation of Texas.

1846: The Oregon Treaty between the United States and Great Britain signed settling boundary dispute. Areas now encompassing Washington state, Oregon and Idaho became undisputed United States territory.

1848: Gold discovered in California.

1848: Treaty of Guadalupe Hidalgo ends Mexican American War. Mexico recognizes United States' annexation of Texas and cedes territory which is now California, Utah, Nevada, Colorado and most of New Mexico and Arizona.

TIMELINE

1850: California becomes the thirty-first state.

1851: Herman Melville's *Moby Dick* published. Melville describes Japan as "that double bolted land."

1852: New York Senator William H. Seward advocates for support of a survey of the Behring Straits, the Arctic Ocean and for American trade across the Pacific.

1852: Ulysses S. Grant arrives to take up duty at Fort Vancouver at the mouth of the Columbia River.

1853: Commodore Matthew C. Perry first sails into Tokyo Bay.

1853: Grant leaves Oregon for California posting.

1854: Walsh Brothers establish an American trading company in Nagasaki.

1854: Perry returns to Tokyo Bay, signs Convention of Kanagawa which provided a limited opening of the ports of Hakodate in Hokkaido and Shimoda. The convention addressed concerns of coal resupply and treatment of shipwrecked sailors.

1858: Treaty of Amity and Commerce, also known as the Harris Treaty, between the United States and Japan signed. This was followed the same year by treaties between Japan and France, Russia, Great Britain and the Netherlands. Collectively these five treaties are known as the Ansei Treaties.

1858: Treaty of Tianjin ends Second Opium War.

1859: Oregon becomes America's thirty-third state.

1859: Yokohama harbor opened for foreign trade. Walsh Brothers, joined by George Hall, establish Walsh, Hall & Co.

1859: Dr. James C. Hepburn, M.D., American missionary, arrives in Nagasaki and relocates to Yokohama. Hepburn later published a still-used Japanese/English dictionary, established the standard for romanization of Japanese, and was a major contributor to translation of the Bible into Japanese.

TIMELINE

1860: Tokugawa mission visits Washington and meets with President Buchanan to formalize Harris Treaty. New York City welcomes the Japanese delegation with massive parade.

1861: Abraham Lincoln inaugurated, appoints William Seward as secretary of state.

1861: Colonel Ulysses Grant and the Seventh District Regiment entered U.S. service as the Twenty-first Illinois.

1863: Shimonoseki Incident when forces of Choshu, the dominant feudal domain in western Honshu, are defeated by British, French, Dutch and American forces. Japan's Tokugawa government is forced to pay a punitive indemnity that becomes a major factor in weakening the Tokugawa government's two and a half centuries of control of Japan.

1863: Russian Arctic fleet winters in New York and San Francisco.

1865: President Lincoln assassinated. Ohio Congressman John Bingham, later longest serving minister/ambassador to Japan, becomes only civilian on prosecution team of the assassins. Seward, wounded by assassins, remains as secretary of state in the Andrew Johnson administration.

1865: Congress authorizes $500,000 to Pacific Mail and Steam Ship company to subsidize American transpacific steamship service.

1867: Pacific Mail and Steam Ship Company transpacific passenger service begins.

1868: Alaska purchase. Referred to by some as Seward's Folly or Walrussia.

1868: Meiji Restoration begins in Japan.

1869: Transcontinental railroad opens linking Omaha, Nebraska to Oakland, California.

1869: Navigation of Suez Canal opens, greatly facilitating European access to East Asia.

TIMELINE

1869: Charles Coffin, noted Civil War journalist publishes *Our New Way Round the World,* an account of his travels just before the Suez Canal opened and which emphasizes his visits to Asian countries, including Japan.

1870: Seward's visit. September 25 - October 14.

1871: Longfellow's stay. June 25, 1871 – March 13, 1873.

1872: William Perry Fogg, journalist from Cleveland, Ohio, publishes *Round the World - Letters from Japan, China, India, and Egypt,* a collection of his letters that had been published two to three years earlier in a Cleveland newspaper.

1872: Iwakura Mission visits the United States. Count Iwakura pays courtesy call on President Grant at the White House.

1872: Japan's first railway opens, linking Yokohama to Shimbashi in Tokyo.

1873: Jules Verne seems to like the name Fogg and uses it for his protagonist Phileas Fogg in *Round the World in Eighty Days.*

1876: Japanese pavilion at Philadelphia Centennial Exhibition is a great success in American press.

1877: Satsuma Rebellion in which disaffected samurai elements staged last military challenge to Meiji rule.

1877: Rutherford B. Hayes succeeds Ulysses S. Grant as America's president in controversial election.

1878: Assassination of Okubo Toshimichi one of the most important early Meiji leaders.

1878: Carnegie's visit. November 16-December 3.

1879: Grant's visit. June 21-September 3.

WILLIAM HENRY SEWARD

WILLIAM HENRY SEWARD

Introduction by Jeff Ludwig

dwig has been the Director of Education at the Seward House m since 2015. In that capacity, his ongoing research into the d family history shapes the Museum's interpretive and program- agendas. He is known for his entertaining and informative tours vard House and Museum and his encyclopaedic knowledge of 'd's political and diplomatic career. Jeff holds a PhD in History the University of Rochester. Prior to his appointment at the Seward ;e, Jeff worked at the Office of the City Historian in Rochester and ght history courses at SUNY Geneseo.

On July 29, 1852, New York Senator William H. Seward rose on the Senate floor to report out a bill from the Committee of Commerce. Seward was asking for support for a survey of the Behring Straits, the Arctic Ocean and for American trade across the Pacific. Eighteen years and two months later, on September 26, 1870, Seward stepped off the Pacific Mail steamship *China* onto the dock in Yokohama, Japan.

The intervening years had been momentous for America and for Seward. Governor of New York, Senator from New York, Lincoln's rival for the Republican nomination for president at the Chicago convention in 1860, Seward was chosen by Lincoln to serve as secretary of state. As secretary, Seward succeeded in the vital diplomatic effort of keeping European nations from recognizing the Confederate government, an accomplishment as critical as victory or defeat on more fabled battlefields of the war. The night Lincoln was shot, Seward was in bed recovering from injuries from a serious carriage accident when an assassin entered his residence and further wounded him.

Though a major player in the most dramatic political events of his generation, a century and a half after his death, Seward's prescient vision and career-long promotion of America's position in the Pacific Basin is perhaps his most impactful legacy. After Lincoln's death, Seward chose to keep his cabinet position in the Andrew Johnson administration. As a senator, he had advocated for construction of the transcontinental railroad, pushed for a subsidy for American operated steamship service across the Pacific from San Francisco, and encouraged the mission to Japan well before Commodore Mathew Perry was given the assignment.

As secretary of state, Seward laid a firm, practical foundation for his Asian aspirations. In 1867, he more or less single-handedly negotiated the purchase of Alaska from Russia. The Alaska purchase, criticized by some in the press as Seward's Folly or more colorfully, Walrussia, was in general well received. And the Sandwich Islands, Hawaii, remained securely in the American sphere of interest. Michael Green, one of the present generation's most prominent scholars of America's role in the Asia Pacific writes, "Seward remained unrivalled as a strategist on the region for a generation."(1)

In 1868, Japan's new emperor ascended the Chrysanthemum Throne. The young Meiji Emperor became the symbolic embodiment and political focal point of Japan's effort to remake its society. Like the contemporaneous Reconstruction Era in the United States, the early years of the Meiji Restoration were a time of social upheaval and political uncertainty. The American diplomatic mission was sparsely staffed and poorly housed. The decade of the 1870s would witness dramatic changes. Seward and his party arrived during this volatile time.

Today, America's two-way trade across the Pacific exceeds its trade across the Atlantic. Alaska and Hawaii have been states for generations. Popular history often focusses on turning points, a key election, a decisive battle. But long term change comes from dogged policy efforts. For this reason, Seward deserves recognition as a major founder of America's Pacific presence.

Popular history also likes to find good gossip. And Seward's trip around the world offered plenty. Seward's wife, Frances, died just months after the end of the Civil War. The next year, his daughter, Fanny, died at age 21. By 1868, Seward was keeping company with a young woman, Olive Risley, daughter of Hanson Risley, a friend and treasury official. Seward biographer Glyndon Van Deusen notes that by 1868 Seward's "attentions to Olive became marked."(2) Olive did not accompany the former secretary on earlier journeys he made to Alaska or

Mexico, but she did join him on the round the world trip.

When the traveling group left Auburn, New York to head for San Francisco, Olive was well chaperoned. Her father and younger sister, Hattie, joined Seward and Seward's servant on the cross country train ride. In San Francisco, the party was joined by former Postmaster General Alexander Randall and Mrs. Randall. Nephew George Seward, off to Shanghai as consul general, and his wife also joined the group as they headed to Yokohama on the Pacific Mail's *China*. Hanson Risley stayed behind and did not sail to Japan. George Seward and his wife, as planned, stayed in Shanghai. And the Randalls, while in Shanghai, decided not to continue the round the world tour but rather returned home. That left sixty-eight year old Seward with two young women in their twenties, an indelicate arrangement for a public figure in 1870. Gossips speculated that Olive Risley might become Olive Seward.

She did. But Olive did not become Mrs. Seward. Instead she became Miss Seward when somewhere between Shanghai the old codger drew up a will and adopted his close companion as his daughter. This diplomatic solution stopped tongues from wagging, calmed nervous relatives and secured a livelihood for Olive. The arrangement also helped make possible William H. Seward's *Travels Around the World*, for which Olive Seward completed the majority of the work—editorial, typographical, and generally providing the intellectual and creative ballast for the project.

Which is not to suggest that Seward himself was not personally invested in bringing *Travels* to print. The book meant a great deal to the retired (and exhausted) statesman, who was still revising his nearly-completed manuscript on the day he died. Seward abandoned work on in-progress political memoirs to dedicate his final months of life to recounting his post-retirement circumnavigation of the globe. Pulling Olive and other family members into the small study of his Auburn home, he leaned on others to help him finish the incredible account— a taxing physical ordeal that, by many accounts, "consumed" him. Dictating his memories while Olive shared her own and served as amanuensis, Seward expended his last energies to bring *Travels* forward in an octavo volume of almost 800 pages. It was published roughly one year after his death.

The final result was an artful and elegant book. With multiple editors

WILLIAM HENRY SEWARD

bidding against each other for the rights to the manuscript, Seward's family negotiated a sumptuously high production value. The winning agency, New York publishing house D. Appleton and Company, bore not only considerable royalties to the Seward estate, but the substantial costs of printing a sprawling tome with over 200 detailed illustrations and a large trifold map inserted in the appendices. The firm was quickly rewarded: the first run of 60,000 copies of *Travels* completely sold out.

A major reason why D. Appleton could afford Seward for its catalog—as well as contemporaries like William T. Sherman and Jefferson Davis— owed to the fortune it made selling titles linked to social Darwinism, then fast emerging as an American vogue. D. Appleton was the leading distributor of texts related to evolutionism. In particular, they specialized in publishing affordable copies of the works of Herbert Spencer who applied Darwinian precepts of natural selection to philosophy and sociology, fastening the phrase "survival of the fittest" into the American mind along the way.

Seward evinced many of these same unfortunate ideas in his own travel writing. Within the pages of *Travels* he both looked down patronizingly at civilizations he deemed "less advanced" and ranked many of the cultures he encountered into a hierarchy. Indeed, Seward viewed all of his experiences abroad through the lens of a man who was at once accustomed to power, comfortable with patriarchy, and invested in empire. Passages of his book read like classic examples of Orientalist western text, with Seward exoticizing otherness. This was often especially true when he confronted differences in gendered roles, with Seward's gaze lingering on sights like erotic dance scenes and harems. Somewhat ironically, at the same time Seward held Olive out as a case study, urging foreign leaders to consider her as the basis for the value of empowering women.

Editor's Note: *In preparing this book, I had access to several versions of Seward's* Travels. *A number of quality reprints are available for sale online. But the real pleasure was seeing, handling, and using an original edition for the scan to make this book. I thank the staff of the archive section of the Carnegie Library of Pittsburgh – Oakland, for allowing me to borrow an original volume through their inter-library loan system. The scans were prepared by a true craftsman, Ryan Tomazin of Tomazin Scanning Services, Bridgeville, Pennsylvania.*

WILLIAM HENRY SEWARD

Notes

(1) Green, Michael. *By More Than Providence: Grand Strategy in the Asia Pacific Since 1783*. Columbia University Press, New York. March 2017.

(2) Van Deusen, Glyndon. *William Henry Seward.* Oxford University Press, New York, 1967.

Additional suggested readings

Sexton, Jay. "William H. Seward and the World." *Journal of the Civil War Era* 4.3 (September 2014): 398-430.

Taylor, John. *William Henry Seward: Lincoln's Right Hand*. New York: HarperCollins, 1991.

WILLIAM H. SEWARD'S

TRAVELS AROUND THE WORLD.

EDITED BY

OLIVE RISLEY SEWARD.

"A mighty maze, but not without a plan."
Pope.

WITH TWO HUNDRED ILLUSTRATIONS.

NEW YORK:
D. APPLETON AND COMPANY,
549 & 551 BROADWAY.
1873.

WILLIAM HENRY SEWARD

CHAPTER II.

FROM SAN FRANCISCO TO JAPAN.

The Vessels of the Pacific Mail Line.—Our Fellow-Passengers.—"The Great Company of the Preachers."—The Chinese Passengers.—The Great Event of the Voyage.—The Moods of the Sea.—A Still Greater Event.—The Loss of a Day.—The Gyascutus.—The Beginning of the End.—The Coast of Japan.—The Ocean-Fisheries.

Steamer China, Pacific Ocean, September 1, 1870.—Our party having received its promised accessions, we embarked at noon. More kind friends could not have come on board to take leave if we had been long residents of San Francisco. If Mr. Seward had been thirty years younger, such a parting would even then have taxed his strength.

We passed the sometimes turbulent, but always majestic Golden Gate, with scarcely a disturbance of the ship's balance, and began our voyage on a calm sea and under a bright sky.

September 4th.—The vessels of the Pacific Mail Line are side-wheel steamers, and in accommodations and appointments are surpassed only by the palatial boats on the Hudson River and Long Island Sound.[1] The China, four thousand three hundred tons burden, is the smallest of them all. We enjoy an uninterrupted promenade seven hundred feet in circuit on the upper deck. We have sixty cabin-passengers, and might carry comfortably twice that number. Among them are General Vlangally, the Russian Minister returning from St. Petersburg to Peking, and half a dozen English civil officers coming from "home" to their posts in Japan and China. "Great," it must be confessed, "is the company of the preachers:" Fifteen American missionaries with their wives and children!—the elder families returning, and the younger going for the first time to fields of labor in Japan, China, Siam, and India; United States naval officers, on their way to join the Asiatic squadron, four English and as many American youths just emerged from college on an Eastern tour; a United States Treasury agent, going to inspect the Oriental consulates; and one American office-seeker, at least, proceeding to lay his claims before the Emperor of China at Peking. The gentlemen amuse themselves with gymnastic games, the ladies with music and books. An expert Japanese juggler entertains us in the cabin. In the steerage, are five hundred Chinese returning home. They pay less than half price, and are fed with the simple fare of their country. Knowing no use of beds, they sleep on the floor. In the middle of their cabin they have made, with canvas, a dark room for opium-smoking. When on deck, they appear neatly clad, and amuse themselves with unintelligible and apparently interminable games of chance. The annual immigration of Chinese to the United States is twelve thousand. They are invariably successful. Half the number go back to China, either on visits or to remain. Our freights consist of Mexican silver dollars, manufactured goods, agricultural machines, carriages, furniture, flour, butter, fruits, drugs, and patent medicines. These go in exchange for teas, silks, rice, and Chinese emigrants.(2)

September 6th.—The great event of the voyage occurred this morning. All were on deck, in a state of pleasant excitement. At seven o'clock, precisely the hour which the captain had foretold, the ship America, eighteen days from Yokohama, appeared in a direct line before us, under full pressure, and with square sails set. Signals were promptly exchanged, and, to avoid collision, each ship turned slightly from its course and stopped. The America has eighty cabin-passengers and four hundred Chinese. The cabin-passengers on either vessel cheered loudly, the Chinese looking on silent and thoughtful. A well-manned gig, with an officer in the stern, came bounding over the waves, and delivered to us Chinese and Japanese (European) newspapers, with a bag of letters from her passengers. We, in return sent on board the latest American newspapers, and a mail well charged with letters to our friends at home. The America's boat was then hoisted to its davits, the walking-beams of the two giant ships

MEETING OF THE STEAMERS IN MID-OCEAN.

gracefully bowed to each other, the wheels gently revolved, the passengers repeated their cheers, and a gun from either deck announced that the meeting was over. Each vessel resumed its course, and in a few moments not even a spy-glass could discover the waving of handkerchiefs or other signal on the deck of the America.*

If we gave to the eastern-bound travellers the first news of the European war, and of the death of Admiral Farragut, they in exchange gave us intelligence of an expected war between the European powers and the Chinese Government, in consequence of the recent dreadful massacre at Tien-Tsin.[3] Every one is astonished that Mr. Seward persists in his purpose of visiting Peking. He says that France, in her present disabled condition, cannot make war against China, and, without the lead of France, no Western nation will.

* The telegraph from Shanghai reports that the America was burned in the harbor of Yokohama, August 25, 1872.

32   UNITED STATES, CANADA, AND PACIFIC OCEAN.

September 14*th.*—Those who would know the sea, have need to study its varying moods and aspects. They must see it in the later hours of cloudless night, when it reflects the bright stars and constellations; they must see it in the morning twilight, when its broad surface seems contracted to a small, dark lake, and then under the illumination of the dawn it resumes its illimitable expanse. Doubtless it is terrible in its more serious moods by reason of its vastness, darkness, and powerful agitation, all elements of the sublime. Happily for us, we have not yet witnessed those moods.

September 16*th.*—It was a mistake to pronounce our meeting with the America, on the 6th, the event of the voyage. A greater one has just occurred. Our last date is the 14th. This note is written on the 16th. The former entry certainly was made yesterday. The chronometer marked eight o'clock at night at Greenwich, at the very hour when our clock, which keeps the running time, marked eight o'clock in the morning. We are half-way around the world from Greenwich, and have lost just half a day. It is quite clear that, if we should continue onward making the same discrepancy of time, we should have lost a whole day on arriving at Greenwich. We might postpone the readjustment of our ship's time until we reached Greenwich, but the scientific world has wisely decided that this readjustment shall be made in every case by compromise on the 180th meridian, and therefore, instead of striking out a half-day here, we strike out a whole one.

If the absolute loss of one whole day out of our lives is a distressing thing to think of, we may console ourselves with Red Jacket's profound reflection. When a missionary had delivered before the Seneca nation, in council, a homily in the usual style on the shortness of life, and the necessity of improving its fleeting hours, he called on them for an expression of their sentiments on that important subject; Red Jacket, having duly consulted with the chiefs, head men, women, and warriors, responded in their behalf: "Red men have all the time there is going; they do not see that white men have any more." **(4)**

THE COAST OF JAPAN.

September 20th.—Four thousand miles from San Francisco. The sea has come down from the long, surging swell of a few days past, and is now smooth and glassy. We have entered the outer belt of the hot circular current which warms the coasts of Japan, Siberia, and Alaska.

A brig under full sail is seen, though at a great distance, moving eastward. Everybody tries the spy-glass to make her out. When all have failed, a passenger, noted for controversialism, pronounces that the brig is the Gyascutus, from Macao, bound for Valparaiso, freighted with coolies. We all start at once, and ask, "How do you know?" "I assert it to be the fact," he replies; "let him prove the contrary who can. If this is not sufficient proof, it is at least the same form of argument that our preacher used in his sermon last night."

September 23d.—The beginning of the end! Every inch of the deck, bulwarks, stanchions, rigging, and boats, has been scoured, tarred, or painted, and the whole ship is clean as a Shaker meeting-house. Our five hundred steerage-passengers are confined within a rope-enclosure on the forward-deck—they appearing in new and shining cotton clothes, with pates freshly shaven. A dozen women are seen for the first time. All are engaged, especially the women, in dropping handfuls of rice and small pieces of colored paper into the sea, to propitiate the gods for a safe arrival. Flying-fish surround us; one white-breasted gull has come to attend us into port; and a whale, the only one we have seen on the voyage, is spouting in the distance.

September 24th.—The coast of Japan rises in a long, gray outline over the dark sea, but Fusi Yama veils his head, and refuses to take notice of our coming. (5)

We have crossed the Pacific Ocean. How much it is to be regretted that we must make such long stretches, and yet see so little! How profitable it would be to study the North-Pacific American coast, the shores of Puget Sound, the Territories on the Columbia River, and Alaska, in a near future the great fishery, forest, and mineral storehouses of the world!—the Aleutian chain of islands hereafter to be the stepping-stones between the two continents. We have lost a sight, also, not only of the Sandwich Islands, but of Australia, a fifth continent on which a kindred people are devel-

FUSI YAMA, COAST OF JAPAN.

oping a state that may at some future day challenge comparison with our own republic.

The Northern fisheries known in commerce are chiefly above the 34th parallel. The United States and Russia own more than half of the coast on both sides of the Pacific, north of that parallel. Mr. Seward left, as a legacy in the State Department, an inchoate negotiation of a treaty for reciprocity in those fisheries. Its importance may be estimated by recalling the controversies and conflicts between the United States and Great Britain, during the last hundred years, which have arisen out of the fisheries on the Atlantic coast.

WILLIAM HENRY SEWARD

Notes on Part 1 Chapter II
Page numbers refer to pagination of facsimile document.

(1) September 4th - (p.29) The title "minister" rather than "ambassador" is used for the Russian diplomat, Vlangally who headed Russian's diplomatic mission in China. He was returning to post in Peking, as it was called then, from St. Petersburg. The title ambassador did not come into use for Western diplomats in Asia until decades later. In the case of the United States, the chief of mission's title in Japan was raised to ambassador in the early 20th century. Concurrently, the designation for the mission, then called legation, was upgraded to embassy.

(2) (p.30) The Mexican silver dollar circulated widely in East Asia from the 1500s, mined in Peru, minted in Mexico, and shipped across the Pacific to Manila in the Spanish Philippines.

(3) September 6th – (p.31) Massacre at Tien-Tsin, now written Tianjin. A riot by Chinese resulting in the death of French missionaries.

(4) (p.32) Red Jacket (1750-1830) Seneca chief known for his oratorical skill.

(5) September 24th – (p.33) Fusi Yama is Mt. Fuji.

PART II.

JAPAN, CHINA, AND COCHIN CHINA.

CHAPTER I.

YOKOHAMA AND ITS VICINITY.

The Bay of Yokohama.—Natives and Foreigners.—Native Costumes.—Japanese Barbers.—The Tokaido.—Japanese Cemeteries, Gardens, and Temples.—Monks and Monasteries.—Kamakura.—The Great Statue of Buddha.—The Daibutz.

Yokohama, September 25th.—Night closed with more than moonless darkness. With a true seaman's solicitude for the good name of his ship, Captain Freeman still promised that we should anchor before midnight. Who could think of sleeping when the lights of our first Asiatic port were so near? We walked the deck around and around, from stem to stern; we tried whist, we drew uncounted symphonies from the piano—but no consolation. The ship scarcely moved, and the equinoctial 24th day of September became the longest of all the days in the year. Time lagged more and more tediously between the hours of eleven and twelve. At last we gave it up, and went to rest. We were wakened by the ship's gun, and the slow dropping of the anchor. The morning brought an explanation. The ship's clock had been retarded, and did not announce the hour of twelve until the chronometer marked half-past two.

The bay of Yokohama is as spacious, and its surroundings are as beautiful, as those of Hampton Roads. The landscape recedes gracefully from the shore, and high above the beautiful scene Fusi Yama's sacred brow reflects the glowing smile of the morning sun. The hills and valleys wear all the freshness of spring. It is Sunday; the harbor is gay with the flags of many nations on men-of-

38   JAPAN, CHINA, AND COCHIN CHINA.

war and merchant-ships, and is made more animated by the quaint Japanese craft and their shouting, grotesque, native managers.

Yokohama, September 26th.—The United States minister, Mr. De Long, Captain McCrea, of the Asiatic squadron, Mr. Shepard the consul at Yeddo, Mr. Walsh, and other American citizens, came on board, and after kind expressions of welcome and congratulation conducted us to Mr. Walsh's residence.(1) (2)

Captain McCrea received Mr. Seward and his friends with national honors on board the United States steamship-of-war Monocacy.

Accustomed at home to the intermingling of all classes, conditions, and races, in subjection to one system of laws and tribunals, with common standards of morals and manners, we are as yet unprepared for the different constitution of society we find here: instead of one community, two, standing side by side, each independent of the other—the one native, the other foreign.

The native population of Japan is forty millions, all of the Mongolian type;* the so-called European population, five thousand, temporarily residing here from various nations, including the United States. These foreigners are gathered upon tracts of land, one, three or six miles square, called concessions, adjacent to native cities in the chief ports of this maritime empire. These foreign settlements are corporations, regulated and protected by the several foreign nations, and are copied in all respects from Western models, while the unpaved native cities, built of firs and cedars, thatched with bamboo and cane, are as perfectly Japanese as if a European had never touched the coast.

It may be conceived that it is difficult for the transient traveller, who always sojourns among his countrymen, and speaks with the natives only through an interpreter, to study Japan or its people. The Japanese, however they may have been heretofore, are not now jealous or suspicious. They labor cheerfully on the wharves, serve faithfully in foreign families within the concessions, and manufacture, in their own districts, articles of furniture and fancy goods for foreign markets. They are polite, sagacious, and skilful traders.

---

* The Prime-Minister informs Mr. Seward that the census recently taken gave thirty-five (35) millions, but that it was erroneous. He estimates the population at fifty millions.

WILLIAM HENRY SEWARD

YOKOHAMA, JAPAN.

September 27th.—The representations of native costumes on the Japanese porcelain and lacquer-work, which are found on our tables and in our parlors at home, are not less accurate than spirited. The coarse, black hair is a chief object of pride and care. The

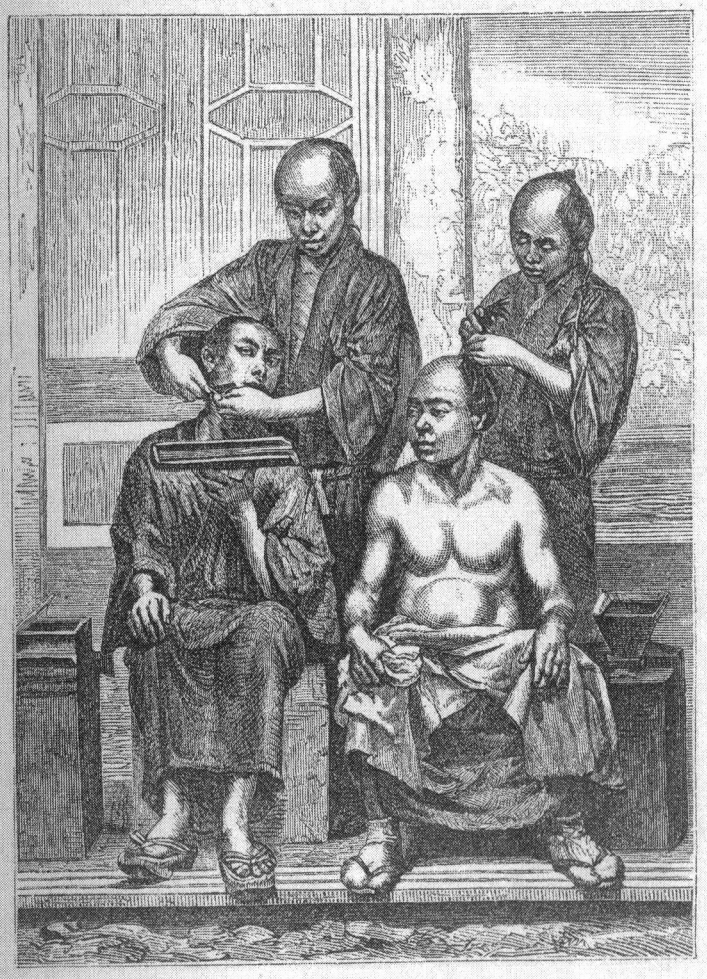

JAPANESE BARBERS.

barber with his scissors, combs, razors, and pomatum, is seen at all hours of the day in the most public places. The women brush the hair away from the temples *à la Pompadour*, and gather it up under a small smooth puff at the back of the head with gilt and vermilion pins. The hair of the men is shorn entirely off the crown, leaving enough at the sides and back to be drawn upward and fastened in a graceless and meaningless knot. The effect is simply shocking. The barber-work being performed only three times a week, care is taken to prevent disarrangement in the intervals. They use, instead of a pillow, a wooden block adjusted to the shape of the neck. The pomatum so lavishly applied is extracted from an herb, which, growing in the eaves of the houses, makes a pretty green fringe for the brown thatched roofs. They say that one of the emperors, for sumptuary reasons, forbade the cultivation of this plant in the fields. Thus the people, while evading the law, beautify their dwellings.

Here, as in Alaska and in ancient Mexico, civil economy re-

JAPANESE GIRLS.

quires that the married and unmarried women shall wear distinguishing badges. The girl, with full hair tastefully arranged, with white teeth, and with the free use of cosmetics, and a scrupulously modest costume, is attractive; when married, her eyebrows are immediately shaven off, her teeth are stained jet-black, the ornaments are removed from her hair, and she becomes repulsive.

JAPANESE CEMETERIES.

Wherever a city of the living is, there is also a greater city of the dead. The Japanese bury on the hill-sides. Though cremation

JAPANESE CEMETERY.

is sometimes practised, the body is more generally interred in a sitting posture, cramped within a plain, white, square box, borne to the grave on men's shoulders. All who attend, wear white mourning-badges. Women do not appear in the processions. Burial is without pomp and pageantry. A black or gray stone obelisk is raised over the grave.

All the cemeteries are crowded, but doubtless this is due to the economy of land required by so dense a population. They are, however, always shaded and green.

September 28*th*.—We made an excursion, by boat, to-day, on the bay of Yeddo, to Kanagawa, and its precincts. The Tokaido, the high-road which traverses the island of Niphon, passes through the town. A crowd of both sexes and all ages gathered and stared at our landing. The architecture of Japanese towns and villages is monotonous. The buildings, public and private, are small and huddled together. It was a pleasing surprise to find the railroad to Yeddo in process of construction. It is undertaken by a native company, using only Japanese capital, credit, and labor. By-the-way, the projectors are becoming timid in prosecuting the work, under an apprehension that, when it shall be completed, foreigners will base extortionate claims on any accidental injuries they may suffer. (3)

Ascending a high hill, just beyond the town of Kanagawa, we enjoyed our first interior view of Japanese rural scenery. Thenceforward we had a path only five or six feet wide, which winds across the plains and around the hill-sides, not on any principle of road-making, but simply for the convenient use of the soil. The hill-tops are covered with majestic cypresses and yew-trees, intermingled with the chestnut, holly, pine, persimmon, and camphor. At their bases are thick groves of the slender bamboo, which, besides being highly ornamental, is the most variously useful of all the woods in the East.

The althea, the lily, the japonica, the arbor-vitæ, the wisteria, the passion-flower, and many other shrubs and creepers, which require so much care and labor in our gardens and greenhouses, are luxuriant here. There is no waste, either by rock, marsh, or jungle; every hill is terraced, every acre irrigated, every square foot of land covered by some tree, cereal, or esculent. Instead of farms, there are small plots, and each is tilled with cotton, flax, wheat, barley, sugar, beets, peppers, sweet-potatoes, cabbages, turnips, and other vegetables, by a single family, with care equal to that which is bestowed on our flower-beds. No allowance is made for even accidental waste of the crop. The individual wheat-stalk which is bent down by the storm is restored and supported. Each head of rice, each particular boll of cotton, is kept in its place until care-

WILLIAM HENRY SEWARD

A JAPANESE GARDEN.

fully removed by the husbandman's hand. There is no loss of time in gathering the crops into garners; as fast as the product ripens, it is harvested and immediately prepared for the market. Despotism, though often cruel, is not always blind. A law of the empire obliges every one who fells a tree to plant another. In the midst of this rich and beautiful landscape, within an enclosure of two hundred acres, stands a Buddhist temple, with an adjoining monastery, surrounded by groves such as Downing might have designed. We came upon the base of the temple by successive flights of steps, each reaching from a platform below to a more contracted one above. The edifices are constructed of wood, which is generally used in Japan, for greater security against earthquakes.

The temple has an overhanging roof and portico, which are unique and graceful. The columns, architraves and cornices are elaborately, though grotesquely carved. The bonzes received and conducted us through the sacred edifices with ceremonious politeness, requiring us to leave our boots at the door, not as a religious observance, but as a regulation of domestic economy. These priests are vowed to celibacy and temperance, and in their tonsure and habit they resemble Carmelite friars, except that their spotless white raiment is not of wool, but of soft silk. The monastery is divided into numerous apartments by sliding paper doors, but all these were thrown open to us. A fine, clean bamboo mat, two inches thick, is spread on every floor, and serves for " bed and board." There is no other furniture. While we were enjoying our collation in one apartment, the bonzes were taking tea and smoking in the next one. Each bonze, before lifting his teacup or bringing his pipe to his lips, brought his head half a dozen times to the floor by way of compliment to his several companions. We inferred that some of the party were pilgrims, enjoying the hospitalities of the house. The temple is a square enclosure, with an open corridor on every side. Nearly the whole floor is covered with a dais, in the centre of which is a large altar, with a smaller one on either side. Over each a carved image—the middle one, Buddha; on his right, the mythological mikado, on the left an apostle or lawgiver. No space is allowed for worshippers. They prostrate themselves at the porch, and are content with throwing small coins into the treasury just within the door. A cemetery near the temple is crowded with monuments of pilgrim princes and saints. Take away from this temple its pagan devices and emblems, and the whole place would seem to be pervaded with the very spirit of religious devotion. It combines seclusion, repose, and silence with solemnity. The good monks dismissed us with many blessings, after having obtained Mr. Seward's leave to visit him at Yokohama. On our return, we found the bay highly agitated. Discarding the life-boats of the Monocacy, we crossed in a native craft, rowed by a vigilant and active though excited and vehement crew.

September 30*th*.—A second excursion, this time overland to Kanagawa, southward on the Tokaido. A hundred years ago, no part of the United States, perhaps few countries in Europe, afforded a road equal to this in firmness and smoothness. At intervals, hot

TEA-HOUSE ON THE TOKAIDO.

tea in tiny cups, with cakes and sugar-plums, was brought out to us by pretty girls, *artistes* in dance and song. The beverage might not be declined, though we were not allowed to pay for it. In many places we found circular benches arranged under trees five hundred years old. This frequent provision for rest and refreshment is due to the circumstance that travel in Japan is principally performed by pedestrians, with the occasional use of chairs. Daimios have always used horses, and recently foreigners have introduced vehicles.

GROUP ON THE TOKAIDO.

The Japanese are a busy as well as a frugal people. Thickly-clustering houses, booths, and work-shops nearly close the road on either side, making it difficult to distinguish where a rural district begins or ends. Occasionally a vacant space opens a beautiful vista. At the end of twenty miles we sent our carriages back to Yokohama, and proceeded in chairs by a narrow path over a lofty hill, and then came down on the ocean-beach. The feet of our coolie bearers sank deep in the sand, but we enjoyed the refreshing spray which dashed in our faces. Then leaving the shore, and following a rugged mountain-path, we came upon a high plain, where once stood the renowned ecclesiastical capital, Kamakura. Practically speaking, Japan has no ruins. An extensive and hand-

TEMPLE AT KAMAKURA.

some temple, which still maintains its prestige, is the only monument of the ancient city. A few miles beyond this temple, we left our chairs, and, diverging from the road, we confronted a high wooden arch, fantastically painted with bright green, blue and yellow colors. On either side of the arch is a carved bronze demon, fifteen feet high, protected by an iron railing. These figures, designed to be terrific, are simply hideous. They are plastered over with moistened paper pellets, which have been cast on them by passing pilgrims. The adhesion of the pellet is taken as an assurance

THE GREAT STATUE OF BUDDHA.

that the monster is appeased, and consents to the visit of a votary. Trusting that the missiles which our bearers had thrown upon the demons had propitiated them in our favor, we boldly entered the gate. Ascending a solid flight of steps, we reached a paved court, three sides of which are graced with monumental shrines of stone and bronze. On a pedestal six feet high, in the centre of the square, is the gigantic statue of Buddha (famous as the Daibutz), sitting with crossed legs, on a lotus-flower. Though description by measurement is not poetical, we must use it to convey an idea of this colossal idol. It is fifty feet high, a hundred

DAIBUTZ.

feet in circumference at the base, and the head is nine feet long; the hands are brought together in front, with thumbs joined; the head is covered with metallic snails, which are supposed to protect the god from the sun. Some travellers find in the face an expression of sublime contemplation; to us it seems dull and meaningless. The statue being made of bronze plates, is hollow; the interior is shaped and fitted as a temple. We are inclined to believe that the Japanese have lost their early reverence for the Daibutz; we find the walls covered with the autographs of pilgrims and travellers. The bonzes invited us to register our own names, and they offer to sell the god to any purchaser for the price of old copper.

JAPANESE BONZES.

WILLIAM HENRY SEWARD

Notes on **Part 2 Chapter I**
Page numbers refer to pagination of facsimile document.

(1) September 26th - (p.38) Mr. De Long is Minister Charles De Long, Grant's first appointee to the Chief of Mission post. During the presidential election, De Long had been important in delivering California to Grant. De Long, in his late 30s at the time, had no diplomatic experience but no lack of enthusiasm. Yeddo (also written sometimes as Yedo or Edo) is an older name for Tokyo. For a thorough treatment of De Long's tenure as minister see Jack Hammersmith, *Spoilsmen in a Flowery Fairyland – The Development of the U.S. Legation in Japan, 1859-1906*.

(2) September 26th - (p.38) Mr. Walsh is Thomas Walsh, head of Walsh and Hall, Ltd. First established in Nagasaki shortly after Japan's opening to foreign business, Thomas Walsh and Francis Hall founded Walsh, Hall & Company. At the time of Seward's visit, Thomas Walsh was based in Yokohama while his brother John ran the operation in Nagasaki. Hall left the company several years before Seward's visit and the Walsh brothers were the most prominent American business leaders in Japan during the last decades of the 19th century.

(3) September 28th – (p.42) Japan's road and internal transportation network before the opening to the West was well developed. The regional lords, or daimyo, were required to maintain residences at the capital, Edo, in addition to the ones in their domains. This alternative attendance requirement was instituted to discourage regional centers from becoming too powerful but also encouraged development of an extensive internal transportation network.

With regard to the work begun on a railroad connecting Yokohama to Tokyo, Olive Seward writes that it is using "…only Japanese capital, credit and labor." In fact the project was largely a British affair but at the time of the Seward visit, a scandal involving the British supervisor of the project had given a ray of hope to minister De Long that this might provide an opening for American participation. It didn't. An excellent recount of these manoeuvrings is in Chapter 3 of Dan Free's book, *Early Japanese Railways, 1853-1914*.

WILLIAM HENRY SEWARD

CHAPTER II.

VISIT TO YEDDO.—INTERVIEW WITH THE MIKADO.

Interview with the Japanese Prime-Minister.—Tremendous Storm.—Some Points of History.—The Mikado and the Tycoon.—Japanese Foreign Office.—Minister Sawa.—The Question of Saghalien.—The Tombs of the Tycoons.—A Speck of War.—The Delmonico of Yeddo.—Sketches of Yeddo.—The Interview with the Mikado.

On board the Monocacy, Bay of Yeddo, October 1st.—On Mr. Seward's arrival at Yokohama, the Japanese Government at Yeddo invited him to a banquet in the palace of the Hamagotên.[1] The Japanese ministry, with other official persons, in all six hundred, were to be present, and the prime-minister was to preside. Mr. Seward excused himself on the ground that the condition of his health and his habits oblige him to forego large assemblies. He wrote, at the same time, that he intended visiting the capital in a private manner, and that it would afford him pleasure if allowed to pay his respects to the Minister of Foreign Affairs. This morning, we set out on the excursion thus proposed, in the Monocacy, accompanied by Mr. De Long; we arrived at the anchorage before Yeddo, at five o'clock, expecting to land immediately, under the ship's salute.

Since our arrival at Yokohama the weather has been intensely hot, and everybody has been predicting some fearful convulsion of earthquake or tempest. A wind with heavy rain gave us a rough voyage; but the sea has now calmed, though the rain continues. Mr. Seward, protesting against delay, asked for boats when the anchor dropped. The ladies shrank from exposure; even the

United States minister became demoralized, and Mr. Seward was overruled; so here we are, lying five miles from Yeddo, under the guns of a long line of Japanese forts, built on shoals, midway between our anchorage and the city. The naval officers are to give up their quarters to us for the night, in expectation of a calm sea and cloudless sky to-morrow; an expectation which Mr. Seward desires it to be distinctly understood he does not share. In the mean time they are entertaining us with music and conversation.

Yeddo, October 2d.—Mr. Seward was right. We retired at eleven o'clock, to the very narrow "regulation berths," imprisoning ourselves with close mosquito-nets, in the smallest of state-rooms, looking through the open ports at a very silvery moon, bright stars, and a smooth sea, the ship drawing nine feet on an anchorage of three fathoms. Between us and the forts, the harbor was covered with vessels, including a large number of Japanese steamers and other boats, as well as Chinese junks. Some of these lay quite near to us. There was no sleep. At four o'clock in the morning, a phosphorescent wave, pouring through the open ports, deluged our state-rooms. At this juncture, the order came down the hatchway, "Close the ports." The steward informed us that there was "something of a high sea." Wrapping ourselves in our now thoroughly-wetted garments, we rushed into the dark cabin, and there overheard low conversation on the deck, which expressed apprehension of a fearful storm.

We were on deck at break of day. The sky wore a copper hue; the air grew intensely hot; the barometer fell from 30° 50′ to 28°; a violent wind seemed to come from all quarters, and, in the midst of a deluge of rain, blew the sea from underneath the ship, causing her continually to bound and rebound on the sandy bottom. It was the typhoon! Nevertheless, we remained on deck, lashed fast in our seats, preferring the open tempest there to the close and nauseating cabin. The captain was self-collected; he ordered the top-masts down, and every spar well secured. Three anchors, the ship's entire ground-tackle, were thrown out; every vessel, and every other object on sea and land, now disappeared from our view.

With confused fears that some ship might be driving against us, or that we might be dragging toward a lee-shore, we put our engines in motion, to keep the Monocacy up to her anchors. The more juvenile officers, of whom, of course there were many, enlivened the dark and dreary hours by whispered accounts of all the ships which had been wrecked, or escaped wreck, in all the typhoons, and all the tidal waves, and all the earthquakes that have raged in Asiatic waters, or in any other seas, within the memory of man.

At twelve o'clock, we were driven from the deck by alarms that the guns were breaking loose from their fastenings, that the bulwarks and stanchions were giving way, and the bending masts and spars would crush us. We took refuge once more in the cabin, uncertain whether the ship was parting her anchors, or breaking to pieces in her berth. All the hatchways being closed, excluding air except through a convoluted funnel, a lethargy came over us, which made some helpless, and nearly all hopeless. About two o'clock, an officer, anxiously and carefully consulting the glass, said in a low voice, "It is rising," and, after a few seconds more, he exclaimed, "It is the end!" And so it was.

In half an hour we were on deck again. The sky was bright, and the sea, though yet rolling, had lost its violence. But the vessels which had been moored in such dangerous proximity were no longer there. The lee-shore was so near that we wondered at our presumption in having anchored there. At five o'clock, a full boat's crew manned a prize-gig, and with bright and merry oars rowed us around the forts to the wharf of the consulate at Yeddo. On the way we passed a crowded steamer, broken directly in the middle, and hanging across the rampart of the upper fort; while a dozen vessels were seen half out of water in the shallow and treacherous bay. When we saw the broken walls, overturned trees and fallen buildings on the shore, we were convinced that our anchorage in the bay was the safer refuge, notwithstanding all its terrors. The Monocacy had neither parted a rope nor started a nail, while the consulate had been beaten and shattered on all sides and in every part.

Sunset came on; while there was no rainbow, all the prismatic colors and hues were painted on the broken and rolling clouds, as brilliantly and as distinctly as they are ever seen in the "arch of promise" itself.

With what grateful emotions did we reflect that the tempest which so often breaks and destroys the stanchest of ships in the Eastern seas, had been in this instance withheld, not only until we had crossed the great ocean, but even until we had found an anchorage from which we had beheld the terrific phenomenon without disaster!

Monday, October 3d.—The Monocacy having done her best to rouse the sleepers of the capital by a salute to Mr. Seward, returned down the bay to Yokohama. Thanks to her brave officers and noble crew, with earnest wishes for their health and promotion.

The damages of the consulate have been repaired sufficiently for our comfortable accommodation. We are guests of the minister and the consul. At an early hour an officer came from the Minister of Foreign Affairs, to learn when Mr. Seward would make his promised visit. He appointed ten o'clock, to-morrow.

Before we go to the foreign office, it may be well to recall some points of history, in order to make our observations on Yeddo intelligible.

The people of Japan, whether indigenous here or derived from Siberia, assumed political organization, according to their own records, about twenty-four hundred years ago, in the two islands of Niphon and Kiusiu. They were governed by an emperor, who, being descended from the gods, was divine and absolute on earth, and when he died was worshipped. Not only was his person too sacred to be looked upon by a stranger, but even the sun must not shine on his head. It was sacrilegious to touch the dishes from which he ate. At his death, his twelve wives and all their attendants committed *hari-kari*. These attributes are still popularly conceded to him. As vicegerent of Heaven, he wears the title of Tenno; as sovereign in temporal affairs, he is the Mikado or Emperor.

Miako, some thirty miles inland, was his ancient capital, and

WILLIAM HENRY SEWARD

AMERICAN LEGATION AT YEDDO. (2)

Osaka its seaport.(3) The Emperor by divine right owned the lands in the empire, and in time graciously divided them into provinces; retaining five or more of these for himself, he parcelled out the others among great lords or princes, called daimios. In the thirteenth century, a rebellion arose in the empire, and the Mikado, remaining at Miako, committed the defence of the state to the richest and strongest one of these daimios, who wore the title of "Tycoon." This military commander, after a short time, absorbed the temporal sovereignty and reigned absolutely. Yeddo thus became a third capital of the empire.

The Tycoon, nevertheless, paid homage to the Mikado, who retained his titular rank, and unquestioned spiritual authority and preëminence. Besides the proper revenues of his own five provinces, the Mikado enjoyed, for the support of his dignity, an annual allowance made by the Tycoon, out of the general revenues of the empire. As he cultivated religion and such science as the age allowed, Miako became the centre of intelligence and learning. It still retains this distinction. Osaka being an alternate residence of the Mikado, it partook of the sanctity of the capital.

By degrees the Mikado, free from all responsibility for administration, grew in the affections of the people, while the Tycoon, exercising his power despotically, and held responsible for all national disasters and misfortunes, became an object of public jealousy and hatred. It was at this juncture that the United States, through Commodore Perry, and the European powers afterward, made their treaties with the Tycoon, in ignorance of any pretensions on the part of the Mikado to temporal power. It was the Tycoon who sent two successive embassies to the United States, one in 1860 and the other in 1868. In 1865, the ministers of the Western powers, residing at Yeddo, wrote alarming accounts of popular discontents with the Tycoon's administration, and of frantic appeals made to the Mikado to resume the sovereign power, annul the treaties, and expel foreigners from the empire. For this object, a party was formed by powerful daimios and fanatical ecclesiastics.

While matters were in this situation, a young daimio, son of the powerful Prince Satsuma, was improving an academic vacation in England, to visit the United States. He went to Mr. Seward, in the Department of State. He inquired of the prince to which of the local parties in Japan he belonged. To Mr. Seward's surprise, he answered, "to the Mikado's." "What," said Mr. Seward, "is the cause of the civil war, and what question does it involve?" He replied: "The Tycoon, who has no title to the throne, but is only a general in the imperial service, some time ago usurped the government, and claims to transmit it to his heirs. This usurpation is intolerable." "How long," said Mr. Seward, "since this usurpation was committed?" "Oh, it is very recent—it is only six hundred years since it occurred."

The revolution was successful, the dynasty of the Tycoon was abolished, and the heaven-descended Mikado in the year 1868, leaving his spiritual seat at Miako, repaired to Yeddo, and fully resumed the throne of his ancestors. He promptly confirmed the treaties, and of course was duly recognized by the Western powers.

October 4th.—At nine this morning a cavalry-escort was placed at Mr. Seward's command. It is attentive and orderly, although, according to our Western ideas, not particularly well mounted or disciplined.

After a diligent exploration of the two or three European livery-stables in the city, the consul succeeded in procuring three well-worn English carriages, drawn by native ponies, like those of our escort. Taking no heed of the suggestion that women are forbidden in Japanese society, and unknown at court, Mr. Seward proceeded to the foreign office with the ladies, the minister, Mr. Randall and the consul. (Mr. George F. Seward and Mrs. Seward have gone forward to Shanghai.) As we drove through the streets, we found them filled with gayly-dressed and merry crowds, and thus learned that Mr. Seward's appointment had fallen on one of the numerous national holidays.(4)

The foreign office is in the centre of a paved court, which is enclosed by a stone-wall twelve feet high. The gates were wide open; Mr. Seward and his friends were received by hundreds of official persons, with profound demonstrations of homage. The inner building is of wood, one story high, surrounded by a broad corridor. The corridor itself is separated from the court by sliding sash-doors, with oiled-paper and silk instead of glass. On the inner side the corridor opens into a succession of chambers constructed like those of the monastery we have before described; the apartments small, the ceilings low and the partitions movable panels. The floors are covered with matting.

We were conducted through the corridor to a room a little larger than the others, perhaps eighteen feet square. Some furniture had been extemporized here. There was a European centre-

JAPANESE OFFICER OF STATE.

table covered with an ornamental cloth, a small Brussels rug spread under the table, and upon it a lacquered box filled with cheroots, and a rich bronze brazier containing live charcoal. We sat on stools in the order indicated by the Japanese usher, Mr. Seward being next the seat reserved for the host. Presently, with great rustling of silks, Sawa, the Minister of Foreign Affairs, entered. (5) He bowed many times very low. He then gave his hand to Mr. Seward in the American fashion, and afterward to the other visitors, as they were formally presented, manifesting, however, some slight embarrassment in exchanging this form of courtesy with the ladies. Well he might, for "be it known unto all to whom these presents shall come" that they are the only women, of whatever nation or race, who, within the memory of man, have been received in an official circle in Japan. The Japanese Government is not behind the ancient court of Haroun-al-Raschid, in the opinion that "women have little sense and no religion." The porch of a temple in the interior has this inscription: "Neither horses, cattle, nor women, admitted here."

Sawa is five feet ten, and stout. He has the features of the Mongolian, with its complexion a little relieved, clear, mild eyes, and an expression at once intelligent and amiable; his hands and feet very small and delicate, his hair gathered up from all sides, elaborately oiled, and brushed and fastened in a knot. On the top of his head rested a curiously-carved jet-black lacquered cap, which by its shape reminded us of a toy-boat. This ornament was fastened under the chin and behind the head, by heavy purple silken cords with tassels large enough for modest window-curtains. His dress was double—an under-tunic and trousers of dark silk reps; the upper garments, of the same cut, though more full and flowing, were of gold and white brocade. He wore spotless white shoes and stockings—the shoe and stocking of each foot being of one piece; at his side a single sword, highly wrought, with hilt and scabbard of ivory and gold. Some show of awkwardness gave us an impression that he found his magnificent toilet, on this occasion, inconvenient and uncomfortable. Looking at Mr. Seward, Sawa, in a very low voice, pronounced, in the Japanese language, what sounded like not one speech, but a succession of distinct sentences. The interpreter Ishtabashi, kneeling at his side, at the close of each sentence signified his understanding of it by the aspirate "Hi! hi! hi!" Sawa having finished, Ishtabashi gathered

JAPANESE INTERPRETER, IN COURT DRESS.

up the sense of these fragmentary speeches, and rendered the whole into English, as follows:

"Mr. Seward, all the ministers of Japan proposed to receive you on your arrival at Yeddo, at such a time as you would appoint. But this is a holiday in our country. It is our custom that at this hour, on every holiday, all the ministers repair to the castle, and pay their homages to his Majesty the Tenno. The other ministers have gone there for that purpose. I have obtained from his Majesty the indulgence to remain here, and receive you in behalf of my associates."

Mr. Seward thanked the minister, and expressed regret that he had unwittingly chosen so unsuitable a day for his visit.

Sawa resumed: "I have heard of you much, and I know you by character. I see your face now for the first time, and I am happy to see it."

Mr. Seward answered, that it afforded him great pleasure to see Japan, and become acquainted with its government.

The Minister: "I am happy that you have arrived safely after so long a journey. I see that you are very old and very handsome. You show high resolution in making so great a voyage. All of us will be glad to avail ourselves of your large experience as a statesman."

We are not a practical reporter, and therefore cannot detail the long and interesting conversation which followed. It was highly deferential on both sides. Some parts of it showed that the profession of politics is the same in Japan as in other countries. Sawa was asking Mr. Seward's good offices to obtain a mediation by the United States Government, to effect an adjustment with Russia of the boundary-question which involves the title to the island of Saghalien. Mr. Seward, hardly willing to assume so grave a responsibility, tried to divert Sawa's attention from it, saying that the United States and Russia were once near neighbors on the other side of the Pacific Ocean, and that a dispute arose between them concerning the right of American seamen to take fish in Russian waters. The controversy, just at the moment when it was becoming serious, was happily brought to an end by the United States purchasing the entire Russian possessions on the American Continent. "What would you think," he added, playfully, "of a suggestion that Japan shall, in the same way, purchase Saghalien?"

The minister hesitated, cast his eyes on the floor, and meditated; then, looking up with a smile of conscious satisfaction, he answered: "All our histories agree that the entire island of Saghalien belongs to Japan now. We could not buy from Russia territory which we own ourselves!" **(6)**

WILLIAM HENRY SEWARD

INTERIOR OF SHEBA.

"That is so," replied Mr. Seward, "and, if the people of Japan are like the people of the United States, you will very soon find out that you can no more sell your own territory to others than you can buy it from them."

During the conversation, tea and cigars, and afterward champagne and cakes, were served by attendants who crouched on the floor whenever they received or executed a command. After an hour and a half passed, Sawa mentioned the places of special interest in Yeddo which he thought Mr. Seward ought to see, and explained the arrangements which had been made for that purpose; then, stipulating a private interview with Mr. De Long for the afternoon, the Minister of Foreign Affairs rose and took a graceful leave by bowing and shaking hands cordially with the whole party.

Yeddo is a singular combination of compactly-built and densely-inhabited districts, with intervening gardens and groves, appropriated to civil and religious uses. When in one of those populous districts, it is difficult to conceive that the whole vast city is not built in the same way; and when in one of the deeply-shaded parks, it is impossible to realize that you are in the heart of a great city.

As Sawa had suggested, we proceeded first to Sheba, the spacious grounds which contain the colossal tombs of the Tycoons who ruled in Japan so many centuries.(7) Some of the tombs are of granite, others of bronze. They surpass, not only in costliness, but in impressive effect, any imperial or royal modern cemetery in the West. The sarcophagus, the obelisk, and the shaft, forms familiar in Western monumental architecture, equally prevail here. The monuments bear no epitaphs, but each is surrounded with many lantern-bearing votive shrines, covered with inscriptions commemorative of the virtues and achievements of the dead, and expressing the affection and gratitude of the princes by whom the tributary structures were erected. The domain is planted with great taste. Each particular tree and shrub has been formed and trained into a shape suggestive of religious sentiment.

By the side of the cemetery stands the Temple of Sheba. What with hideous devices of the great red dragon of Japan, with his forked wings, flaming mane, and powerful claws, the monstrous

TOMBS OF THE TYCOONS.

transformations of Buddha into lions rampant and roaring, peacocks proud and strutting, and sagacious storks stalking and prophesying, the interior of the temple is a weird combination of the mythic and the terrific.

Though we have experienced neither menace nor insult, our guard is nevertheless indispensable to protect us against intrusive curiosity. The crowds gather around, and follow us wherever we alight and wherever we go. Perhaps the escort might be needed in case of sudden excitement or tumult, such as is liable to happen in every great city.

That was not only a seasonable but a pretty and pleasant breakfast which Sir Harry and Lady Parkes gave us at the British legation. It did not need the after *divertissement* of native legerdemain. The zeal and efficiency of Sir Harry Parkes, as minister, are well known. Lady Parkes is not less distinguished for the spirited manner in which she sustains him in his diplomatic studies and labors. (8)

We left the British legation in compact procession, as we had entered it, Mr. Seward and Mr. De Long leading in a pony-carriage,

BRITISH LEGATION AT YEDDO.

Mr. De Long driving. Three other carriages followed, attended by the consul, and the whole surrounded by the escort. For a time the carriages in the rear had the forward one in full view, while its occupants, frequently looking back, exchanged greetings. Mr. Seward and Mr. De Long at length reached the high stone bridge, built

BRITISH LEGATION, YEDDO.

across one of the canals, and famous in Japanese history as the Nippon-Bas.(9)There they became aware that the other carriages had fallen out of sight. The street which intervened was filled with holiday crowds, drawing huge, painted idols, mounted on low trucks. These crowds were rapidly moving in the direction of the missing carriages. The guards who surrounded the forward carriage gesticulated, in a manner betokening alarm. Mr. De Long, a Western gentleman, becoming excited, said to Mr. Seward, "There is a fight; the ladies are attacked!" With this exclamation, he sprang from the carriage and rushed back at the top of his speed, his long whip in his left hand and a Colt's revolver in his right, determined to effect a rescue. Mr. Seward remained sitting in the little pony-carriage on the Nippon-Bas, attracting a constantly increasing native crowd. Mr. De Long, scattering the natives right and left, found the carriages in the clear, open street, a hundred rods distant from the bridge and vacant, while, upon the matted floor of a silk-merchant's "go-down," he found the ladies with the consul, sipping tea, a ceremony always introductory here to the cheapening of Japanese crapes and gauzes. Without saying a word, the minister pocketed his revolver, and, lowering his whip in the most pacific manner, walked quickly back to Mr. Seward, whom he found safe on the bridge. Even at this hour of writing, it remains uncertain what was the sentiment which overpowered Mr. De Long at this discovery, whether it was one of satisfaction at finding his *protégées* in safety, or of mortification at having so impulsively yielded to groundless alarm. Neither the advance-guard, nor the main body of the procession, has been able to discover what was the occasion of the Japanese excitement which produced so much trouble.

October 5th.—A busy day, but less eventful. We have visited the Hamagotên and its palace, where Mr. Seward was to have been feasted. The palace, built and ornamented in Japanese style, is luxuriously furnished in the European. One of the saloons is appropriately called the Cool-room, its walls and ceilings being decorated exclusively with huge pictured fans, in many different positions, and so well executed that you might fancy that you feel the air stirred by their motion. The grounds are as extensive as those of Central Park in New York, and not less elaborately embellished. There are quaint bamboo summer-houses, with pretty scroll roofs,

WILLIAM HENRY SEWARD

NIPPON-BAS, YEDDO.

WILLIAM HENRY SEWARD

HAMAGOTĒN.

covered with hundreds of creepers, known to us only in our greenhouses, standing in the midst of lakes well stocked with gold-fish. There are groves of mulberries, chestnuts, persimmons, and oranges. Stately shade-trees, cut and twisted into the shapes of animals, castles, and ships, crown hundreds of high knolls which overlook the smooth bay of Yeddo.

From the Hamagotên, we drove to old Osakasa, where we wonderingly examined a temple which surpasses all the others we have seen. Superstition, though abating in Japan, is nevertheless far from being extinct. They show at Sheba, in the court of the temple, a bowlder, in the top of which a deep, smooth, circular basin has been made, which is filled with water, and kept carefully covered with a stone lid. It is an accepted belief that this water rises and falls with the ocean-tide. At Osakasa we were required to look with reverence upon two native ponies (one cream-colored, the other brown), both nicely trimmed and groomed, and superbly caparisoned, occupying apartments neat as a parlor. They remain in perpetual readiness for the equestrian exercises of the gods. The beasts are maintained by pious contributions of pilgrims. Ecclesiastics in Japan, as sometimes they do elsewhere, resort to questionable expedients for raising money. The highly-ornamented grounds of Osakasa are rented for tea-houses, theatrical exhibitions, jugglers' entertainments, and other popular amusements. (10)

A dinner was ordered for us at a tea-house—the "Delmonico's" of Yeddo. Leaving our carriages with the escort in the streets, and our boots at the door, we were ushered up a very steep, but highly-polished wooden staircase into a chamber, or rather a dozen chambers divided by sliding-doors. Here we sat down on the clean matted floor. A lacquered table was set before each person. It was eight or ten inches high, and large enough for two small covers. Tea in little cups without saucers was served, clear, and piping hot. After the tea, *saki*, a liquor distilled from rice, fiery and distasteful, was poured from a porcelain vase into such small, shallow, red, lacquered vessels as we sometimes mistake for tea-saucers. Our hostess, a middle-aged matron, was assisted by eleven pretty girls, their ages varying from twelve to sixteen.

JAPAN, CHINA, AND COCHIN CHINA.

These attendants, by the elegance of their costume and abundance of white cosmetics, had enhanced their beauty to the degree that, in Oriental speech, it would be said that "every one of them was a temptation to the servants of God." One of them went down on her knees beside each guest, and remained there until it was time to bring on, with the tiniest of delicate hands, a new course. Their actions were graceful and modest, their voices bird-like. They manifested childish delight at every compliment we gave them, and their pleasure seemed to rise to ecstasy when permitted to examine our watches, fans, parasols and other articles of dress or ornament.

JAPANESE MUSICIAN.

A SELF-DENYING ORDINANCE.

The dinner, however, was rather a self-denying ordinance. There was a vegetable soup flavored with *soy*, raw fish in thin slices with horse-radish, petty bits of game, various preparations of rice, and many dishes whose composition was unascertainable. These courses were intermingled with sweetened fruits and confectionery. *Saki* was offered with every course, and always with great ceremony.(11) All the dishes had one common flavor, which we could not analyze. Even the sugar had this raw, indescribable taste. After the entertainment, the girls, sitting on the floor, each with a rude instrument, in form a compromise between the banjo and the guitar, played and sang, and at intervals rose and danced. Though the airs were not without melody and harmony, they were so crude and monotonous that the highest expert in the "heavenly art" could find no musical meaning in them. The posturing and gesticulation were artistic, though the dancing was conducted on no rules of the ballet. Great skill was displayed in the dance, the long and heavy dresses of the performers always covering the feet, and most of the time even the hands. Night overtook us before we left this "haunt of delight," and the performers accompanied us from the banqueting-floor to our carriages in the dark street. Their grateful gestures and speaking smiles were intelligible, though their soft and gentle words were not.

We needed to drive with much care through the crowded streets, now dimly lighted with an occasional paper lantern. But our dragoons were men "dressed in brief authority;" they dashed furiously forward, and, with shrieking shouts and screams, startling myriads of bats from the thatched roofs, they drove the people, returning from their daily occupations, or listening to theatrical amusements, into the open doors or alleys.

October 6th.—The day began at Yeddo with an audience given by Mr. Seward, at the consulate. The visitors were Japanese who have acquired some knowledge of foreign nations. Mr. Seward inquired for the Tycoon's ambassadors, Ono Tomogoro and Matsmoto Judaiyu, with whom he had negotiated in Washington. But there has been a revolution. The Mikado, then only a nominal sovereign, is now absolute at the castle. The Tycoon is a prisoner of state; Ono Tomogoro is also a prisoner, nobody knows where, and Matsmoto Judaiyu is a fugitive—some say at Shanghai, others at San Francisco. It seems to surpass Japanese comprehension that a new administration of the Government of the United States has come in, and that Mr. Seward has gone out of place without losing his head or public consideration.(12) (13)

While Mr. Seward was holding his audience, the ladies shopped. The Japanese artisans contrive to produce exquisite articles of taste and *vertu* from cheap materials, and with an infinitesimal proportion of the precious metals. Their modern porcelain is inferior to the Chinese, but they excel in ornamental lacquer-work and fans of all sorts. Their designs in bronze are exceedingly curious, but their execution inferior to that of Europeans. In painting they are unsurpassed in the imitation of all forms of animal life. With a keen sense of the ludicrous, they may yet come to be employed as caricaturists in our presidential elections!

There is no special manufacture at Yeddo. It is an emporium for the whole empire. We have found it impossible to ascertain the districts in which particular classes of articles are made. The shops are small and closely packed with wares. The indifference assumed by the merchants would be provoking, if it were not for their extreme politeness. If the buyer means to obtain a fair bargain, he must affect equal reserve and indifference. The entire family look on, half a dozen men and three or four women busying themselves in every sale. Indeed, the house and the shop are one. Four feet square of matting in the centre of the shop is the common dining-room and bedroom. Must they not eat and sleep by turns?

The United States minister was recalled to Yokohama last night. Captain Bachelor put the reins of two fine American horses into our hands, to drive in a light New-England phaeton down the Tokaido to Yokohama. Mr. Randall conveyed the other ladies in a carriage drawn by Mr. De Long's mottled native ponies. Each carriage was attended by two *bettos*, quick-footed boys, whose service is to run like coach-dogs by the side of horse or carriage, warning everybody out of the way, and they are ready to seize and hold the horses at every stopping-place, or in any case of alarm. The road was literally crowded, and hilarity and merriment displayed themselves on all sides. The crowds were labyrinthian. The activity and songs of the *bettos*, and the ejaculations and imprecations of our mounted guard, with the clangor of their arms, made our rapid drive a very exciting one, while a bracing air with genial sunshine was exhilarating. But all pleasures have their drawbacks. Neither the *bettos* nor the dragoons were capable of understanding our requests or remonstrances. They wanted rest at every tea-house, or, what was the same thing, they sought favor at the tea-houses by bringing us up at the doors. The guard dismounted, and, with the *bettos*, took the refreshments profusely offered them, while we, though declining any, were obliged to wait. When we had made twelve miles, half the distance to Yokohama, we brought up at a hostelry, with a stable. Our horses were taken out to be fed and groomed. From open windows in an upper chamber we saw in the court a huge brass caldron sunk in the ground over an oven. The horses were brought to it. Four grooms took possession of each horse, and rubbed him thoroughly from head to hoof with wisps of straw dripping with hot water, and afterward dried him with as much care as the human patient receives when he comes out of a Turkish bath. We improved the time by a Japanese dinner, which, when we were completely surfeited, we left unfinished, very much to the disappointment of the music-girls. Once more on the road, we indulged a faint hope of reaching Yokohama before midnight. We came, after three or four miles, to the bank of a river twenty rods wide. There was one rough flat-boat on the other side, worked by an endless chain. We awaited its tedious arrival and delivery of passengers multitudinous and various. Then our beasts were led separately into the boat and crossed. It returned to our shore, and, as in the riddle of the fox, goose and peck of corn, took the dragoons and the carriages. "Last came joy's ecstatic trial." We hurried on board, and, reaching the opposite bank, found the vehicles there, but not the horses. We were obliged to walk forward a quarter of a mile, to a place where the *bettos* and cavalry were taking tea and smoking, as if they

WILLIAM HENRY SEWARD

A BOOK-STORE AT YEDDO.

had fasted the whole day. Then they went back and brought up the impedimenta. A brilliant, full-orbed moon expanded into majestic size every object that we passed, and lit up the waters of the bay as we approached Kanagawa. Mr. De Long's native ponies, after frequently giving out on the way, fell in climbing the sharp, high hill, and it taxed our own horsemanship to get over this difficult part of the road. The other carriage was drawn over the hill by the *bettos* and dragoons, and the ponies were then reattached. Meantime *bettos* and dragoons lighted each his variegated paper lantern. They made the suburban streets of Yokohama resound with vociferous shouts, thus exciting the astonishment and perhaps the fears of this inoffensive people. We arrived at Mr. Walsh's hospitable gate, much to the satisfaction of our friends within, who, owing to the lateness of the hour, had become apprehensive for our safety.

Steamship New York, off the Coast of Japan, October 8th.—We have embarked, without having had time on shore to record the latest and most striking incidents of our visit at Yokohama. Mr. Seward was not allowed to leave Japan without a marked demonstration from the government, as well as an expression of respect from the foreign residents. On our return from Yeddo, on the 6th, he received an invitation to an audience of the Mikado. This ceremony is usually distinguished by procrastinations and formalities even more tedious than in European courts. The time being shortened, however, in this case, the invitation was accepted. Yesterday morning, we were awakened from sleep, which was quite too short after our drive on the previous day, by an infinite clatter of mechanics, upholsterers, and decorators, who were engaged in constructing with canvas, all around Mr. Walsh's very large house, a broad suite of saloons, dancing-halls, waiting-rooms and supper-rooms. The whole was completed during the day, decorated with flags and tropical shrubbery, and flowers, and softly lighted by fanciful lanterns. The band of the German naval squadron played "Hail Columbia," and the ball was opened at ten o'clock. All the diplomatic and consular corps were present, as well as the naval

WILLIAM HENRY SEWARD

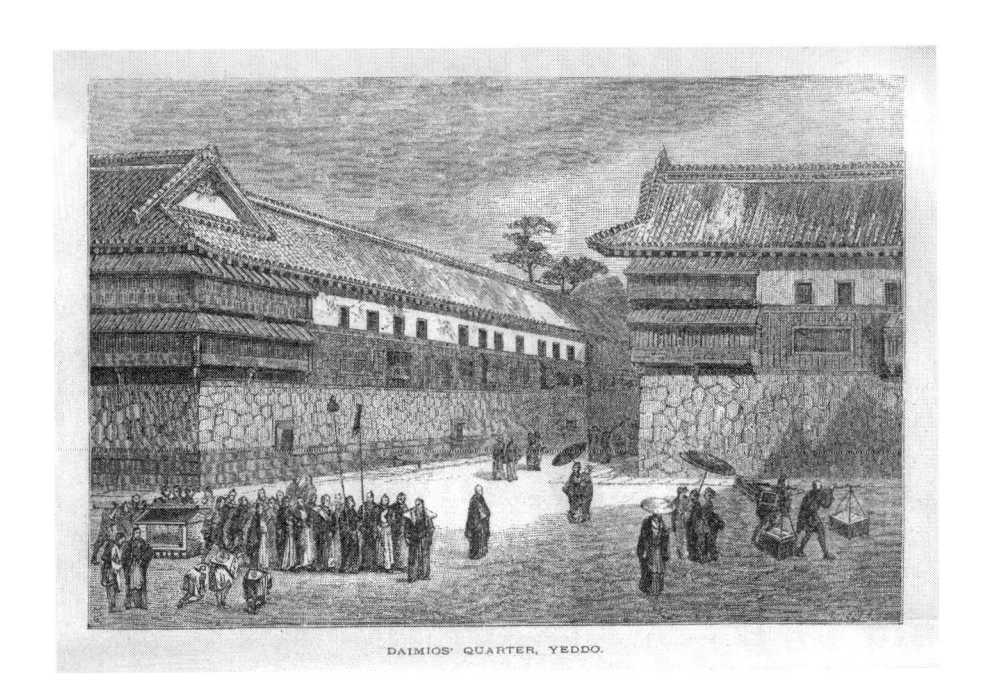

DAIMIOS' QUARTER, YEDDO.

officers of the United States and other nations, and foreign residents. Of course, not one Japanese of either sex was there, for, as we have before intimated, there is no social intermingling of the two populations. Caste and race are unrelenting antagonists to universal civilization. This beautiful ball crowned most gracefully the generous hospitalities of which we were recipients during our sojourn with Mr. and Mrs. Walsh.

At two o'clock yesterday morning, while the merry dance was yet going on, Captain Bachelor brought to the wharf, in front of Mr. Walsh's compound, then so highly illuminated, a little steam-yacht and received Mr. Seward on board, who, against all remonstrance, persisted in keeping his engagement, although in the midst of a driving wind and rain. He was accompanied by Mr. De Long, Mr. Shepherd, and Mr. Walsh, and at six o'clock, after grounding three or four times on the way, they were safely landed at Yeddo. At eight o'clock, Mr. Ishtabashi appeared in rich official Japanese costume, and, profoundly bowing, said, with measured words: "I am waiting for the honor of conducting Mr. Seward to the great castle, where he will be received by his Majesty the Tenno; (14) not in the customary official manner, but in a private audience, as an expression of personal respect and friendship. I am particularly commanded to make this explanation of the character of the proposed audience."

At nine o'clock the party proceeded in two carriages, with an enlarged mounted escort. They were conducted, whether by design or not, through streets bordered by immense walled enclosures, which are the strongholds and barracks of the several daimios who, under the Tycoon's administration, were required to reside during alternate periods, with their armed retainers, at the capital. The discontinuance of this usage, since the restoration of the Mikado, is a singular illustration of the same advance toward a more popular system of government which was made by the kings of Europe when they reduced the feudal barons to subjection. The barracks vacated by the daimios' soldiers are now occupied by imperial battalions. The feudal soldiers of the Tycoon must have been a ferocious crew, if they were more savage than these rough and ill-looking guards of the Tenno. The citadel, called "The Great Castle," crowns an eminence in the centre of the city. It is a triple fortification, nine miles in circumference, consisting of three concentric forts, each by itself complete, with rampart, inner embankment, ditch, bastion and glacis, parapet and double gates. The outer fort stands on a level with the plain, the next higher, and the central one higher still, overlooking the country and the sea. The walls of each are fifty feet high, built of granite blocks, more massive than those of the Rip-Raps, off Old Point Comfort. The imperial palace is in the centre of the inner fort. It is a low structure, differing from the temples and monasteries which we have before described, not in material or style of architecture, but in the arrangement of its apartments. The area which surrounds it is tastefully planted and adorned with lawns, winding gravelled walks, small lakes, and what we would call summer-houses, and tenements for attendants and servants. The areas of the other two fortifications are similarly embellished. In any past stage of military science, the citadel must have been impregnable. We cannot learn its history.

When Mr. Seward and his friends had reached the gates of the outer fort, they were received with a salute at each of the double portals, and were permitted to pass through in carriages to the gates of the second. They were received here with similar honors, and passed to the gates of the third. Entering these with salutes as before, they were received by one of the eight Ministers of Foreign Affairs, who, having requested them to dismiss their carriages, conducted them, with much obeisance, across the lawns to a sheltered place, where they rested on lacquer stools. Here a second Minister of Foreign Affairs joined the party, and, making new compliments, led them to seats on the shore of a small lake. Here the minister informed Mr. Seward that Mr. Walsh, being an unofficial gentleman, could proceed no farther, and that the same rule excluded Freeman. They stopped. At this juncture Sawa, chief Minister of Foreign Affairs, met Mr. Seward, and conducted him to a summer-house more spacious than the others, which overlooks a larger and deeper lake. On the way thither, he obtained a view of a part of the imperial stud. A rail twelve or fifteen feet long is fixed three feet above the ground, on supports. Several iron-gray Japanese ponies, unattended by grooms, stood at this rail, in readiness for his Majesty's use at the close of the proposed audience. When the party had arrived at the summer-house, the prime-minister, the Chief Minister of Finance and the heads of the other departments, were found waiting, and they were severally presented by Sawa to Mr. Seward. The whole party then sat down at an oblong table, the prime-minister presiding, and Mr. Seward and the other visitors on his left hand, the Japanese ministers on his right. The prime-minister first, and after him each of his associates, addressed Mr. Seward in words of courteous welcome, to which he briefly replied. A pleasant conversation now ensued, during which tea, cakes, confectionery, cigars and champagne, were successively brought in by attendants, who prostrated themselves on the ground at every offer of their service. The prime-minister then, in a very direct but most courteous way, said to Mr. Seward: "It is the custom of his Majesty the Tenno to receive official visits upon business affairs in an edifice which is built for that express public purpose, and called among us a court; but his Majesty on this occasion recognizes you as a special friend of Japan, and a man devoted to the welfare of all nations, and he therefore proposes, by way of showing his high respect for you, to receive you, not at a public court, but in a private lodge of his own, to which he will come down from his palace to meet you."

Mr. Seward answered that he appreciated his Majesty's condescension and kindness. While this conversation was going on, Mr. Seward, looking through an open window, saw at a long distance his friend Mr. Walsh, and Freeman, walking within the precinct which had been appointed them. Presently, an officer came hurriedly into the presence of the grave international council at the summer-house, and announced an intrusion. The prime-minister, upon Mr. Seward's explanation, directed that the supposed eavesdroppers should not be interfered with, but they must come no farther.

When half an hour had passed, a chamberlain announced his

Majesty's arrival at the summer-house. Sawa and Ishtabashi remained with Mr. Seward; all the other ministers took leave to join the Mikado. A final summons came to Sawa; he rose and conducted the party some distance along a smooth, narrow walk, till they came to a high, shaded knoll, conversing by the way. The minister and Ishtabashi now stopped, and, making low genuflections, announced, in subdued and almost whispering tones, that his Majesty was to be in a summer-house directly behind this hill. After this, there was no word spoken. When they had gone round the knoll, the lodge which now contained the heaven-derived Majesty of Japan came to view. It stands five feet above the ground, is one story high, and consists of four square rooms of equal size, with sliding partitions, the ceilings six feet high, and the whole building surrounded by a veranda. All the rooms were thrown open, and were without furniture. The visitors entered the apartment, which was at their left, and, looking directly forward, saw only Ishtabashi surrounded by a crowd of official persons, all crouched on the floor. Having reached the exact centre of the room, Mr. Seward was requested to turn to the right. He did this without changing his place. The United States minister and the consul stood at his right hand. In this position he directly confronted the Mikado, who was sitting on a throne raised on a dais two feet above the floor. The throne is a large arm-chair, apparently of burnished gold, not different in form or ornament from the thrones which are used on ceremonial occasions in European courts. All the cabinet ministers and many other officials had arranged themselves below the dais, and behind and around the throne. The Mikado was dressed in a voluminous robe of reddish-brown brocade, which covered his whole person. His head-dress differed in fashion from that which was worn by Sawa in our audience with him, only in this, that a kind of curved projecting prong was attached to the boat-shaped cap, and bent upward, the corresponding appurtenance of the minister's cap being shorter, and bent downward. What with the elevation of the dais, and the height of his elongated cap, the emperor's person, though in a sitting posture, seemed to stretch from the floor to the ceiling. His appearance in that flowing costume, surrounded by a mass of ministers and courtiers, enveloped in variegated and equally redundant silken folds, resting on the floor, reminded Mr. Seward of some of the efforts in mythology to represent a deity sitting in the clouds. His dark countenance is neither unintelligent nor particularly expressive. He was motionless as a statue. He held a sceptre in his right hand, and at his left side wore one richly-ornamented, straight sword. What the Mikado and his court thought of the costumes of his visitors, with their uncovered heads, square, swallow-tailed dress-coats, tight white cravats, tighter pantaloons, and stiff, black boots, we shall never know. Who shall pronounce between nations in matters of costume? The Mikado raised his sceptre, and the prime-minister, kneeling, then announced to the United States minister, by the aid of Ishtabashi, also kneeling, that he might speak. Mr. De Long advanced a step or two, and, bowing three several times, said: "I hope I find your Majesty in good health."

The prime-minister, kneeling again, presented to the Mikado a written paper, open, and as large as a sheet of foolscap. The Emperor, after looking at its contents, touched it with his sceptre. The prime-minister read it aloud in Japanese. Ishtabashi, again kneeling, brought his head to the floor, and, then raising it, read, from a translation which lay before him on the floor, his Majesty's gracious answer: "I am very well; I am glad to see you here."

Thereupon Mr. De Long, thus reassured, said in a distinct voice, worthy of a Western orator as he is:

"I have the honor to present to your Majesty, William H. Seward, a citizen of the United States. Your Majesty having been pleased to invite him to this audience, it is unnecessary for me to speak of the achievements or of the character of this eminent American statesman."

The interpreter, having rendered this speech into Japanese, Mr. De Long resumed his place. In accordance with an intimation from the prime-minister, Mr. Seward now advanced, and said: "I am deeply impressed by this gracious reception by the sovereign, at the capital of this great, populous, and emulous empire. I desire to express earnest wishes for your Majesty's per-

74   JAPAN, CHINA, AND COCHIN CHINA.

sonal health and happiness, and for the peace, welfare, and prosperity of Japan."

The prime-minister held before his Majesty another paper, which, being read by him, was then rendered by the interpreter as follows:

"I am glad to see you now for the first time. I congratulate you on your safe arrival here, after the very long journey you have made. The great experience which you have had must enable you to give me important information and advice how to promote the friendship that happily exists between your country and my own. If you would please to communicate any thing in that way, you are requested to make it known to my prime-minister, and I invite you to express yourself frankly and without reserve."

Mr. Seward replied: "I thank your Majesty for this gracious permission to confer with the prime-minister on international affairs. A citizen of the United States, I am visiting Japan and the adjacent countries on the Pacific coast, as a traveller and observer. I wear no official character, and I bring no message. The President, however, and all my countrymen, will expect me not to leave any thing undone which I can do, to promote a happy understanding between those countries and the United States, as well as also the advancement of civilization in both hemispheres. With this view, I shall, with great pleasure, avail myself of the privileges which your Majesty has granted me."

The Emperor, with his entire court, remained in place until the visitors had retired, after an exchange of salutations. They were conducted back to the summer-house. All the Japanese ministers soon entered and resumed their places around the table. Refreshments were served, and Mr. Seward was informed that his audience was the first occasion on which the Mikado has completely unveiled himself to a visitor. Not only the prime-minister, but all his associates, discussed with Mr. Seward at much length the political relations of Japan with foreign powers. The minister desired him to take notice that the government, in dealing with the vanquished Tycoon's party in Japan, at the close of the late revolution, had copied the example of toleration given them by the United States.

They carefully inquired concerning the machinery employed in the United States in taking the decennial census, and also the details of the system of collecting and disbursing public revenues.

They wrote a letter on the spot, addressed to their ambassador at Peking, and, delivering it to Mr. Seward, solicited his aid of their interest at that court. Mr. Seward was deeply impressed on two points: First, that although the administration of justice in Japan is conducted in a manner widely different from that of the Western nations, yet that the public mind entertains not the least distrust of its impartiality. Second, that the administration of the Mikado is sincerely emulous and progressive. Again, if there is any danger in the near future, it will arise, not from a retarding, but from a more rapid acceptance by the government of Western ideas and sentiments, than a people so rude can at once understand.

The ministers had assigned the whole day for the high consultation. They expressed much regret when Mr. Seward announced that he was obliged to depart at the earliest moment for Yokohama, where the steamer was waiting. Waiving invitations to examine the citadel and the imperial palace and grounds, Mr. Seward returned to the Consulate, and thence proceeded down the bay, directly to this steamer, bound for Hiogo.

A box followed him which contained all the cake, fruit, and confectionery, which remained from the entertainment at the Castle. The ladies noticed that the varieties of cakes were not merely colored externally, but through and through—crimson, yellow, purple, and indigo. The supply sufficient for the voyage to Shanghai.

It ought not to mar the effect of the Mikado's courtesy, if we state that the audience, in its minutest details, was projected and perfected in the Japanese cabinet, with the concurrence of Mr. De Long. All European governments, and even that of the United States, adopt a similar precaution in regard to official executive audiences.

Japan has especial reasons for prudence. The empire is a solitary planet, that has remained stationary for centuries, until now it is suddenly brought into contact with constellations which, while they shed a dazzling light, continually threaten destructive collisions.

WILLIAM HENRY SEWARD

Notes on Part 2 Chapter II
Page numbers refer to pagination of facsimile document.

(1) October 1st - (p.49) In 1870 the Meiji government took possession of Hamagoten, a residential compound and garden site used by the Tokugawa Shogun's family. A palace on the compound, Enryokan, was used as a guest house for important visitors. The Enryokan no longer stands and the compound grounds are now a park, Hamarikyu Gardens. To meet with Japanese government officials the Seward party had to travel to Tokyo from Yokohama. They made the short trip in the American naval ship, *Monocacy*.

(2) (p.53 picture of Legation) Olive Seward often refers to the consulate when talking about the American diplomatic residence in the capital. In fact, at that time, there was a consulate in Yokohama and Minister De Jong often stayed in Yokohama and came up to Tokyo (Yeddo) for official business. The formal residence and office for the American diplomatic mission was the legation located in Azabu, in what was then the southern portion of the capital. See picture on page 53.

(3) (p. 52) Miako, more often written Miyako was an older term for Kyoto.

(4) October 4th – (p. 54) George F. Seward was William H. Seward's nephew. George Seward was appointed consul in Shanghai in 1861 and became consul-general when the position was upgraded in 1863. He served as consul-general until 1876 and remained in that position until 1880 when he left office under a cloud of scandal. His appointment and retention in China posts is an indication of his uncle's commitment to strong Asia Pacific engagement.

(5) (p.56) The Japanese Minister of Foreign Affairs Sawa Nobuyoshi, died at the age of 38 in 1873.

(6) (p. 58) Saghalien now Sakhalin

(7) (p.59) Sheba is now rendered in roman letters as Shiba.

WILLIAM HENRY SEWARD

(8) (p.60) The British Minister Sir Harry Parkes was first among equals in the diplomatic community, reflecting his outgoing personality, years of experience in East Asia, and Britain's dominant presence in the region.

(9) (p.61) Nippon-Bas now Nihonbashi

(10) October 5th – (p. 63) Osakasa, the name of a temple and a district of Tokyo now written as Asakusa.

(11) (p. 65) Saki is sake.

(12) October 6th – (p. 66) Department of State, Office of Historian, a February, 1867 letter from then United States Minister in Japan, R. B. Van Valkenburgh to Secretary of State Seward requests the secretary to meet these representatives and provide assistance to facilitate Japan's purchase of ships of war for the Tokugawa government. For more on Van Valkenburgh's tenure as American minister see Hammersmith, *Spoilsmen in a Flowery Fairyland* mentioned above with De Jong.

(13) (p.66) Ono Tomogoro and Matsumoto Judaiyu had been members of a Tokugawa delegation that had visited Washington, D.C., in 1860. The delegation met with President Buchanan in May of that year. At that time, Seward was a senator from New York. For more information on the mission see: Masao Miyoshi. *As We Saw Them*, the First Japanese Embassy to the United States. Paul Dry Books: Philadelphia, 2005. Both gentlemen's portraits are displayed at Seward House in Auburn, New York

(14) October 8th - (p. 68) Seward's meeting with the Emperor took place on October 7th. The term Tenno referring to the Emperor is familiar modern usage.

WILLIAM HENRY SEWARD

CHAPTER III.

FROM YEDDO TO SHANGHAI.

Hiogo.—The Place of Massacre.—A Japanese Steamer.—The Gulf of Osaka.—A Harem on a Pic-nic.—The City of Osaka.—The Tycoon's Castle.—Japanese Troops.—Nagasaki.—Beautiful Scenery.—Christians of Nagasaki.—Japanese Character.—Departure for China.—Concluding Reflections on Japan.

Hiogo (Kobe), Monday, October 10*th.*—A voyage of thirty-six hours, in which night and rain have prevented all observation, has brought us to this southeastern port on the island of Niphon. The United States Consul, Mr. Stewart, and the agent of the Pacific Mail Line, came on board in the early morning. They were surprised when Mr. Seward pointed out to them with minuteness and accuracy the several places of interest in the port. "This," he said "is the European settlement, that place behind it the native town of Hiogo: the road which divides them is the one on which the Mikado's army was moving northward at the time when it fired upon and massacred the foreigners in 1864: this is the field through which the foreigners were pursued by the Japanese soldiers on that occasion: it was in the bay here on our right that the natives massacred the French naval surveying party in their boats: was it not in the building which I see on that hill that the Mikado's officers, who were condemned to death for those atrocious outrages, committed *hari-kari*, and that the foreign ministers interposed after seventeen such self-executions, and said, 'It is enough?' On this knoll is the place where the offenders were buried."

The official reports of those painful transactions which Mr. Van

UNITED STATES CONSULATE, HIOGO.

Valkenburgh, the United States Minister, made to the Department of State, had left this distinct and ineffaceable impression on Mr. Seward's mind. It is five years since those massacres occurred. We now find that the people, obeying the instinct of nationality, have erected a monument over the grave of each of those victims, and on that monument have recorded his voluntary death as an act of civil and religious martyrdom. So true to country and to God are the impulses of our common nature everywhere. (1)

Hiogo is twenty miles distant from Osaka, and bears the same relation to that great southern metropolis of Japan that Yokohama bears to the central one of Yeddo. Hiogo, opened quite recently (2) to foreign commerce, is not especially successful. Since the opening of Japan, the population of Yeddo has been reduced from three millions to one million, chiefly by removals to Yokohama. On the contrary, Osaka has not materially declined, nor has Hiogo considerably increased. The foreign population of Hiogo is at most two hundred. The importance of its harbor is due to its double advantages as a port of Osaka and a gateway to the Inland Sea of Japan.(3)

October 11th.—We dined yesterday with Mr. Senter's amiable family, and slept in the Japanese bungalow, now occupied as the Consulate, by the side of its pretty lotus-garden. Although the lotus has been held sacred from time immemorial as a divine symbol throughout the whole East, it is nevertheless indigenous only in tropical and semi-tropical climates. We now for the first time see in perfection on its native soil this magnificent flower, of which, "whosoever eateth wishes never again to depart, nor to see his native country, if it groweth not there."

Here the intelligent Japanese governor passed two hours with Mr. Seward, explaining the system of provincial administration, which seems very effective. He learns also that education of all classes is compulsory, and that the schools are maintained by taxation, which is remitted in behalf of the poor.

We went, this morning, on board a small coasting steamer, which was built in the United States for Japanese owners, and is managed exclusively by natives. The gulf of Osaka has pictu-

78   JAPAN, CHINA, AND COCHIN CHINA.

resque shores, thickly studded with villages, clustering at the water's edge. The sloping hills are terraced and irrigated, and their summits are planted with forests. The Temple of the Moon, standing on the highest peak of the mountain, reflected the morning sunlight

TEMPLE AT OSAKA.

from gilded roofs, resting on snow-white columns. The moon in Japan is a masculine deity. Is this exceptional idea due to the native jealousy of the gentle sex? Or is it owing to the fact that it is a man's face and not a woman's that is seen in that benignant orb? *Quien sabe?*

It is the bar at Osaka which forces the ocean-trade to a harbor so distant as Hiogo. Our countryman, Admiral Bell, lost his life two years ago, in sounding it. Our steamer could not cross, though drawing only four feet.

Osaka, as early as the sixteenth century, became a great commercial city. Its temples, surpassing those of Yeddo in number, vie with those of spiritual Miako. As we approached the bar, we saw a gay Japanese yacht, of perhaps two hundred and fifty tons, moving slowly out to sea under a light wind. The sails were quaint, like the form of the vessel they impelled, which was brilliant with scarlet and blue paint and gilding. A daimio sat at the stern on the upper deck, gorgeously arrayed in silks and lacquer, surrounded by numerous retainers and a bevy of highly-painted and elegantly-dressed young women, who were entertaining him with a concert of guitars, flutes, and drums. Manifestly the daimio was giving his harem a picnic.

We were transferred here to a small, neat, flat-bottomed bamboo barge, with a canopy overhead and a deck covered with mats, in which we floated over the bar, and up to the great sea-wall of the city.

The confluence of two rivers with the sea makes the harbor of Osaka, like that of Charleston. The rivers are formed into canals, and connected at convenient intervals by cross-canals. Venice is not more noticeable for its gondolas and barges, nor Amsterdam for its pleasure-boats, than Osaka for its picturesque shallops covered with bright awnings of various colors. It is perhaps from the amusements of the regatta that the women in Osaka have acquired the fame of being the prettiest in the empire. Time served us to traverse only three or four of the thirty or forty canals, but sufficient to enable us to reach the more important monuments and institutions of the metropolis, to notice the regularity of the streets, the grace and lightness of the hundred cedar bridges, and to wonder at the immense traffic carried on by families who dwell in the vessels they navigate. The wealth and enterprise of Japan being in the southern part of the empire, Osaka is the domestic main emporium.

While, for centuries, state policy required the daimios to reside a part of each year with their armed retainers at Yeddo, the political capital, the same daimios made their metropolitan homes in commercial Osaka. Here, on the banks of the canals, they erected palaces, with storehouses and wharves and offices. Here they received their rents in kind, and exchanged them in trade.

Between these palaces the canals are lined with cheaply-built dwellings, two stories high, with a veranda around the first story.

STREET IN OSAKA.

The lower story is a mercantile convenience, being washed with the tides and floods. The people seen in the streets here, as well as elsewhere in Japan, wear wooden shoes and dress coarsely. The nudity, so frequent at the north, becomes here more common and offensive. Crowds followed us with a curiosity which shows that few foreigners visit Osaka. Notwithstanding the mean appearance of dwellings and people, the city contrasts favorably with

Yeddo, in show of prosperity and affluence. Some of the temples are built within the areas of the princely palaces. More commonly, however, they are independent and spacious, and; like the palaces, accessible through canals and basins. They are on the same model with those at Yeddo, but more lavishly ornamented with allegorical carving, and statuary in granite and bronze. Men are seldom seen in or about the temples in Japan, but woman, poor, meek and ragged, though forbidden, steals in there, reverently paying her devotion to the gods and pitifully asking alms. How could woman endure existence anywhere on earth without the solaces of religion?

"From all ancienty to the present time," as a stump-orator, we once heard, expressed it, the Japanese have made their irregular and grotesque coins with the use only of the hammer. The government has just now established a mint at Osaka, with machinery of the latest invention, and equal, it is claimed, to the Philadelphia Mint. Here they are making new coins similar in form and device to those of the Western nations, the value being based on subdivisions of the Mexican dollar.

Livy has given us what he says was the speech of Romulus when he had founded Rome: "If all the strength of cities lay in the height of their ramparts or the depths of their ditches, we should have great reason to be in fear for that which we have now built." The Japanese might be excused if they should reverse this sentiment, and speak with great confidence of the security of the empire derived from ramparts and ditches. As with Yeddo, so with Osaka. Its boast is its castle, an imperial residence and fortress of mikados and tycoons. We tried ineffectually to obtain a measurement of some of the granite blocks of this structure. We think it safe, however, to say, that one of them is thirty feet long, fifteen feet high and five feet thick. No one knows where, when or how, such immense stones were riven at the quarry, and brought to the summit of the lofty hill, which overlooks the city of Osaka. The Tycoon in the late civil war, however, took possession of the castle with his forces, only to find it a prison, and insecure at that. He was dislodged by the Mikado's army, and made his escape on a United States steamer. Before leaving the citadel, he destroyed its defensive works, so as to render it unavailable to the conqueror. Now used as a camp of instruction, it is as jealously closed against visitors as the castle at Yeddo. Instructions having come down from the capital to the Governor here, as well as to the one at Hiogo, to show consideration to Mr. Seward, we were conducted through the castle, and allowed to witness the drill, and at the same time were honored with a serenade from the trumpeters, which consisted of European artillery and cavalry calls jumbled together on French horns. The din and discord may be imagined. The bronze-faced native Japanese troops, lower than European in stature, and bow-legged, but dressed in French uniforms, recalled our recollections of the first organization of negro troops in the late civil war. The Japanese are not less docile and orderly, and they went through evolutions and drill, according to French tactics, commendably.

The Japanese umbrellas are the best as they are the cheapest in the world, but they could give us no protection from the rain-storm which overtook us in the dilapidated castle. Captain Kinder's family being the only European one in Osaka, took us in and dried our clothes, and gave us all we had time to take, "a hasty plate of soup." When we reached our yacht, black night with high winds shut out from us the beautiful gulf-shores, and so passed away Osaka, to be seen no more by us, for we have taken care not to eat of the "fruit of destiny," the lotus. The heaving of the steamer on the now roughened sea was uncomfortable, but the tossing and pitching of the small boat which conveyed us from the yacht to the side-ladder of the New York was dangerous and frightful.

Nagasaki, October 13*th.*—As Hiogo commands the southeast, so Nagasaki commands the northwest entrance of the Inland Sea. That sea is a tortuous passage, flowing between the North Pacific Ocean on the east and the Yellow Sea or Straits of Corea on the west coast of Japan, separating the northern island of Niphon from the southern islands of Toksima and Kiusiu.(4) How and when was this channel made? Were the three mountain-islands which it separates once compact land, and did the ocean force its passage through? Was all Japan once submerged, and were the islands thrown up in their present form? Who can say? Not we. Perhaps Agassiz might.(5) We must content ourselves with writing that,

ENTRANCE TO NAGASAKI.

like most inland seas, this of Japan is marvellously beautiful. Four hundred miles long, of varying width, everywhere deep, it washes the shores of the main islands in some places, while in others it is broken into twenty narrower channels which break on the shores of uncounted lesser islands. In this the Inland Sea resembles our own Lake of the Woods, which takes its strange name from the fact that the island-surface enclosed within its shores exceeds in area the water-surface of the lake. These islands of the Inland Sea are said to be three thousand, but we are inclined to think that islands in groups like these are never accurately counted. Everybody speaks of the Thousand Islands in the St. Lawrence, without remembering that they are reckoned at eighteen hundred.

84   JAPAN, CHINA, AND COCHIN CHINA.

The channel twists around and among the islands in all directions, so that the headlands which we pass seem as fleeting as the clouds, producing ever-varying scenery. During one hour, we are making our gloomy way under the deep shadow of a naked precipice four thousand feet high. In the next, we are passing terraced hill-sides, covered with sunlit orchards, flowery plains and fields, and forests in which the bamboo, the tulip and the cypress commingle. It seems as if the busy population of the whole empire has clustered on these romantic shores. Manufacturing towns alternate with

NAGASAKI HARBOR.

fishing-villages, and every nook is filled with quaint and miniature shipping.

Night set in, and the bell summoned us to dinner as we were beginning to round a jutting promontory of the western shore. Shall we ever forgive Mr. Randall for beguiling us with his humorous stories until we were brought suddenly to our feet, by the dropping of the anchor, and the firing of a gun, which announced to us that we had arrived in port?

A moonlight view of Nagasaki; fitting sequel of a two-days' voyage through the Inland Sea. We forgive Mr. Randall; the first view of Nagasaki ought to be by moonlight. The bay is small; we almost know, without being told, every object around us. These vessels on the larboard are Japanese ships-of-war. This steamer directly before us is a German man-of-war; this ship on our starboard quarter, with its black funnels and its stubbed masts, is the British admiral's flag-ship; and this long, narrow steamer is a Russian corvette. Beyond the area thus occupied by armed vessels are two American merchant-ships and forty awkward but seaworthy Chinese junks. On encircling hills, which rise two thou-

TEMPLE OF BUDDHA AT NAGASAKI.

sand feet out of the sea, are the temples and groves of Buddha. Those dark shades below them are hanging gardens in which the consulates and the merchants' residences are embowered. This ravine which stretches from the shore upward on the hill-side is the ancient native town; this quay on our right is the seat of active trade; this island just before us, hardly broader than a flat-boat, is the famous Decima, for two hundred years the mart and the prison, (6) the boast and the shame of the Dutch traders in Japan; those terraced hill-sides opposite the town are the city of the dead; and this

VIEW OF DECIMA.

high, conical rock, which seems to close the passage to the sea, is Papenburg, memorable as the scene of the martyrdom of the early Jesuit teachers and converts in Japan.

What does this scene want to perfect its magic? Only music! Instant with the thought, the band on the German frigate delivers its national hymn, "Des Deutsche Vaterland;" then come swelling forth from the British flag-ship the inspiring notes of "God save the Queen;" and these only die away, when the solemn national anthem of Russia, " Thou pious and gentle leader, shield of the church of believers, God be the protector and defender of our great Czar," grander than all, rolls over the sea.

Is not this glorious concert, under the flags of these great Christian nations, in these distant and lonely waters, suggestive? Mr. Seward answered, "Yes, but deceptive." The German is here lying in wait for his French enemy; the British admiral is here to intimidate the semi-barbarous races; and the Russian admiral is guarding the eastern gate of his master's empire, which towers behind and above Asiatic and European states on both continents. So it is that jealousy and ambition breathe in the notes of this majestic serenade.

October 14th.—It is because we cannot swim that we fear the deep. It is because we delight in climbing that we admire the high. While the flat is dull, the circle is our chosen form for the beautiful. Thus the amphitheatre, with its circular and lofty walls, was adopted for the Pantheon as well as for the Coliseum; though it has since been sometimes discarded from the temple, it remains nevertheless universally associated with the stage and the hippodrome. If we must live in a town, give us one which, like Nagasaki, is an amphitheatre, whose base is the sea, and whose towering walls are green and terraced mountains. It was under an inspiration like this that Peter on the mount said: "Master, it is good for us to be here. Let us make three tabernacles, one for thee, one for Moses, and one for Elias." The preaching of Christianity here by St. Francis Xavier, in 1549, was followed by such success that, within fifty years afterward, Nagasaki was surrendered by its native prince to the Portuguese, and became at once the see of an episcopate, and an emporium of Portuguese trade. But Xavier little apprehended that the Order of Jesus, which he was introducing, would become so arrogant and ambitious as to contest with the native sovereign absolute dominion within the empire. The Portuguese Christians thus becoming obnoxious to the government, all foreigners were within the first hundred years excluded from Japan, under pain of death, while persecutions more cruel than those of Nero were visited on the teachers and converts alike. A few Protestant merchants from Amsterdam, renouncing their religion, joined the government in the persecution of the Christians, and were permitted, under humiliating surveillance, to replace the Portuguese at Nagasaki. This truly pitiable colony was found here on the arrival of the United States squadron in 1853. It was understood, at that time, that the Christian faith had been effectually extirpated by the massacres at Papenburg. The world was astonished, however, in 1867, by a discovery that the Christian religion was still living in the province of Nagasaki, and that a large number of natives were condemned to death or servitude for their clandestine adherence to that faith. The Western nations interposed in their behalf. The government contented itself with forcibly deporting twenty-seven hundred of the offending Christians from their homes, and distributing them through the more distant provinces of the empire. This new persecution being thus arrested, it is manifestly the intention of the government now to adopt the principle of universal toleration.

It would be pleasant to dwell on the hospitalities of Mr. and Mrs. Mangum, and on the courtesies of the foreign fleets. (7)

Yellow Sea, October 15*th.*—Leaving Nagasaki yesterday morning, we carefully examined Coal Island and the other islands which close the magnificent harbor. Nor did we omit to notice that marvellous rock, which, having been dropped nobody knows how or from where, is lodged like a wedge between two naked natural abutments. Our parting view of Japan was a sunset glimpse of the Goto Group, the western outpost of the Island Empire.

It is hardly more satisfactory to quit Japan after a residence of only twenty days, than it would have been to leave it altogether unvisited; nevertheless, there is Peking before us, "a bourn from which no traveller" can "return" later than November, and so we must onward. Let us set down our memories, such as they are, while they are fresh.

Although society in Japan is divided, as it is in every other country, into high classes and low classes, classes wearing two swords, classes wearing one sword, and classes wearing no swords at all, yet the people are universally docile and amiable. We saw not one act of rudeness, and heard not one word of ill-temper, in the country. Heaven knows that, in the arrogant assumption by foreigners of superiority among them, the people have provocations enough for both! One of the Japanese ambassadors to the United States in 1867 was robbed at Baltimore of a richly-mounted sword. Neither he nor his government made any complaint. Mr. Seward fortunately recovered and restored it, with a national apology. Foreign residents in Japanese cities are often timid, jealous, and suspicious. Some are prone to exaggerate inconveniences into offences. Others are dogmatic and contemptuous. Even one of the most generous of American citizens, when driving Mr. Seward through the streets of Yeddo, could not forbear from cracking his whip over the bare heads of the native crowd. Mr. Seward endured this flourish silently, but he vehemently and earnestly implored his impetuous friend to spare a litter of sleeping puppies which lay in the way. Women and children shrieked as they caught up the mangled brutes behind the carriage-wheels, but the relentless charioteer only said: "It will never do to stop for such things; let them learn to keep their streets clear." Intimidation and menace naturally provoke anger and resentment. European and American fleets are always hovering over the coasts of Japan. Though the eye of the Japanese is long and curved, it sees as clearly as the foreign eye, which is round and straight. Human nature is the same in all races. Who could wonder if the Asiatics fail to love, where they are taught only to fear?

It would be manifestly unfair to judge the Japanese by the standard of Western civilization. Measured by the Oriental one, it cannot be denied that it excels the Asiatic states to whose system it belongs. The affections of family and kindred seem as strong here as elsewhere. There is no neglect of children; there is no want of connubial care; no lack of parental love or filial devotion. Nor is it to be forgotten that, in regard to domestic morals, we are giving the Japanese some strange instructions. On this very ship on which we have embarked, there is a German merchant who, after a

90 JAPAN, CHINA, AND COCHIN CHINA.

short but successful career in Yokohama, is returning rich to his native land; with him his child, a pretty brunette boy, two years old. The father brings him to us to be caressed. We ask, "Where is the Japanese mother?" "I have left her behind; she would not be fit to bring up the boy, or to be seen herself in a European country."

No one denies that the Japanese have both the courage and the politeness which belong to an heroic people. They are accused of practising fraud, cunning, and cruelty in war. Are they more vicious in this respect than other pagan or even Christian nations? Do not the records of war on our own soil contain a melancholy catalogue of similar crimes? Are not the pages which record Napoleon's great campaigns sullied by deeds alike unworthy of our race? The Japanese are sanguinary in civil war. Are they more so than the French were in their first great Revolution?

The painstaking culture which extends from the water's edge to the mountain-verge; the tedious manipulation practised in mechanism; and the patient drudgery of the coolies in the cities, in labor elsewhere performed by domestic animals, show that the Japanese are industrious. Though the empire has, from its earliest period, been isolated from the civilized world, yet the silks of that country were found among the richest freights of Venice. A Japanese bazaar is seen in every modern European city; and there is no drawing-room, museum, or palace in the world, which is completely furnished without Japanese fabrics.

They have no legislature, yet they have uniform laws, and these laws are legibly inscribed on tablets at every cross-road and market-place. Although science and literature in the West have borrowed little or nothing from these islands, the Japanese are nevertheless a reading and writing people. We hardly know whether Boston, Philadelphia, or New York shop-windows display greater number or variety of maps, books, charts and pictures, than the stalls of Yeddo, Osaka, or Miako.

Japan is populous, whether we allow it twenty millions, as some of our missionaries do, or fifty millions, as the prime-minister claimed in his conversation with Mr. Seward. Nevertheless, mendicity, though unrestrained by law, is less offensive than in Naples, or even in New York.

It would be a curious study to inquire how and when the severe feudal model of the middle ages of Europe obtained a place in Japan, or how it has continued so long among a people so mercurial, and yet so thoughtful. While in theory the Mikado is sovereign proprietor, the whole domain practically belongs to the daimios, who are rich. The revenues of many of them are not less than the public revenues of some of the States of our Federal Union. Though the peasantry are poor, we nowhere heard a complaint against rents or taxes, or the price of labor. Moreover, the Japanese, while they encourage immigration, never emigrate. We infer from these facts that, if not a happy people, they are at least a contented one.

They were a religious people when they accepted the Mikado, and gave him their reverence. They must have been a religious people, when they accepted from the Mikado the teachings of the Sintu sect; they must have been a religious people, when the doctrines of Buddha supplanted so generally the dreamy mysticisms of the earlier faith. Xavier found them a religious people, willing to accept the teachings of Christianity. But the religious age in Japan has passed. Confucian philosophy has undermined all mythological creeds, and left the Japanese a nation of doubters. Government now makes no provision for the support of religious orders. Their revenues, derived from ancient foundations, are diminishing. The priesthood is as inoffensive as it is poor. It may be expected that under this toleration the Christian faith will now, for the first time, come into public consideration in Japan in the way it ought to come, that is to say, in connection with the science, literature, and art, and the political, moral, and social institutions of the Western nations.

The Japanese are less an imitative people than an inquiring one. They are not, however, excitable concerning the events of the day, but rather diligent in studying what is useful. All their dramatic representations are didactic; and, though they have a fondness for legerdemain, they enjoy it not because it is amusing, but because it makes them think from power to product, from cause to effect.

The most unpropitious feature of Japanese society is the grossness of the popular sense in regard to woman. Among the common people neither sex maintains decency in dress, and they use the public bathing-houses promiscuously. In Japan, as elsewhere throughout the East, there indeed is marriage, but it is marriage without the rights and responsibilities of that relation. This debasement of woman has tainted and corrupted the whole state. We are obliged to conclude that domestic virtue has not a prominent place in the morals of Japan, although some glimpses which we have had of life in the upper classes have inclined us to believe that among them vice is not altogether free from restraint.

Japanese history derives many of the institutions and much of the science, literature and morals of the country, not from China, but from ancient Corea, which seems to have taken precedence of China in civilization, as the Pelasgian civilization took precedence of the Grecian. The Japanese may, however, be considered as a distinct and independent Mongolian race, which has matured its own civilization, without having been deeply affected by intrusion from any quarter. In this respect the Japanese seem to have enjoyed a fortune like that of the Aztecs of Mexico. That people had developed a unique civilization, and were maturing it, when they came into conflict with European nations. The Mexican nation went down under the violence of the shock, and altogether disappeared. The Japanese had in like manner effected and were maturing a civilization of their own when they were reached by the Western nations. More advanced than the Aztecs, they more clearly apprehended the danger of the contact, and with great promptness and decision they effectually resisted and defeated European intervention. Having thus isolated themselves, they remained so nearly three hundred years. If they did not advance during that time, they did not fall back. That isolation, however, has at last come to an end; steam, the printing-press, and the electric telegraph, have brought the Western nations on all the shores of Japan. It is manifest that the two distinct and widely-different civilizations cannot continue in such near contact. The great problem now is, whether the European civilization can be extended over Japan, without the destruction, not merely of the political institutions of the country, but of the Japanese nation itself. The Japanese are practically defenceless against the Western States. If they are to be brought completely into the society of those nations, it must either be by the application of force, or by that of persuasion and encouragement. The interests of both require that the latter mode should be adopted, but it yet remains to be seen whether Western civilization has reached such a moral plane as to secure its voluntary and peaceful adoption.

There is much of discouragement in the prospect. Few stationary or declining nations have been regenerated by the intervention of states more highly civilized. Most such have perished under the shock. On the other hand, there are some reasons for hope. Mankind seem at last to have risen equally above the theory that universal conquest is beneficent, and above the theory that it is possible. Commerce has largely taken the place of war, and it is now universally felt that interest and humanity go hand in hand. It is the distinction of the United States, and we may hope fortunate for Japan, that they have come to the front of the Western states as tutors of the decaying Asiatic nations.

If the tutorship of the United States in Japan is to be made successful, it must be based on deeper and broader principles of philanthropy than have heretofore been practised in the intercourse of nations—a philanthropy which shall recognize not merely the distinction of strength and power between nations, but the duties of magnanimity, moderation and humanity—a philanthropy which shall not be content with sending armies or navies to compel, but which shall send teachers to instruct, and establish schools on the American system, in which philosophy, politics and morals, as well as religious faith, are taught, with just regard to their influences in social and domestic life.

WILLIAM HENRY SEWARD

Notes on Chapter III
Page numbers refer to pagination of facsimile document.

(1) October 10th – (p.77) Selected to head the American mission in Japan by fellow New Yorker Secretary Seward, Van Valkenburgh had arrived to take up the post of minister in August 1866. He had previously served two terms as a congressman. The best account of Van Valkenburgh's tenure as minister is Jack Hammersmith, *Spoilsmen in a "Flowery Fairyland."* p. 61-79.

(2) (p. 77) Hyogo was often romanized as Hiogo and refers to the area around the modern city of Kobe.

(3) (p 77) The population figures given here, Yeddo (Tokyo) losing 2/3 of its population as people relocate to Yokohama is wildly inaccurate. Certainly Yokohama was growing but not approaching Yeddo's population of the time which was in the neighborhood of 1 million.

(4) October 11th (p. 82) Kiusiu is now romanized as Kyushu. The author refers to Shikoku as Tokshima. Now written Tokushima, it is one of four prefectures that make up the island of Shikoku.

(5) (p. 83) Harvard professor Louis Agassiz (1807-1873) was a Swiss born American biologist and geologist.

(6) (p. 86) Decima is Dejima.

(7) October 14th – (p. 88) The American consul at Nagasaki was Willie P. Magnum. From a prominent North Carolina political family, Magnum had served as an officer in the Confederate Army, reaching the rank of brigadier general. See Kidder, *Of One Blood All Nations*, p. 197.

CHARLES APPLETON LONGFELLOW

Photo courtesy of National Park Service
Longfellow House-Washington's Headquarters National Historic Site
Cambridge, Massachusetts

Charles Longfellow's Twenty Months in Japan:

Introduction by Professor Julie Joy Nootbaar

Julie J. Nootbaar is a tenured professor in the Global Studies Department at Oita Prefectural College of Arts and Culture and an adjunct professor at Oita University in Oita, Japan. A graduate of Mt. Holyoke College with an M.A. degree from Sheffield University, Professor Nootbaar has over two decades of experience teaching, advising and supervising students on overseas study programs in six countries. Lecturing in both Japanese and English, she has long been interested in researching the experience of Charles A. Longfellow, one of the earliest Americans to immerse himself in Japanese culture. She has published her research on Longfellow's experience which is available in both Japanese and English.

The son of Henry Wadsworth Longfellow, America's most famous poet of the time, Charles Appleton Longfellow landed in Japan just after his 27th birthday in 1871. Charley, as he was called by family and friends, would end up staying in the country for twenty months on this trip and returning two times afterward for extended visits. With no profession or any professional aspirations, Charley's affluent background and family connections afforded him the opportunity to live his life as he pleased, and he took advantage of this privilege wholeheartedly. Having been exposed to the exotic country of Japan by relatives, friends, and the media attention this newly opened land was enjoying at the time, Charley appears to have departed on his Japan adventure quite suddenly, first mentioning it to his father by telegraph the day he set sail from San Francisco. Upon arrival in Japan, he falls quite easily into the select expat community through family introductions and his illustrious name and is swept along by his status to such diplomatic affairs as an audience with the Emperor Meiji and a tour through the as yet undeveloped Ainu territory of Hokkaido.

At the same time, he lives a life of leisure, immersing himself in the local culture and society, spending his days and nights in tea houses and in the company of geisha, relaxing in kimono, and being extensively tat-

CHARLES APPLETON LONGFELLOW

tooed in the traditional irezumi style. Along the way, he amasses quite a collection of arts and crafts, photographs, and interior items, which he will ship back to Boston to display and disperse, exemplifying his love and respect for the country in which he quite possibly left his heart. Among the many European and American travelers to Meiji Japan, Charley was not only one of Japan's earliest and longest sojourners but was deeply immersed in and enamored by the country and its people.

Charles Appleton Longfellow was born to Henry Wadsworth Longfellow and Frances Elizabeth Appleton Longfellow in Cambridge, Massachusetts on June 9, 1844. He was a rambunctious and adventurous child, and though his parents showed great affection for their eldest child, they struggled with his discipline and education. His parents were, however, committed to imparting to their children a broad knowledge of the world beyond their circle of society in Boston. Having traveled extensively in Europe themselves, they fostered in their children a love of traveling and curiosity about the world through reading and storytelling, both by themselves and through their well-traveled relatives and friends.

At the time, with the so-called opening of Japan to the West by Commodore Perry in 1852, Japan was the topic of the day, and Charley would have been exposed to many aspects of this emerging yet exotic nation through the literature, art, and other cultural influences which had seeped into New England society. The Longfellow family also had direct connections with Japan, having connections with two members of Perry's expedition, as well as several others who would travel to Japan in the years soon after. Most significantly, the Longfellows were neighbors with Richard Henry Dana, Jr., who spent two weeks in Japan in 1860 among his other travels and from whom Charley often heard stories.

One can only imagine how exciting the tales and trinkets of these adventurers must have been to a teenage Charley. The writings of Dana as well as Raphael Pumpelly, a Harvard professor and acquaintance of Henry's who lived and worked for the Japanese government in Hokkaido in 1862-1863, include snippets about Japan that may have piqued Charley's interest, including everything from geisha culture to the frontier of Hokkaido and the aboriginal Ainu people. Charley would also have been influenced by the trend in Europe and America at the time, a rush to see the old Japan before it lost its exotic charm to modernity combined with improvement in travel such as steam ships and the Suez Canal, inciting a boom in travel to the heretofore secluded land of the Mikado.

But before Charley could depart on any travels to explore this or other faraway lands, he ran off to join the army and fight in the Civil War. This was his first attempt to escape the constraints of his family and circle of society, and after recovering from the wound which took him out of the war in 1865, he takes up yachting for more adventure. The following year, he makes a transatlantic crossing with his uncle and continues on to Paris and Russia, then two years later in 1868 sets out on a Grand Tour of Europe with his family before going off on his own to India and the Himalayas for the next couple of years. At the same time, the Meiji Restoration takes place in Japan, and along with the restoration of imperial rule, Japan enters itself into the world of modern nations, embarking upon a rush to join the civilized world. This news would have reached Charley on his travels and been the talk of society, so it is no surprise that soon after his return to New England in 1870, he would be setting his sights on Japan.

Soon after Charley arrived in Japan on June 25th, 1871, he became acquainted with the U.S. Consul Col. Shepard, and through him meets the Prince of Tosa, Yamanouchi Yodo. He also becomes acquainted with a New Yorker named Jaudon who worked at the Japanese Foreign Office and with the U.S. Minister to Japan Charles De Long. It is through these early connections that Charley was introduced to not only the beautiful scenery of places such as Mount Fuji and Hakone, but also the many pleasures of tea houses, pleasure boats, and geishas. In more than one letter home, he is effusive about these charms, but he leaves out what is noted in detail in his unpublished notebooks, the great amount of time he spends with geishas and prostitutes in the pleasure quarters and at his home, a former samurai residence in Yedo (Tokyo), and with several young women in particular.

However, Charley's life in Japan was not limited to idle evenings in pleasant company along the Sumida River. His family connections and new acquaintances also put Charley in a position of prominence among other expats in Japan at the time. During his stay, Minister De Long invited Charley on a five-week expedition to Hokkaido for official business, where he was also able to explore Ainu country for fifteen days. Charley would have been particularly excited for this adventure far beyond the Treaty Ports to which foreigners were restricted, and his writings reflect the depth of his observations of the Ainu people upon direct contact on several occasions.

De Long also made it possible for Charley to be included in an audience with the Emperor Meiji and a state dinner, something unheard of for a regular visitor or foreign resident of Japan, by appointing him acting secretary of the Hawaiian mission to form a treaty of friendship and commerce with Japan. His rare account of this event can be considered significant due to its detail and uncensored nature, and his observations are indeed enlightening to scholars of Emperor Meiji and the state of palace affairs at the time. Subsequently, and although Charley had never set foot in Hawaii, upon a second audience with the Emperor, he was offered the office of American and Hawaiian Consul in Yedo (Tokyo), which he refused.

So, it is clear that Charley's pursuit of pleasure and adventure does not preclude an interest in diplomacy, politics, and trade. Along with his observations on the Imperial Court, his interest in politics is also evident when he expresses some disdain upon the ineptitude and of the corruption of Japanese officials at all levels, when he is critical of the Japanese for being untrustworthy and untruthful, and in his comments on the surface level of the modernization which is rapidly taking place around him. He gives his commentary of the relatively higher position of the British mission in comparison to the American, and the obstacles the U.S. emissaries face in attempting to make equal progress in the eyes of the Japanese officials, showing avid interest in the state of diplomacy between Japan and his home country of the United States.

The longer Charley is in Japan, and given his close contact with diplomats and businessmen, the more he understands about what he sees and experiences. He appears to have good days and bad, as some days he is almost rhapsodic in his musings upon the natural surroundings or the nature of his companions and the society in general, while other days he takes a decidedly more restrained and even scathing tone towards the people and the surface-level of progress. This can be expected of anyone spending any amount of time in one place, and perhaps more so for Charley, who has no real purpose for being there. At times his romantic view of the traditional culture and ways of the people become eclipsed by what he sees being lost due to progress.

CHARLES APPLETON LONGFELLOW

In the end, however, Charley concludes that the longer he stays, the better he likes Japan. He makes repeated effort to extend his sojourn, however, his financial pipeline eventually runs dry, and he is forced to return home. In the context of the period, Charley's 20 months in Japan may mean nothing except to himself. Aside from filling a seat next to U.S. Minister De Jong at some important (and rather not so important) occasions, Charley did not contribute in any way to diplomacy or politics, nor to commerce or industry, or to any specialized field for which foreigners were being brought into Japan. His sojourn there can be considered merely an act of folly by a young man of privilege and wealth.

However, his writings, which were not published until 1998, offer a rare unfiltered and unedited glimpse into the experiences of an American in early Meiji Japan. Because he had no official capacity and no intention to publish his journal or letters, he is unguarded in his honesty and the frankness of his accounts. Charley Longfellow experienced Japan on his own terms, jumped at any and all opportunities of import and adventure, and enjoyed the pleasures of life to the fullest. He made his home in an old samurai residence, away from the expat communities, attempted to learn the language, wore kimono, and got extensively tattooed. He embraced the arts and cultural traditions. And he spent his days and nights with the local people in the pursuit of enjoyment. What better viewpoint can there be to get an uncensored view of the real Japan as it was in the 1870s, just as the country emerged from feudalism and embarked upon joining the modern world?

Editor's Note: *The good people at Longfellow House – Washington's Heaquarters in Cambridge, Massachusetts, have been wonderful in their willingness to help with this project. They kindly supplied their scans of Charley Longfellow's journals and letters, shared photographs in their possession and patiently talked me through how to use the materials they provided. Longfellow House's excellent book edited by Christine Laidlaw,* Charles Appleton Longfellow: Twenty Months in Japan, 1871-1873, *published in 1998 is, and will always remain, the vital source on Longfellow's stay in early Meiji Japan.*

The text in this book and the notes and comments are just a portion of Charley's more extensive papers. I have not included many items, most notably the journal of the trip to Hakodate (Hokkaido or Yesso) and back and the descriptions of the Ainu, the aboriginal people living in Hokkaido. These

CHARLES APPLETON LONGFELLOW

sections will be fascinating to those with an anthropological bent and I can only suggest getting a copy of Twenty Months. *I have tried to focus more on documents that illuminate politics and introduce people who show up in other research on Japan and America's early relationship.*

I have tried to follow the transcriptions by the Twenty Months *editorial team with slight variations. Where there are words or passages in parentheses, those were included by Longfellow himself. Words or passages in square brackets, [xxx] were added by the editors of* Twenty Months in Japan. *In several instances in* Twenty Months, *words or texts are contained in curly brackets {xxx} indicating the editors changed the verb tense or rearranged the word order. Alternative or contemporary writing of Japanese words, place names and personal names were mostly added by the editors of* Twenty Months, *except for a few cases where I was able to add something to try to help the modern reader.*

I have omitted some of the footnotes from Twenty Months *and added others. When the text of the footnote comes from* Twenty Months, *I have so indicated. I have tried to remain true to the texts as rendered in* Twenty Months, *but admit and accept responsibility for any mistakes or oversights.*

Finally, in preparing this section I want to pass along special thanks to Kate Hansen-Plass archivist of the Longfellow House – Washington's Headquarters. Without her patient help I would not even have been able to even begin this project. And finally, another thank you to John Bell, Administrator, Friends of the Longfellow House whose special efforts made it possible to include the Charley Longfellow section in this book.

Suggested readings

Laidlaw, Christine Wallace. *Charles Appleton Longfellow: Twenty Months in Japan, 1871-1873*. Cambridge: Friends of the Longfellow House, 1998.

Longfellow, C., translated by Yamada, Kumiko. *Ronguferou Nihon Taizaiki-Meiji Shonen, Amerika Seinen No Mita Nippon (Longfellow Japan Journals-Early Meiji Japan as Seen by a Young American)*. Tokyo: Heibonsha, 2003.

Nootbaar, Julie. 大分県立芸術文化短期大学研究紀要 第52巻(2015年)
(in English)

Arrival in Japan and Life in Yokohama

Western Union Telegraph Co.
San Francisco, Cal. June 1, 1871

To H. W. Longfellow, Cambridge[1]
Have suddenly decided to sail for Japan today.
Good Bye. Send letters to the Oriental Bank Corporation, Yokohama.
                C.A.L.[Charles Appleton Longfellow]

On board *Japan* 400 miles from Yokohama
June 23rd, 1871

My dear little Edie,[2]

    I was so much surprised and pleased at having a line from you in Alice's last that I have hardly recovered yet from the pleasant surprise.

    There is a very meagre chance that we may meet a steamer today on her way to San Francisco, so I take the chance of writing a few lines. At any rate I can send these after the arrival by the next steamer which sails in a month.

    We had a very pleasant passage for the first two weeks, but since then it has rained every day and is muggy and sticky to the last degree. We have all got sick and tired of each other.

    We have two cliques on board who hardly speak to each other, and the amount of scandal, storytelling and "sells" is appalling. There is a Mr. [Elisha E.] Rice[3] on board, who on account of his size – weighing two hundred and sixty – is called General. He is consul at Hakodate, and a fine double-faced sinner he is. First singing psalm

CHARLES APPLETON LONGFELLOW

tunes with the missionaries and then coming among us, getting the last scandal, adding to it and regaling it all over the ship – much to the discredit of certain young men, or "boys" as he calls us. On being accused of this the other day, he became excited and has threatened that the last day on board he will reveal terrible mysteries and exterminate us "boys" generally, worldly and physically. We await our doom with fortitude....

I guess we can hold out until tomorrow night when we ought to be in at any rate. If you never hear of me again, you will know that the General has sat on me.

With lots of love to the dear ones at home.

Your loving Charley

Please send my letters to Russell & Co., Shanghai, until further notice. Write again soon, "sweet little one."

Charles Journal:

Sunday, June [25]

Arrived in Yokohama. Fine entrance to bay, green shores. People come on board. [Samuel Kirkland] Lothrop[,Jr.][4] turns up, takes me to his hong [trading establishment], Walsh, Hall & Co.[5], a nice place on [the] Bund [esplanade]. Spend day and evening strolling about town, very pretty shops, elegant streets, bright wood houses.

Thursday, July 6th

Started for Miyanoshita in the mountains near the foot of Fujiyama about 50 miles from Yokohama. Our party consisted of Col. [Charles O.] Shepard[6], U.S. Consul, [W.F.A.] Torbet, paymaster of the *Idaho*, [S. Howard] Church and Manilla Austin. We drove to Fujisawa the first day along the *Tokaido*, or grand road through the island. Good road, beautiful scenery, so green. Large trees along the road side, tea houses, pretty girls. Everybody polite and good natured. Had an escort of two yakunins [officials] in European clothes. Wonderful how horse boys keep up. Five miles from Fujisawa [is] Daibutsu, an enormous god. We were nearly eaten up by mosquitoes at night. Nothing but eggs, rice and fish to be had at these teahouses. One has to take his own chow with him.

Friday, July 7th

Drive on to Sagami, where we had to get permission of headman of town to have our traps [luggage] ferried over river, which had risen too high to be forded. At Odawara river [crossing], left traps and were carried over on stretchers. Water breast high. The town [is] quite large, a Daimio place. Rested for lunch. Then on to Miyanoshita in kagos [sedan-chairs], a sort of basket hung on a pole. Well in the mountains now, fine large teahouse, some Johnnies.[7] About 1,500 or 2,000 feet elevation.

Saturday and Sunday

Spent mostly lazing off on mats. Took a walk over to Ashinoyu, four miles off. Hot sulphur springs, lots of native patients there for their health. Forlorn place reeking with sulphur, half a dozen teahouses or hospitals properly speaking. Buzz women [?]very amiable, invited [us] to come in bathing with a mama, two daughters and small son.

Monday July 10th

Price of Tosa [Yamanouchi Yodo][8] arrived at Nara-ya's teahouse where some of us are [staying]. Sent the Consul [Shepard] two bottles of champagne, spent evening and dined with him. Had singing, music and dancing by his own girls. Fleas! Fleas!! Fleas!!! Spent quiet day in house as it rained. Climate so far, anything but bracing. Musical entertainment given by priest, such noises. Nice people.

CHARLES APPLETON LONGFELLOW

Wednesday, July 12th

Walked over to Hakone Lake [Lake Ashi] and town, 3 hours via Ashinoyu. Last part along Tokaido under fine old moss-grown trees. Found Ashinoyu to be 1,300 feet higher than Miyanoshita, and Hakone 1,000 [feet higher than Miyanoshita]. After delicious swims in the beautiful lake and tiffin [lunch] in the teahouse overlooking it, walked down Tokaido to Hata. Quite a town where some Englishmen had a row last year.[9]

Tokaido very steep [descending], 1,100 feet. Large smooth stones for paving come down through the Hakone pass, the dividing line between north and south in the last rebellion, before the Mikado got his rights.

Yokohama July 20th, 1871
My dear little Alice[10]

Tomorrow's steamer is the first to leave here for a month, hence my reticence.

Among the first fellows who boarded the *Japan* on our arrival here was Kirk Lothrop, an old friend and now partner in Walsh, Hall & Co. He and one of the other partners live in the nicest house in the place, with gardens round it and looking out over the harbor, with his little schooner yacht moored within hail of the house. L. insisted on my living with him which you can imagine has been very pleasant.

The weather has been very good since my arrival here, between eighty and eight-five most of the time. I have not as yet bought any things. There are so many, and they are all so lovely, that one gets perfectly dazed strolling through the Japanese town. But before leaving, I must make a foray and capture a few of these pretty things for you and the "brats."

CHARLES APPLETON LONGFELLOW

The other day I made a week's trip back into the country among the mountains to the foot of Fujiyama, the holy [mountain] of Japan. We were four Yanks, one our consul, and we had a mounted guard of two men – more to spy upon us than protect us, I expect, as in all cases where Europeans have been attacked the native guard has "left very sudden." We all kept a revolver in our belts and didn't have the least trouble. The Japanese being, I should say, from what I have seen of them a mighty nice people and very good natured – except an occasional soldier or retainer of some swell Daimio or prince, who when half tight tries his hand at carving a stranger.

We had a charming trip, and the day after I got back, I started off with some other fellow to another place along the coast for a few days and only got back yesterday.

Japan is without any exception the prettiest country I have ever seen. It beats England for greenness, and it is all broken up into hills and plains covered with the most luxuriant verdure. And there are vistas along the Tokaido, under the great trees covered with moss and creepers, as at every turn in every direction. But best of all [was]our view from the teahouse verandah at Enoshima. With the bay in front, with a few junks here and there and the green mountains in the distance, with the barren peak of Fujiyama to cap it all, it was lovely. Earny [Longfellow][11] ought to come out here for six months. He would make sketches enough for the rest of his life. Even a Johnnie the other day allowed that Japan was the England of Asia, the wonderful conceit!!

I think I shall stay here, that is Japan, another month as it is too hot in Shanghai at present.

With lots of love to all
Your loving brother Charley

I send by this mail some views of the Korea taken while the fighting was going on or just over.[12]

CHARLES APPLETON LONGFELLOW

Notes and Comments

[1] Note in Laidlaw, Christine Wallace. *Charles Appleton Longfellow: Twenty Months in Japan, 1871-1873* indicates that the telegram cited and the following letters from Charles to Henry W. Longfellow: December 22, 1871; July 19, 1872; October 23, 1872; and February 10, 1873 are in the Houghton Library, shelf mark bMS Am 1340.2 (3503). Published with the permission of the Houghton Library, Harvard University.

[2] Edie is Edith, Charles' middle of three sisters, eighteen years old at the time. Their mother, Fanny Appleton Longfellow, had died in 1861.

[3] Elisha E. Rice – Earlier trade agent and later American consul at Hakodate. Hakodate is a port in Hokkaido and was among the early ports to open because of fishing and fur interests and also its usefulness as a coal port for steamships.

[4] Samuel Kirkland Lothrop, Jr. The young Lothrop was the son of Boston clergyman, Samuel K. Lothrop, Sr. (1804-1886), family friend of the Longfellows. The younger Lothrop's date of death is unclear. Another son of Samuel K. Lothrop, Sr., Thornton Kirkland Lothrop (1830-1913) was a noted author who in 1899 published a biography of William Henry Seward.

[5] Walsh, Hall & Co. was the most prominent American company in Japan at the time. Thomas Walsh had hosted the Seward party a year before Charley Longfellow's arrival in Yokohama.

[6] Charles O. Shepard was a Civil War veteran and came to Japan as Consul General in 1868. Shepard was the first American diplomat in the Meiji period to be stationed full time in Tokyo.

[7] Johnnies are English, i.e. John Bull.

CHARLES APPLETON LONGFELLOW

[8] The Prince of Tosa was Yamanouchi Yodo. The Tosa domain in Shikoku played an important role at the end of the Tokugawa and beginning of the Meiji periods.

[9] From Laidlaw, *20 Months*, the speculation is that the row was over not paying their bill.

[10] From Laidlaw, *20 Months*, Alice was the oldest of Charley's three sisters, in her early twenties at the time of this letter.

[11] From Laidlaw, *20 Months,* Earny Longfellow was Charles' younger brother. Earny was an accomplished painter.

[12] While Japan was opened and making adjustments to foreign trade and contact, Korea remained closed. In 1871 ships of America's Asia Squadron sailed to Ganghwa Island, off the mouth of Korea's Han River. The Americans were fired on by Korean shore batteries and in the ensuing fighting several hundred Koreans were killed. The American expedition withdrew and Korea remained closed. It was not until 1882 that the United States was able to sign a treaty with Korea.

Charley Goes to Yedo

Charles' Journal

Yedo [Tsukiji] Hotel [is] enormous [and] empty – very bad hotel. No servants to be found. [The] gatekeeper pays 60.00 year for [the] privilege of showing Japanese over it as a curiosity and [a] specimen of the way Europeans live. [A] rum idea they must get of us. They pay 6 cents a head for this glimpse of the outside world.[1]

Drove to Atagoyama (fire god)Teahouses on hill, [you] go up by steps. Then round [the] Mikado's castle, crossing three moats. Some parts [of Yedo are]]like country. [I] never think myself in center of a large city. Daimios' residences [are] surrounded by barracks. Lots of store rooms.

Had stunning dance in evening under [Payton] Jaudon's[2] wing. Four musicians, two dancers. [They] played games with their hands. Three very pretty.

Temple of Ueno [contains the] tombs of Tycoons, endless stone carp stands.[3]

[We went to] Asakusa…

Curious city by night. Colored paper lanterns. Crowds half-naked. Street vendors of toys, sweetmeats, etc. Paddled up [the] Sumidagawa to teahouse. [Charles E.] De Long wouldn't take his shoes off, so [they] wouldn't let us in. Tried another [with] better success. River [was] covered with pleasure parties in covered boats – singing and girls playing on the *samisen* (guitar). Charming way of spending hot evenings.

CHARLES APPLETON LONGFELLOW

Yedo August 3rd, 1871
My dear Alice

There is an extra steamer this month which gives me the chance of writing you sooner than I expected.

A few days after my last letter was written, I came up here with the idea of staying two or three days only, as most of the people I had asked about Yedo said, "Oh, it isn't much. You will have all you want of it in three days and the hotel is very bad." It shows how we mustn't take other people's ideas about a place, as I have had a splendid and most interesting time here and don't know when I shall leave. It is quite different from any city I have ever seen, covering miles and miles. One constantly is thinking that he is in the country, when in reality he is perhaps in the center of the city. There are lots of canals and five moats surrounding the Mikado's palace, the last two of which one is not allowed to cross.

It has been very hot the last week, over ninety most of the time, but still Jaudon (a tip-top New Yorker, now in the Japanese Foreign Office) and I would start out in jinrikisha (large perambulators drawn by a man) and cut about the city. Besides the scenes in the streets which are always curious and interesting, there are a great many magnificent temples to visit and tea gardens where the "young Japan" delight to spend the day lazing off on cool straw mats in loose dressing gowns, smoking, singing, reading aloud to each other, and listening to the singing girls they often bring with them. Our evenings have been spent drifting about on the river, which is most refreshing after the heat of the day and is most amusing – as the water is covered with hundreds of boats, each one lit by a large round paper lantern and filled with pleasure seekers. I must say the Japanese know how to enjoy themselves most rationally. But I must describe one of these evenings which is a fair specimen for nearly all, that is for me – as with this child's usual luck I have seen more of Yedo and Yedo's pleasant side than some fellows who have been out here several years.

CHARLES APPLETON LONGFELLOW

Through a friend of mine, I have got acquainted with some swell Japanese merchants, officers of Tosa – one of the most powerful princes in this "section." Unfortunately they don't speak a word of English, but with the two or three Japanese words I know, by signs, and occasionally the help of Lepper[4] who speaks very well, we get on capitally. The second or third evening I was here, Iwasaki [Yataro][5] asked us to go up the river with him in his boat. So after dinner we took our "jinrikishas" and drove to his house through a maze of streets lit up with paper lanterns of the brightest colors, and filled with stalls selling sweetmeats, toys, fruits, flowers, etc., and crowded with people – men, women and children – who had come out to walk in the comparatively cool evening air and who were too poor to own or hire a boat to lie on the river in. Under every bridge, there would be a laughing and splashing and bobbing of black heads of fellows swimming in the canals.

After a mile and a half of this, we came to Iwasaki's, our host's house, and found him already in his boat directly on the other side of the street. There were three or four of his friends with him, and we just made a nice party. Of course, before getting into the boat, we pulled our shoes off so as not to dirty the beautiful mats with which the center of the boat was spread, under a roof. These boats are capital for this sort of work, long, flat bottomed, of unpainted pine, and spotlessly bright and clean. The two sailors in the stern soon were sculling us rapidly down the canals to the river.

At every turn, we would meet other parties like ourselves bound for the more open water of the river, which we emerged on in about twenty minutes. It is about a quarter of a mile broad, and as we glided along among the other boats to the bright moon light, with the cool evening breeze refreshing us, the shores lit up from the rows of the lanterns hung out from the teahouses, the sound of many "samisens," and snatches of song and laughter that came floating over the water from the hundreds of boats gliding about looking like fire flies with their paper lanterns…was charming – and I thought of the remarks of my acquaintances in Yokohama, that Yedo didn't amount to much. I don't know what *they* want but I know such evenings are only too short for me.

As we got higher up the river, the boats got thicker and many would be lashed together, friends evidently taking this pleasant way of seeing each other with their families.

We landed at one of the teahouses near the second bridge and were ushered upstairs to a large corner room overlooking the river and the animated scene upon it. Here our friends took off their swords and clothes and put on loose dressing gowns to be more at their ease, while the teahouse girls place in front of each of us beautifully lacquered trays filled with sweetmeats, cakes and a lot of queer things, which I couldn't make out – but several kinds of fish were apparent and strips of cold whale – and everything served in the neatest and most appetizing way. We each of us squatted on the mats, each one behind his own collection of little trays.

And then was heard a great tittering and laughing, and in trotted twenty-five singing girls, their bright eyes sparkling and white teeth shining as they came forward, knelt down, and bent down until their foreheads touched the ground. They knelt in front of us while we ate, helping us in the most graceful way, and going into fits at my bungling way of handling the chopsticks. But one took my education in charge, and soon got the hang of it and [ate] my raw whale like a man. Then a girl would present you with a tiny tea cup and fill it with sake, a very mild spirit made from rice and drunk warm. After which if you like the girl and want to be gallant, you dip your cup in a bowl of cold water to clean it and hand it back to her. When she touches it to her forehead with a low bow, you fill it for her, and she drinks. This is the correct thing, and we did it at intervals throughout the evening.

While we were thus engaged, some eight or ten of the girls ranged themselves in a row at the other side of the room, tuned their samisens and soon began to play and sing –- the rest joining in the chorus – while two of the smallest began to dance. This dance is impossible to describe, a series of movements of arms, body and feet twisting about, singing and clapping of hands. It would be very ugly badly done, but the grace of every movement of these girls is such that it is fascinating – though it has none of the voluptuous movement of the Indian dancing. One is on the point of exclaiming all the time, "You little cunning!" And they are, as all their ways are charming, and as for manners they take the shine out of us Westerners completely. And so we spent the evening, listening to the songs, watching the dancing, and enjoying the cool breeze as we reclined on the straw mats.

The next evening we passed in the same way, only going three or four miles higher up the river and, having besides the dancing, some actors and jugglers and a dinner served European fashion – sent from the hotel for the benefit of Mr. De Long, our minister to Japan, who can't eat Japanese chow-chow. The girls were very curious to taste our food, and they would put little bits of bread in their pockets to take home to their mothers as great curiosities – as most of these girls had never seen Westerners before, except perhaps at a distance.

Their fellows try to make them think we are brutes and that, if we spoon them, it is to get a chance to suck their blood, which is supposed to be our ruling passion. But our girl friends told us they didn't think we were so bad after all. And some of them we met out at a teahouse in the country yesterday showed such a fondness for our society that their "fellows" took them off to another part of the house where they were out of talking distance. Our guards seemed to think we should get into a row and tried to get us away, but nothing happened. Perhaps a large revolver laid on the floor had something to do with it. If they had gone for us, I shouldn't have blamed them, as in no country is it pleasant to have your girl chaffing [jesting] with strangers.

Mr. De Long asked me the other day if I would go with him to Hakodate by sea, into the interior of Yesso[6], and then cross over to the northern shore of Nippon[7] and march across country to Yedo. No Westerner has ever done this, and you can bet I said yes. There are hundreds of fellows who would give all their old boots to do this, but

CHARLES APPLETON LONGFELLOW

my luck had got me into it without asking. I got another invitation this afternoon from some fellows to join them on another, but shorter, trip to the interior – also a part as yet unvisited by Europeans. I shall go with them, too, if it doesn't interfere with De Long's trip. He is a rough and ready Colorado man[8] who would shine more in the field than the cabinet, but seems a very good fellow. I am going down to Yokohama in a day or two to see if he really wants me, and if so, when we are to start. So you can see, my dear Alice it begins to look as if I should spend a month or two in Japan more than I expected.

It seems half like Nahant as I sit at the open window and look out over Yedo bay lit up by the moon. I hope you are all having a first rate time and that the *Alice* has been doing herself proud.[9]

> Direct my letters care of Russell & Co., Shanghai
> With lots of love to all the family
> Your affectionate Charley

CHARLES APPLETON LONGFELLOW

*Longfellow House-Washington's Headquarters National Historic Site
Cambridge, Massachusetts*

CHARLES APPLETON LONGFELLOW

Nahant Aug 9, 1871
My Dear Charlie,

We have been delighted to receive your letters from the Pacific Steamer and are now looking for tidings from Japan, to tell us that you are well, and well-satisfied with your journey so far. Miss Dora Clark tells us that Arthur [Clark][10] thinks of coming home soon, on a visit. I hope he will not have left China before you reach there. It would be pleasant for you to come home together.

I am a little anxious about your money-matters. Your balance in Bank, Aug 1. was $1916.37 which Mr. [Ebenezer] Snow has remitted to Baring Bros. You will have to limit your expenses as much as possible.

We have had thus far rather cool and uncertain weather at Nahant this Summer. Uncle Tom [Appleton] has been as far as Portland in the *Alice*, towing the *Wyvern* down for Wad. [Longfellow][11], who is beside himself with joy...

I have forwarded your papers regularly, also two letters from W[illiam] Fay, who is laid up with a lame knee. He is consoled by having a son and heir born at Lynnmere.

Good bye and God bless you.

Always affectionately,
H.W. L.[ongfellow]

Charles' Journal

Aug 10th

Spent evening in Japanese theatre. [the seating area is divided into] little pens 4 ft. sq. Lights on poles held in front of actors, part of [the] stage running through [the] pit. Girl killing. Ronins. Daimios, Yohama san in box[?]. Shifted scenes by [a] turn table, whole stage [was] one. [The] audience [was] half naked. [The play] lasted from

CHARLES APPLETON LONGFELLOW

noon to 11 P.M. Had a spread and geishas at teahouse opposite afterwards. Whole [evening cost] 15 ryos.[12]

Sunday Aug 13

Drove from Yokohama to Yedo with Mr. De Long, our minister. I acting as secretary.

Yedo August 14th, 1871
My dear Alice,

The last letter I wrote you, and which should have been on its way to the States now, by some mistake did not arrive in Yokohama in time to catch the intermediate steamer. So that this one will come at the same time.

One day about a week ago – just as I was starting for another short trip to the mountains – I received a note from Mr. De Long, our Minister to Japan, saying he wanted to see me. So I rode up to his house, and almost the first thing he said was would you like to see the Mikado. Of course I said yes, and he appointed me acting secretary of the Hawaiian mission – of which he is the head – to form a treaty of amity and commerce between Hawaii and Japan. So that if this is badly written, you must excuse it on account of my new nationality. Mr. De Long's suite besides myself was composed of three of the officers of the *Idaho*.

We came up here day before yesterday, so as to be ready to leave the hotel at noon of the next day for the Mikado's castle. In the morning [August 14th], De Long and I arrayed ourselves in full dress – swallow tails, white chokers and even stove pipe hats. At quarter past twelve, we got started amidst the admiring gaze of the natives. First came nine mounted yakunins then the carriage of the staff officers with a native swell in charge of them, then this child and Mr. De Long in his carriage, and the rear brought up by ten more yakunins. It is about two miles from the hotel to the Castle, and at every hundred yards or so, at every bridge or street corner along the line of march, was a guard who presented arms as we passed – but evidently took the Navy officers in their bright uniforms to be the minister and suite, and De Long and myself in our black coats as undersecretaries or something of that sort. Along the Tokaido the crowd was kept back by ropes stretched across the side streets. After half an hour of this, slowly working through street after street and across two of the moats that surround the castle, we arrived at a third bridge where our yakunins dismounted. The only foreigners ever allowed to cross beyond here are ministers and their suites. We drove over the bridge through two massive gates and alighted to walk over the last bridge of all – no one ever being allowed to cross it except on foot – through another massive gate, and we were in the Mikado's castle.

We crossed a nicely pebbled courtyard, the guard presenting and bugles blowing, and at the gate of a large pavilion were met by the court interpreter. A few steps further on, we met Terashima [Tozo], vice minister of foreign affairs, and at the head of the steps leading to the pavilion, Sawa [Nobuyoshi] appeared.[13] After shaking hands all round, we were ushered into a large perfectly plain room, with a long table running down the length of it covered with a gay silk table cloth. We were soon seated on silken ottomans, the Japanese on one side and we on the other, according to rank – and while Mr. De Long and the ministers talked about the recent changes in the government, we were helped to tea by gorgeously attired servants who glided about silently and with low bows and trembling hands served us. One fellow outdid himself and trembled all the tea out of my cup over the fine table cloth. Each one also had in front of him a large box of candy and sponge cake[14] of native make and lacquered trays with pipes and tobacco.

It was interesting to watch Terashima's wily face during this interview. He is of low degree, a doctor by education (one of the lowest positions in Japan), but often when all the other ministers are at fault and said their say, he comes quietly out of his corner and by his cleverness unravels the knot.

After a few minutes conversation [through the interpreter (though Terashima understands and speaks English quite well, but was thereby gaining time to think)][15] and very little information gained, the council of state came into the room headed by Iwakura [Totomi], the real Emperor of Japan, and whose word is law.[16] He had a bad face, hooked nose and deep-set wicked looking eyes. They were presented one by one to Mr. DeLong, who had a word for all, and then to us, who hadn't a word for any. A few minutes talk standing up and they retired.

But I have not yet described the court dress. They wear on their heads tied under the chin by a white cord, a queer little black silk skull cap with a high knob at the back, from which a strip of figured crepe hangs like a plume. Their hair is drawn up under this. They wear a sort of undergarment of white, over which is a loose sleeved tunic of embroidered gauze silk or crepe, all black, and enormous silk trousers of different quiet colors embroidered with flowers. These look more like petticoats than trousers, though they now come no lower than the ankles – the old fashioned way of having them trail out behind, so as to give a man the appearance of walking on his knees, having been done away with I was told.

And now a faint wailing sound comes floating through the air like an Aeolian harp growing stronger and stronger. This music is made by a reed band in the vestibule and announces to us barbarians that the Mikado is ascending his throne. A few moments later, and we are conducted along a corridor upon which open three large rooms thrown into one – polished wood floor and framework with vents, and tinted walls – and that is the audience chamber. At the end of the central room is a sort of rose-colored satin tent or bonbon box, in the centre of which is seated a young man of twenty, with an oval and not particularly brilliant face, a queer sort of conical cap strapped on his head, and arrayed in heavy silken robes – red and straw colored, if I remember rightly. This was the Mikado, who a few years ago was not visible to human eyes, except those of a few priests – his own princes being only allowed to know that he was on one side of a screen while they stood on the other.

We stepped a few paces into the room. Mr. De Long made his bow and recited a very short and appropriate speech, while I held the letter from the king of Hawaii [Kamehamea V] and handed it to him at the proper moment. He then advanced and gave the letter into the Mikado's own hand, who rose to receive it, and in turn handed his prime minister, who stood at the side of the tent, a large document which he read aloud in a subdued voice and was then handed to Mr. De Long and C.A.L. Mr. De Long then introduced us one by one to the Mikado, while the two rows of councillors and courtiers on either side of us stood like statues. I could hardly keep from laughing out at being introduced as Hawaiian secretary. After this, we all backed out of the room and retired to our sweetmeats and pipes again for a short time. As we moved away the wailing music announced that the audience was over. After a little more talk, we retired as we came, bugles, salutes, guards, etc.

All the officials shake hands with Europeans, except the Mikado. The audience chamber in which we were received is kept on purpose for European audiences, we not having entered the real palace which is sacred. But there is more work to be done before the treaty is ratified. Next day the treaties had to be written out with the amendments, four copies being needed. So at midnight, Mr. De Long and I drove down to Yokohama, spent a day, and then went back in style [on August 18] in the *Cathrine*, Lothrop's yacht – flying the American flag at the fore, having the minister on board. We had a glorious run up with single reefs in, doing the twenty-two odd miles in two hours and twenty-four minutes. The next afternoon at four, we drove to one of the Mikado's gardens called Hama-go-ten[17] where in a large pavilion we met the Japanese ministers, and the treaty was formally ratified and sealed. These swells have a clerk to sign their names, they only affixing their seals.

CHARLES APPLETON LONGFELLOW

After these formalities, we had a state dinner in the European fashion. On sitting down, each of us found a tray in front of him, on which was two kinds of dried fish with sugar in little saucers, a preparation of rice, chopsticks and a jar of sweet *sake*. These had been sent from the Mikado's own table, it being his first course. This is considered a great mark of attention. After drinking the Mikado's health in sake, all standing, we went on with the dinner which was quite good. Some of the officials were almost as awkward with their knives and forks as we should be with chopsticks, but they seemed to like our food very much. With the champagne, Sawa (Minister of Foreign Affairs) rose and proposed the health of the king of Hawaii, which we all drank. It was a very pleasant dinner, Sawa being a jolly old bird who enjoys fun more than business and like most Japanese is a great story teller. De Long is very good at that, too. So after dinner they got at it, and we had a very good time until our carriage came. They even let us look at their swords and draw them, a thing seldom done.

We have been flying the Hawaiian flag since we have been here, and tomorrow there is to be a royal salute fired in honor of the treaty. The day after our dinner, we had a very pleasant sail back to Yokohama in the *Catherine*.

Since I have seen so much of the official life out here, I see what very uphill work it is for one of our ministers to hold his own with those of other nations – the English for instance, who have the greatest influence here without doubt, though the U.S. has twice the trade and derives [space left blank] million dollars revenue a year from its trade with Japan. The English minister is a trained diplomat in the first place. Then he never moves without his mounted escort. He has several companies of soldiers at his disposal and, above all, he has had a dozen of his countrymen trained and acting as interpreters. So he is sure that what he says or hears is correctly translated, while our minister never knows that his ideas have been properly conveyed to the authorities – the native interpreters not daring often to translate literally and fully what our ministers tell them – so that in this respect, the English and other nations have an immense advantage over us. Besides an interpreter has hundreds of opportunities of telling and hearing things unofficially, which would help to guide the ministers in their policy and give them an idea of the animus of the Japanese on various subjects.

And even this matter of keeping up some style with guards, etc., counts immensely in these Asiatic countries. How can they compare the ministers of two countries, one with his uniform, fine turnout and guards, the other coming to the capital of Japan in a seedy hack or a broken down steamboat – with coolies bumping against him, not knowing who he is. I think it is a great shame. We may have and do have some very clever men, but they must be immensely superior to the others to have a chance against all these obstacles. It places the U.S. in a false position, and Orientals cannot understand that a country which lets its officials go about like any cobbler and trusts its business to the interpretation of foreign interpreters, can amount to much or be very powerful. It hurts our pride to see it and has riled me a good many times out here and elsewhere. Mr. De Long, I believe to be an able man and an honest man and interested in his work, but he has got "a mighty hard row to hoe" to keep square with the Johnnies.

We leave here on the 1st of September for Hakodate and shall be gone over a month, as I wrote you in my last.

I get a good deal of yachting out here and have licked every boat in Yokohama, big and little, in the *Catherine*. Lothrop lets me have her whenever I want, if he is too busy to go. There was a schooner here about two months ago which was warranted to run round the *Catherine*, but somehow the boot got onto the other leg.

I am in hopes of lots of letters by the *America*, who will be in in a few days from the States, and to hear that you have had a jolly old time in the *Alice* this summer.

How does Wad get on with the *Wyvern*? All right, I hope. And by this time I have no doubt he can handle her like "one o'clock."

I send you a group of Japanese taken by a native artist.

CHARLES APPLETON LONGFELLOW

With lots of love to all from the child that thinks of you all very often.

Charley

Notes and Comments

---

[1] The hotel described was in Tsukiji which had only recently caught on as an area in Tokyo where foreigners lived and worked. Most non-Japanese including Europeans, Americans and Chinese had settled in Yokohama. Within a few years, Tsukiji became a bustling community but in 1871 it was still rustic.

[2] Peyton Joudon. From Louisiana, Joudon came to Japan in 1868 and in 1871 joined the Ministry of Foreign Affairs as a language teacher and assistant. He remained in Japan until his death in 1896. At the time of Charley's visit, the foreign community in Tokyo was much smaller than in Yokohama and consisted of many who were employed by the Meiji government.

[3] From Laidlaw. *20 Months*. This is Toshogu Shrine built to honor Tokugawa Ieyasu, founder of the Tokugawa government. Other Tycoons are also buried there.

[4] Thomas Lepper was an employee of Walsh, Hall & Co.

[5] Iwasaki Yataro (1835-85) was president of a Japanese shipping company. In 1873, two years after first meeting Charles Longfellow, Iwasaki changed the name of his shipping company to Mitsubishi and in the next decades became famous as one of the Meiji era's most successful business leaders.

[6] Yesso is Hokkaido. Travel outside the treaty concession zones could only be made with the permission or in the company of the treaty country's diplomatic mission. The primary purpose of De Long's visit to Yesso was to look into "alleged irregularities" with Consul Rice's management of the Hakodate Consulate. (see *Japan Weekly Mail*, September 9, 1871) Rice, whom he describes as " a fine double-faced sinner," was Charley's fellow passenger on the *Japan* on the trip out from San Francisco.

CHARLES APPLETON LONGFELLOW

[7] Nippon in this case refers to the largest Japanese island, Honshu.

[8] De Long was born in New York but had relocated to California and spent time in Nevada. For an excellent, overall account of De Long's background and his time in Japan, see, Hammersmith's *Spoilsmen in a Flowery Fairyland*.

[9] From Laidlaw, *20 Months*. The *Alice* was a sloop Thomas Gold Appleton had built for himself and Charles. She was named after Alice Longfellow.

[10] From Laidlaw, *20 Months*. Arthur Clark is a sea captain and his daughter is Eudora (Dora).

[11] From Laidlaw, *20 Months*. Wad is cousin Alexander Wadsworth Longfellow, Jr., who was sailing Charly's boat, *Wyren*, while Charlie was gone.

[12] From Laidlaw, *20 Months*. One *ryo* was worth about a dollar in 1871 currency.

[13] Terashima Munenori (also called Tozo, a childhood nickname) was an important figure in the Meiji government. Ten years earlier he had studied briefly in London. He became foreign minister in 1873. Sawa Nobuyoshi had become head of the foreign ministry in 1869.

[14] Lauren Malcom (1943-2015), who spent years living and teaching in Japan and was long associated with Longfellow House and an expert on Charles Longfellow, suggests the sponge cake is castella, rendered in Japanese as *kasutera*, introduced by the Portuguese and a still popular confection.

[15] From Laidlaw, *20 Months*. This is Charley's insertion supposing that the time for interpretation provides an opportunity to consider one's response.

[16] Iwakura Totomi, Powerful Meiji leader. Led a mission of senior Japanese officials to the United States and Europe in 1872-3, a major watershed event in Japan's engagement with the wider world.

[17] See note in Chapter II for Seward.

CHARLES APPLETON LONGFELLOW

Editor's Note: *Charles Longfellow next begins a trip to Hakodate on the coastal steamer* Ariel. *He then spends time in Hokkaido before returning from Hakodate to Yedo overland. His journals give a rich description of the Ainu people on Japan's most northern main island. His detailed account of the return trip, mailed to his family in Cambridge, is a vivid picture of a rural and small-town Japan that had been explored by very few Westerners. In the concluding section, dated Saturday November 4 with an addendum on November 22, he says he is considering settling in Japan for the winter and is in negotiations for "a nice little Japanese house."*

Back From the North Country

Yokohama Dec. 22nd 1871
Mr dear Edie

You don't know how delighted [I am] to see you adopting such good resolutions and writing me each steamer. I only wish Annie would do too, but when you all write at once it must puzzle you to discourse on different subjects.

Since my last note I have been to see the Mikado again.[1] And have been offered the berth of American and Hawaiian Consul at Yedo, but my hatred of being tied down even in idea keeps me from accepting them.[2] I feel the compliment however.

The steamer takes over to the States about fifty swell Japanese among them some of the most distinguished men in Japan, Iwakura being the real king almost. They are going to travel and study in the States and Europe and have a few young ladies with them, who are going to school in the Great Republic.[3] I offered to take charge of two of these princesses and take them to Cambridge, but their guardians didn't seem to see it.

CHARLES APPLETON LONGFELLOW

Mr. De Long is going over for a few months by the same steamer, and I hope he will get to Cambridge as I should like to have you see him. It is owing mainly to him that I have seen so much and had such a good time out here. He is rough and unpolished, but clever, clear headed and, I believe, thoroughly an honest man. I should like to have him know Mr. [Senator Charles] Sumner, as he is a strong Republican, and they might arrange things better out here a little.[4]

I have been trying to get a Japanese house in Yedo and think of spending the next five months out here. I can't leave the nice old place, and in a year or two it will be all spoilt. They are beginning to imitate Europeans in dress and manners and remind one of monkeys. There are three small Japanese restaurants run on European principles in Yedo now, a dozen barber shops with striped poles, a few boot blacks, etc. All these are innovations since my arrival in the country. And three nights ago, we were astonished while coming home from a teahouse to find all the gates dividing the different precincts wide open and the guard quietly housed. This is a great improvement, it being a nuisance to have a guard stop you and poke his paper lantern in your face.

In future please send my letters to Walsh, Hall & Co., Yokohama – as at present my letters all go to Shanghai and come back making them three months old when I get them.

[Gustavus] Farley[5] has offered to take home a small box of nick-nacks for you all. It contains 1 pr. bronze sleeve buttons for the Gov[ernor]. And the other things you had better raffle for among you, letting Hattie [Longfellow], Cora and Erny have a hand in it. This is a miserable letter, but the natural reaction after the last.

Good bye and God bless you all
Charley

It was only 3 days ago that I got your letters written Oct 19th.

CHARLES APPLETON LONGFELLOW

Mrs. De Long, and five Japanese girls pose for a group portrait. The Japanese government sent these five girls from samurai families to be educated in the United States. The young girl in the center is probably Tsuda Ume who was sent to live with Henry Longfellow's friends the Lanhams in Georgetown, D.C. After her return to Japan she established Tsuda Daigaku, a top ranking college for women in the Tokyo area.

Photo courtesy of the National Park Service
Longfellow House-Washington's Headquarters National Historic Site
Cambridge, Massachusetts

CHARLES APPLETON LONGFELLOW

Yokohama Dec. 22nd
My dear father,

    I take great pleasure in introducing you to Mr. C.E. De Long, American Minister to Japan, and of whom I have so often written you. He is home for a few months and thinks of visiting Boston. If he does, I know you will try [to] make his stay pleasant, if only on account of the kindnesses he has shown me out here.
    Give Mr. De Long a letter to Mr. Sumner. I know he would be pleased.

Yours most affectionately,
Charley Longfellow

Henry Wadsworth Longfellow on the right with close friend, Senator Charles Sumner

*Photo courtesy of National Park Service
Longfellow House-Washington's Headquarters National Historic Site
Cambridge, Massachusetts*

CHARLES APPLETON LONGFELLOW

Cambridge Jan 19, 1872
My Dear Charlie,

It must have been a great annoyance to you to have all your letters and papers go by you to Shanghai, without the power to stop them at Yokohama. But I trust you have had them sent back to you. Otherwise there will be such an accumulation of them as to make them more of a burden than a pleasure.

We see the arrival of Mr. De Long at San Francisco, but the Steamer's letters have not yet reached us. We always have to write a day or two before we get yours, which is a great pity. Pray let us know if any of ours have reached you.

I enclose an account of the remittances made to Baring Bros. so that you may know how you stand. They have not sent me as yet the year's accounts. So much for business matters.

We are all delighted with your Journal of your journey through the interior of Nippon. It was read aloud at the Library, with Mr. [George Washington] Greene among the audience. He takes a great interest in your travels, being himself of a roving disposition. Mr. Augustus Gilman…was here a day or two ago, and confirms all you say about the beauty of Japan.

I had a visit also, not long ago from Anamori Mori [6], the Japanese Ambassador, and we have in the Law School a very nice youth from Chiguko [Province], Japan by the name of Eneas Yamada. So we are pretty well informed about matters in that remote region…

All send much love.

         Ever affectionately
         H.W.L.

CHARLES APPLETON LONGFELLOW

Osaka Jan 22nd, 1872
My dear Edie,

You may think that I am on my way to China, now that I ha[ve] left Yedo. But I have only come here on a visit while my house is being finished and shall go back in a month and not go to China at all. That is [I] shall probably come home first and take a fresh start.

You have no idea what fun I have been having in Yedo during Christmas and New Year's weeks. The Japanese happened to be having a grand festival at the same time. And in fact with Japanese parties, processions, dinners and pleasant fellows and planning for my new house, over which I am much excited, the time has passed very nicely.

I came down here a few days ago on the *Nautilus*, an old steamer that used to run from Boston to New York. We had such bad weather that we had to put up in Omaezaki for 24 hours, and of course all went ashore, as no Japanese stays a minute longer on a vessel than he can help.

It is beastly cold here, one feeling it much more than at home as fire places are rare and paper windows airy. There is skating over at Kobe where Mr. [Arthur O.] Gay is, some twenty miles from here.

By the way, why do you all insist on sending my letters to Shanghai, when I wrote home 3 or 4 months ago that I was going to stop here and that Walsh, Hall & Co. were my agents in Yokohama? I expect to stay here a few weeks and be back in Yedo by the time my shebang is ready.

I am pegging away at Japanese as hard as I can, but it is very difficult as you can imagine when there are over ten different ways of counting to be used only in their proper places and for every European word they have half a dozen.

I feel awfully stupid tonight and am ashamed to send you such a miserable return for your nice letters, but I write more to tell you that I am always thinking of you all at home, though fascinated with this country.

CHARLES APPLETON LONGFELLOW

We had a New Year's Eve dinner in Yedo with some nice fellows, and as the clock struck twelve drank to "absent friends" – which in fact we always do out here, it being the only toast we drink. You can imagine where my thoughts flew, my dear Edie.

I miss Mr. De Long very much and hope you have seen him, as he was a great friend of mine out here. I hope he will turn up soon again. Send me any accounts of the Japanese mission you may see in the papers.

With lots and lots of love to the dear Governor and all of you.

Your loving Charley

Editor's Note: *In addition to Osaka, on his trip outside Yedo, Charles also visited Kobe and Nagasaki. Returning from Nagasaki, he spent time in Osaka, Kyoto, and sailed for a week with British friends on Lake Biwa.*

Kioto June 17th 1872
My dear Edie,

I have been here in this lovely place ever since [I] last wrote. [I] have been meaning to go every day, but some new thing of interest would turn up, and so on I have stayed. I am very sorry to have to write you such a short and hurried note, but I have only just discovered in this out of the way place, that by sending a special messenger at once over the fifty miles between this and Kobe, he will just catch the steamer which connects with the mail at Yokohama.

I got back two hours ago from a week's cruise on Lake Biwa (7 miles off) in a Japanese boat with two very nice English fellows, Glover and Gower. We enjoyed it very much, going which ever way the wind

CHARLES APPLETON LONGFELLOW

took us and putting up at night in nice Japanese teahouses, often in very pretty places. The lake is some 45 or 50 miles long by 15 or 20 broad surrounded by mountains with several islands in it. And one great beauty was that foreigners were almost unknown to the inhabitants of the towns around its borders.

We of course dined on Japanese chow, which now I can manage like a native, and all together enjoyed it very much.

There are rumors here that a war between England and America will very likely break out within a few days.[7] I hope not, it would be a very stupid thing.

It seems funny that in a few days I shall have been out here a year. How the time has flown, and interestingly. Why does not Erny come out here?

My plans are about as fixed as usual. That is I don't know whether I am coming home in three months or six. But inside of a year, you can be pretty sure – as I want to see you all very much and often think how pleasant it will be – as it always is half the fun of traveling the getting back and telling you all about it.

With lots and lots, and lots of love to you all
Your affectionate
Charley

CHARLES APPLETON LONGFELLOW

Yedo July 19th 1872
My dear Father,

    I hardly ever write you, because in writing to any of the girls, it is the same as writing to all of you – the only difference being the address on the envelope.

    I wrote some months ago about a new letter of credit, but have not as yet heard anything from Baring Bros.

    I wish sometime when you are in Boston, you would see their agent and arrange to have a new letter for two thousand pounds sent me as soon as possible. This seems large to you, no doubt, and I probably shall not use half of it (or even a quarter) before coming home. But still there is no harm in being on the safe side. And another thing is that in the present state of the country and with the chances I occasionally have with the people I know here, I might do a little business. But that is only a possibility, as I am very skittish about business transactions without the profit nearly a dead sure thing.

    Please arrange this matter for me and get them to send me the new letter as soon as possible. I suppose you will have to sell some stock to meet the old account, but I will fix that all right when I get home.

    I imagine you will get this letter while still at Nahant. I should like awfully to drop down there for a few weeks, notwithstanding it is so charming here in my little house, the thermometer at 85 – but I like that temperature now – and the south wind off the bay of Yedo rustling the leaves of the trees in my funny little Japanese garden.

    We are expecting De Long soon, when I hope I shall have another chance to tour in the interior. I am now trying to go with one of the English legation. The trip is from here to Hakodate and up among the Ainus, then by vessel down the west coast of Japan to Sado and some other places of interest, and then back to Yedo overland. It is a capital trip, and I only hope I can get leave.

CHARLES APPLETON LONGFELLOW

I hear by the last mail from Osaka that Kioto has been again closed to foreigners. I always thought the Kioto government not over intelligent, and now I feel sure of it.

Hoping you are all very well and happy

Ever your loving son
Charley

P.S. Please don't forget the money.

Nahant July 23, 1872
My Dear Charley,

At Nahant things are going on as usual at Nahant, though I fear you would find it rather dull. Yesterday came your letter to Edie, and enlivened us a little…the Clarks have been here and told us about Arthur, with all the particulars of his shipwreck.[8] You must have had a pleasant meeting in the Yedo Club-room [9], and a pleasant tour together…

Next Friday the Boston Board of Trade give a Banquet to the Japanese Ambassadors, on their way to England.[10] I think I shall not go, though invited. It is too hot.

On the 12th of the month Mr. Snow deposited to your credit $2,500 so that you will be pretty well in funds.

Did the box of arms sent by [blank] arrive safe and in season?

All send much love.

Affectionately Yours
H.W.L.

CHARLES APPLETON LONGFELLOW

Yokohama Oct. 23rd 1872
My dear Father,

Ned Haven and I have just returned from a short cruise down the eastern coast of Japan in Lothrop's yacht, and as usual, I am sorry to say, have put off writing you until the last moment in hopes there would be more things of interest to tell you of. Not that there is any lack of them here, but where to begin is what troubles me. I find the longer one goes without writing, the harder it is. And I am constantly ashamed of myself for not writing home oftener, but what can I do. I am off in the interior or in Yedo, which is nearly the same thing – only not quite as civilized.

Notwithstanding all the rubbish you see in the newspaper about the progress of Japan, it is only on the outside. They seem to think that European clothes and beer-drinking is going to make men of them, but so far it has had rather the contrary effect – their conceit increasing (if possible). And that [is], of course with an exception at very, very long intervals, the only effect. If you only knew the utter despot that the smallest government official, from a policeman up, is, and the powers they have for arresting and torturing the unofficial class without one earthly reason, except perhaps their personal spite – and without the latter having any means of obtaining redress, there being no such a thing as a court of justice in the country – you would smile at the wonderful accounts of Japan you have seen from time to time. And the strange thing is, that the very men who have lived several years in foreign countries are amongst the worst when they return to their own lovely Japan – for it is a lovely country, without a doubt.

The latest event of interest here was the opening of the railroad from Yokohama to Yedo – a horsecar'y affair of twenty miles in length, single track, across a flat country, only one cutting and two small bridges to be made. And [it] has only taken two years to build, the distance being twenty-two miles, and costing enough to have built nearly one hundred miles of railroad in the U.S. It was built for them by some Englishmen, but the Japanese think it very fine.

And it was opened officially with great pomp by the Mikado in person a few days ago.[October 14, 1872][11] Haven and I went in De Long's suite and saw the thing capitally. It was very interesting to see the courtiers all turn out in their old court costumes (by order), and they looked very well and at home in them – instead of like a lot of hand-organ monkeys as they do in their everyday European clothes.

My remarks in this letter are confined to the present government officials. Nearly entirely the followers of the old Tycoon, of Tokugawa people, were gentlemen by birth and education, while among the present officials, there are more than half almost [who] have been picked up from the gutters and placed in high positions for having done some dirty piece of business with a rascal's cleverness for the present government. I don't speak of lying, because, though these fellows are adepts at it, all the Japanese are pretty good hands at it. And one can never believe more than half [of] what they say, if even that, but you soon get used to that.

I send you the newspaper accounts of the opening of the railroad and also a lot of photographically illustrated newspapers which are not bad at all.

I am waiting anxiously for my new letter of credit which I wrote you about, and when it comes shall think of my return trip.

I should like to write you some more, but we have been beating up the coast all day against a strong northeast breeze, and my eyes are full of salt.

Please write soon. I got no letters by the last mail, only papers – but am looking forward to the next, due day after tomorrow with great hope of a large batch.

With lots and lots of love to all the dear ones at home,

Your loving Charley

CHARLES APPLETON LONGFELLOW

Yedo Feb. 10th 1873
My dear Father

The mail is just in from San Francisco, but I have not yet received my letters. But they are probably waiting for me in Yokohama where I shall go tomorrow, as I have made up my mind to tear myself away from Japan. It has been a hard struggle, as the longer I stay and [the] more I know of the language, manners and customs, the better I like it. I sail on the twelfth for Shanghai and, after a week there, for Hong Kong, and expect to be in Cambridge by the end of June in time to go with you all to Nahant.

Walsh, Hall & Co. have taken over my house, which I found some difficulty in getting rid of at first – as among about a dozen people who were very anxious to get it when I had no idea of selling, when I wanted to part with it and it came to the point, they all backed out.

I think you will be rather astonished when my curios arrive, there being now in Walsh, Hall's godowns [warehouses] eighteen large cases waiting for shipment by sailing vessel to New York, enough to fill two or three large express wagons. Where we shall stow them when they all arrive, I can't imagine. And such lots of rubbish among [them] too, but I am fond of them as being thoroughly Japanese.

I am awfully sorry to hear that Nate has got into such a scrape with his banking. The failure of Bowles Bros. has hurt American interests a good deal out here as, of course, the English papers seize the occasion to warn the Japanese against investing their money in these firms of "American adventurers" and point out the advantages of the Oriental Bank – which at the present rate will soon have (virtual) control of Japan, the government having just borrowed of them an enormous sum and giving for security the whole internal revenue of Japan.

There is a friend of mine in Yokohama named Charles O. Shepard who has lived in Japan now nearly four years, as American consul in Yedo and Yokohama, and was a Col. Of Volunteers during

CHARLES APPLETON LONGFELLOW

our [Civil] War. He is from N.Y. State, Albany I think. He has written two lectures on Japan. And as he proposes returning to America next October for six or eight months, he thinks he would like to deliver these lectures in two or three of the principal cities of the Union…and in that way help pay his expenses while travelling about. And he would like to deliver these lectures in Boston, if the people there took enough interest in the subject, but he does not know who to communicate with. So I said I would write to you for advice…

I don't know how good a lecturer he would make, but a good straight-forward one I should think, as he has plenty of practice in addressing public assemblies in his political career. And his position out here [as] Consul for four years, [and] as Charge d'Affaires during Mr. De Long's absence, {has} given him opportunities of seeing the interior of the country and also of getting an insight into the Government, which a person not holding an official position can not easily get.

His lectures would have one good effect at least, that of giving the people some idea of the state of things out here, which the letters I see published from here do not - most of them being entirely false or written by men who only see skin deep…So much for Mr. Shepard…

I have not yet quite decided whether to visit the Vienna exhibition or not, as I am going to try travel on a strictly economical basis, as I see I have been spending a great deal too much. But there is one comfort. Whatever happens I have always the pleasant reminiscences of my stay in Japan to fall back on.

Please tell the girls I have got them some of those "nice warm Japanese dressing gowns." I think they are anything but nice, but one can never tell what girls will like….

Hoping you are all as well and happy as I am

Your very affectionately
Charley

I enclose two photos taken the other day.

CHARLES APPLETON LONGFELLOW

Notes and Comments

[1] Minister De Long had two public audiences with the Emperor that might fit this time period. The first audience was to introduce 20 officers of the *Alaska* and the *Colorado* on November 17th. Led by Admiral John Rodgers, the Asiatic Squadron had been involved in a battle with Korean forces in June. (See note 13 in first section above). At Ganghwa, an island near the mouth of the Han River that flows past Seoul, the American group was attacked by Korean shore batteries. In the ensuing battle several hundred Koreans were killed and although the damage was not major, the American force did not press forward.

De Long's second audience, on December 2nd was to officially inform the Emperor that he would be leaving the country to accompany the Japanese Iwakura Mission to the United States and that Consul General Charles Shepard would assume the role of Charge d'affaires ad interim in his absence. It is most likely that, in his Hawaiian role, Charley attended the first of these two audiences. (*Japan Weekly Mail*)

[2] The State Department had another idea. Eugene Miller Van Reed had come to Japan in 1859, served at the U.S. Consulate and was named Kingdom of Hawaii's consul general before the Meiji Restoration.

[3] See Kidder, *Of One Blood All Nations*, p. 164-5. And for a fuller treatment, Janice Nimura. *Daughters of the Samurai*. Norton and Company, New York, 2015.

[4] Senator Charles Sumner of Massachusetts. The National Park Service's Longfellow House website calls Sumner Longfellow's closest friend. Sumner had been Chairman of the Senate Foreign Relations Committee since 1861 but at the time of Charles' letter was no longer chairman.
https://www.nps.gov/long/learn/historyculture/charles-sumner.htm

[5] Gustavus Farley was an acquaintance Charles made in Japan. Farley was from New England and visited the Longfellow family and

CHARLES APPLETON LONGFELLOW

along with his sisters became friends with Charley's sisters. In one letter dated March 17, 1873 Charles' sister Edith writes that Eunice (Una) Farley is heading out to Japan. So by then it appears that we have Gustavus and Eunice as Farley family in Yokohama.

[6] Father Longfellow is a bit confused on the spelling and the titles. Mori Arinori was Japanese minister, the title, ambassador, for Japan's chief of mission in the United States was not used until early in the 20th century.

[7] The American government had demanded compensation for damages to American commercial shipping during the Civil War by Confederate vessels built in British shipyards. The most notable of the war ships was the *Alabama*. Another, the *Shenandoah*, was responsible for dramatically reducing the number of American whaling vessels in the Pacific. Resolution of the *Alabama Claims* by the Grant administration ushered in a period of much improved relations between Great Britain and the United States.

[8] In an earlier letter – February 24th, 1872, Charley describes the shipwreck of the *Suwonada*, captained by Longfellow family friend Arthur Clark. The *Suwonada* struck a rock about 60 miles south of Shanghai and Clark had to run her into a sandbar to save the passengers. The ship was then attacked by pirates who were driven off by the ship's guns and small arms.

[9] The Club-room would have been at the Yokohama Club. No comparable facility was located in Tokyo at that early time.

[10] The Ambassadors Henry Longfellow refers to are members of the Iwakura Mission.

[11] The rail line from Yokohama to Shimbashi in Tokyo was officially opened on October 14, 1872.

CHARLES APPLETON LONGFELLOW

Leaving Japan

Photo courtesy of National Park Service
Longfellow House-Washington's Headquarters National Historic Site
Cambridge, Massachusetts

Shanghai April 4th 1873
My dear little Alice

It has just struck me that it is about a year since I have written to you, and I am very sorry that I have been such a bad correspondent to the family generally.

At last I have managed to tear myself away from Japan, and I have had the blues ever since and been a dozen times on the point of going back to the dear old place – especially as the weather has now got warm and the charming open-air life in the country has begun, but having once got away I had better keep away if I ever expect to get home again.

I left Yedo the end of February after selling out everything, spent two days in Yokohama which I left with a fever, so that when I got to Nagasaki it did not take much persuasion from H.A. Howe and Robert Walsh[1] to get me to stop with them until I was better. In three weeks they patched me up, and I was never better than I am now...

[On March 13, 1873, I left Nagasaki by the Pacific Mail steamer *Ariel* at eight in the morning, for Shanghai. I was very blue at leaving Japan, where for 20 months I have lived so pleasantly][2] As we steamed out of Nagasaki harbor, and the well-known hills, islands and little villages began to get farther and farther astern, I felt almost like blubbering. And if I had had command of the steamer should have turned her round and gone back, but as I couldn't I set to work to make a list of the Japanese words I had learnt for future reference should I ever come back...

[The *Ariel* is the worst boat on the line, bar the *Relief*, an old English steamer bought by the PM.S. Co. from the Japanese for a song after the typhoon of 1871 in Yokohama when she was piled up. But the *Ariel*'s officers are old chummies of mine: Capt. Newell, Chief Engineer Rossiter, and Paymaster Smith. We had as passengers Mr. Adams and A. Kassburgh, storekeepers in Nagasaki, the captain of a Russian man-of-war now in dock at Nagasaki refitting, a mysterious French woman, and the Japanese Consul to China, Mr. Ida, with two interpreters, one of whom, Ban Shinzaburo, I had met at Jaudon's in the *Gaimusho*[3] at Yedo. We had a very smooth passage]

I have spent three weeks since my arrival in one round of dinner parties, concerts, private theatricals, etc...

This gaiety is all very well in its way, but give me back my quiet, free, life in Japan...

CHARLES APPLETON LONGFELLOW

    Lots of love to all. Keep on sending my letters to Yokohama as I may any day return there.

                                             Your affectionate
                                             Charley san

Editor's Note: *Charles Longfellow spent four months in China, visited ship captain and family friend Arthur Clark in Hong Kong, went to the Philippines for two months where he was injured in a shooting accident, and returned to Hong Kong for several months to recuperate. In February 1874 he visited Saigon and Bangkok on his way to Singapore. In March he sailed for home on the* Agate *and finally arrived in Cambridge on June 22nd. Charley returned to Japan in 1885 and again in 1891. His collection of Japanese art was likely the largest in Cambridge. He died at age 48 in 1893.*[4]

Notes:

[1] Robert Walsh was the brother of Thomas Walsh. Robert managed the Nagasaki office of Walsh, Hall & Co. and Thomas ran the Yokohama operation.

[2] From Laidlaw, *20 Months*. This and the next passage in brackets are not part of the letter but are from Charles' notebook from March 13.

[3] *Gaimusho* is Ministry of Foreign Affairs.

[4] Information from this passage comes from Laidlaw, *20 Months*, p. 186.

ULYSSES S. GRANT

Julia T (Dent) Grant (1826-1902); Ulysses Simpson Grant (1822-85), Union Army General, 18th President of the USA; Colonel Frederick Dent Grant (1850-1912) (albumen photo), Taber, Isaiah (1830-1912) / American Antiquarian Society, Worcester, Massachusetts, USA / © Courtesy, American Antiquarian Society / Bridgeman Images. Photo taken several days after the Grant's return from Japan, the last stop on their extended world tour.

ULYSSES S. GRANT and JULIA DENT GRANT

Introduction by Edwina S. Campbell

Growing up in the baby boom heyday of World War II books, movies, and TV shows, Edwina began to wonder at an early age why good American relations with Germany and Japan in the nineteenth century descended into global war in the twentieth. Trying to find the answer to this question led her to study German, Japanese (and French) in college; to a Fulbright fellowship in Germany for her M.A. research on Franco-German rapprochement after 1945; and to becoming a US Foreign Service Officer in 1974. She left the Foreign Service to write her Ph.D. dissertation, after which she taught US foreign policy with a focus on NATO Europe for the next 30 years at the University of Virginia, National Defense University, and Air University, while remaining a practitioner of public diplomacy in western Europe for the US Information Agency and Department of State. Over those decades, she answered her initial question about German-US relations (see: Germany's Past and Europe's Future, *1989). Belatedly, an encounter with a photo of Ulysses S. Grant meeting the Meiji emperor in 1879 brought her back to the question of what led from there to Pearl Harbor 62 years later and to her 2016 book,* Citizen of a Wider Commonwealth, *about Grant's post-presidential diplomacy.*

"For history," wrote Wallace Stegner, "is a pontoon bridge. Every man walks and works at its building end, and has come as far as he has over the pontoons laid by others he may never have heard of."(1)

Those working at the building end of US-Japanese relations today are building on work done in the 1870s by two men few Americans have heard of and by one US president: diplomats Yoshida Kiyonari and John Bingham and Ulysses S. Grant. A high point of their achievements was the former president's visit to Japan in the summer of 1879.

Unfortunately, to this day, Grant's presidency (1869-77) is underrated, indeed, largely ignored, for its foreign policy accomplishments, but this was not the case among his contemporary world leaders. When the former president circumnavigated the globe from 1877-79, theoretically as a private citizen, but often aboard ships of the US Navy and with State Department support in the countries he visited, he was welcomed from London to Tokyo as the leader of a country that had demonstrated its political and military clout from 1861-65 and settled its disputes with the United Kingdom in the 1871 Treaty of Washington. Throughout Europe and Asia, Grant's reception by monarchs and ministers reflected their expectation that the United States had the potential to become a formidable future global power.(2)

In June 1879, the former president arrived in Nagasaki aboard *USS Richmond*, after more than a month in China. He was met by Yoshida, Japan's minister in Washington since 1874, who had been brought home especially for the visit, and by Bingham, US minister to Japan since 1873. Grant was the guest of the Meiji emperor, whose "restoration" to political power in 1868 with the defeat of the Tokugawa shogunate, had inaugurated a new era in Japanese history. While Grant was still in the White House, Yoshida had told him that the young emperor (26 years old in 1879), his ministers, and the Japanese people would "be exceedingly glad & happy to welcome him," should he visit Japan after leaving office.(3)

Throughout his years in office, Grant had taken an active interest in Japan, maintaining a lively correspondence with Bingham and developing a personal friendship with Yoshida. Through his secretary of state, Hamilton Fish, the president supported Japan's efforts to free itself from the "unequal treaty" regime imposed on it (as on China and other countries) by the European powers; the education of Japanese students at American universities; and enhancement of the US diplomatic and consular presence in Japan.(4)

Arriving in Asia in February 1879 after 18 months of travel throughout Europe, Grant had visited India, Burma, Thailand, Singapore, Hong Kong, and China before his arrival in Japan. China's foreign policy leadership, Prince Kung and Li Hung-chang, had asked the former president to use his good offices to mediate the ongoing Sino-Japanese dispute over control of the Loo Choo (Ryukyu) islands, including Okinawa. While Grant told them that "my position here and my position at home are not such as to give any assurance that my good offices would be of any value," he agreed to discuss the matter with the Japanese emperor.(5)

For its part, Japan's highly orchestrated reception of Grant was one tactic in its broader foreign policy strategy: to demonstrate to the Western powers that it was the "non-China" of Asia, a country that embraced modernization and westernization and deserved admittance on an equal footing to the "club" of global powers. With its victory over the Confederacy in 1865, the United States had been recognized as a potential member of that club, but both its desire and its readiness to join were still up for debate in 1879. Nevertheless, for the Imperial government, Grant's visit provided a golden opportunity to attract American and European attention to Japan's achievements over the previous decade. European diplomatic missions in Tokyo reported to their home governments about Grant's visit, and at home in the United States, there was widespread interest in his travels. He was thought likely to be the Republican nominee for president in 1880, and John Russell Young's *New York Herald* articles reporting on Grant's reception abroad since 1877 were widely disseminated throughout the country.(6)

Grant stayed in Japan for over two months, his longest single visit to one country, giving his hosts the opportunity to showcase their nation's achievements since 1868. The former president visited schools, colleges, military academies, and factories, writing in his diary that, "Every day and almost every hour of the stay was taken up in entertainments which ... were very instructive as to the rapid progress made by the Japanese Govt. & people." Always a proponent of universal, free primary education, he was particularly impressed by the "very perfect school system which enables all classes, male and female, to get a fair education." Many people, both men and women, "dress in European style," and the Japanese were "altogether the superior people of the East."(7)

But Grant was equally impressed by the likelihood and the impact of China's eventual rise to global power. The country was "on the eve of a great revolution," he had written while in Nagasaki, "that will land her among the nations of progress." It had all "the elements of great wealth and great power too and not more than a generation will pass before [China] will make these elements felt." In his discussion of the Loo Choo dispute with Meiji and his ministers, Grant wanted to impress on them his assessment of China's future and encourage the peaceful settlement of Sino-Japanese differences, as Britain and the United States had settled theirs in the Treaty of Washington. He suggested to the emperor "that Japan in a spirit of magnanimity and justice should make concessions to China" and settle the dispute "in a manner honorable to both, and lay the foundations of a lasting peace."(8)

Bur Grant's counsel was ultimately not taken to heart by Japan. In the short term, in part because of his good offices, there were negotiations with China, but in the decades that followed, Japan saw its path to great power status through military conquests on the Asian mainland and Pacific islands. In the context of the late nineteenth century, when, as John Russell Young wrote, "no advancement is sure without gunpowder," that conclusion was, unfortunately, not illogical. But it led to tragic consequences for much of Asia in the early twentieth century and, ultimately, for the world and Japan itself in 1945.(9)

Grant left Japan on September 3, 1879, aboard the Pacific Mail steamer *City of Tokio*, bound for San Francisco. Her departure from Yokohama was a grand affair, accompanied, as she left the port, by a Japanese man-o-war with Meiji's cabinet ministers on board to bid farewell to the former president. The emperor's admiration was sincere. He was "said to have been impressed in his forty-four-year reign by no one more than by the unassuming bourgeois Civil War hero and president." And Grant's appreciation of Japan's accomplishments was accurate; in late October 1879, he described Japan's army and its navy yards to a reporter from the *Sacramento Record Union*, declaring that "within a single generation" Japan would be "a first-class power."(10)

Bingham summed up the grandeur and the significance of Grant's visit in his report to Secretary of State William Evarts on September 2, 1879, when he wrote that "no such imperial and popular reception . . . was before given in this Empire to any foreign visitor." As he concluded, Japan's "extraordinary attentions" to "our illustrious citizen" had been "in honor of the Ex-President and of the Government and People of the United States of America."(11)

ULYSSES S. GRANT

Editor's Note: *As with William H. Seward's* Travels Around the World, *I am grateful for the reference librarians at the reading room of Carnegie Library of Pittsburgh in Oakland for allowing me to read and enjoy their original edition of John Russell Young's book. The Carnegie Library system also allowed me to use their originals so that Ryan Tomazin of Tomazin Scanning Services, Bridgeville, Pennsylvania, could prepare the scans.*

Notes

(1) "Child of the Far Frontier," in Page Stegner, ed., *Marking the Sparrow's Fall: Wallace Stegner's American West*, New York: Henry Holt and Company, 1998, p. 10.

(2) On Grant's travels and their diplomatic significance, see Edwina S. Campbell, *Citizen of a Wider Commonwealth: Ulysses S. Grant's Postpresidential Diplomacy*, Carbondale: Southern Illinois University Press, 2016.

(3) Ibid., p. 229, note 9.

(4) Early in Grant's presidency, in 1871, Thomas Walsh, a prominent American businessman in Japan, urged the president to show that "this Republic is not less concerned in its foreign affairs than are the Monarchies of Europe, that it is . . . careful of its interests in Japan, and that it can afford to maintain its dignity there." Bingham's appointment was a start in the right direction. See Ibid, pp. 148-152.

(5) Ibid., pp, 142-143.

(6) Young (1840-99) was instrumental in encouraging Grant to travel and in informing the American public about the former president's experiences abroad from 1877-79. Based at the *Herald*'s Paris office, Young accompanied Grant on many of his travels in Europe, and in January 1879, he departed Marseilles with him for the voyage "east of Suez." Somewhat revised, Young's dispatches to the *Herald* were published in 1879 in two volumes as *Around the World with General Grant*. Young was US minister to China from 1882-85, and from 1897 until his death, the seventh Librarian of Congress.

(7) Campbell, pp. 156-157.

(8) Ibid., p. 157, 161.

ULYSSES S. GRANT

(9) Ibid., p. 158.

(10) On Meiji: Juergen Osterhammel, *The Transformation of the World: A Global History of the Nineteenth Century*, Princeton, NJ: Princeton University Press, 2014, p. 502. On Grant's Sacramento interview: Campbell, pp. 182-184.

(11) US Legation Tokyo to US Department of State, No. 956, September 2, 1879; see Campbell, pp. 169-170.

ULYSSES S. GRANT

CHAPTER XL

Editor's Note: *This chapter begins on p. 454 and before giving first impressions of Grant's landing at Nagasaki, contains Grant's reflections noted in the table of contents as: The Surrender of Lee, Lee as a General, Jefferson Davis, Army of the Potomac, Ingalls and Halleck, Frank Blair, and Shiloh.*

NAGASAKI.

FOREIGN SETTLEMENT OF NAGASAKI.

The battle was out of his hands, and out of that of his army. What won the battle of Shiloh was the courage and endurance of our own soldiers. It was the staying power and pluck of the North as against the short-lived power of the South; and whenever these qualities came into collision the North always won. I used to find that the first day, or the first period of a battle, was most successful to the South; but if we held on to the second or third day, we were sure to beat them, and we always did."

On the 21st of June we found our ship threading its way through beautiful islands and rocks covered with green, looming up out of the sea, and standing like sentinels on the coast —hills on which were trees, and gardens terraced to their summits, and high, commanding cliffs. Through green and smooth tranquil waters we steamed into the bay of Nagasaki, and had our first glimpse of Japan. Nagasaki is said to be among the most beautiful harbors in the world. But the beauty that welcomed us had the endearing quality that it reminded us of home. For so many weeks we had been in the land of the palm, and we were now again in the land of the pine. We had seen nature in luxuriant moods, running into riotous forms, strange and rank. We were weary of the cocoa-nut and the brown, parched soil, of the skies of fire and forests with wild and creeping things. It had become so oppressive that when our course turned toward the north there was great joy. The Providence who gave us our share of the world no doubt considered this, and made it happen that some of us should rejoice under the tropical and others under the temperate zone. I have come to the conclusion that a longing for green is among our primitive and innocent impulses, and I sometimes think that if Adam had only had a good supply of grass—of timothy and clover—in the Garden of Eden, and less of the enticing and treacherous fruits, there would have been no trouble in his family, and all would have gone well. There is temptation in sunshine. One has a feeling of strengthened virtue as the landscape draws near and unfolds itself, and you have glimpses of Scotland and the Adirondacks and the inland lakes; and the

474   *CONVERSATIONS CONTINUED—ARRIVAL IN JAPAN.*

green is an honest, frank, chaste green, running from hill-top to water-side, and throwing upon the waters long, refreshing shadows. It was this school-boy sense of pleasure that came with my first view of Japan. All the romance, all the legends, the dreams I had dreamed and the pictures I had seen; all the anticipations I had formed of Japan were immersed in this joy-

STREET AND TEMPLE, NAGASAKI.

ful welcome to the green that I had not seen since leaving England—our own old-fashioned green of the temperate zone. This is not a heroic confession, and I should have thought of some fitting emotion with which to welcome this land of romance and sunshine. But I can never get into a heroic vein, and my actual impressions, as I go around the world, are often of so homely a character that I ought not to confess them. How much grander it would be to intimate that my feelings overcame me and I was too much affected for speech. This would sound as a more appropriate welcome to Japan. All that I saw of the coast was the beauty of the green, which came like a memory of childhood, as a memory of America, and in which I rejoiced as in a mere physical sensation, like bathing, or swinging on the gate, or dozing under the apple-trees in the drowsy days of June.

And yet if I could only rouse myself out of this mere boy's feeling of seeing something good—good in the sense of sight and food—there are memories, even around this harbor of Nagasaki, of grand men and heroic days. Here we come again upon the footprints of Francis Xavier. The shadow of that saint rests upon Asia—or perhaps I should say halo rather than shadow, as a word more befitting a saint. Francis was never a favorite of mine, for I have a choice collection of saints with whom I hope one day to be in a closer communion, and the stories of his gifts of tongues and his taking part in the cruel wars of the European against the native were beyond me. But as I pass from land to land, and see the nature of the field in which he labored, and mark his insatiate devotion to faith and duty, he grows in my esteem, and I bow in adoration of his devotion and genius. Perhaps Xavier had no more interesting field than Japan, and one can picture him, the pale, concentrated priest, walking under these green, impending hills. This is the scene of his mission to Japan. Here began that strange movement of the Japanese people toward Christianity. Here it began, and here, also, it came to an end. This height which we now pass, and where the people of Nagasaki come to picnic, is the hill of Pappenberg. It is an island as well as a hill, and runs up like a cone and is arrayed in winning green. It is written that when the Japanese government resolved to treat Christianity as a crime, and extirpate the faithful, that thousands of the Christians were taken to the brow of the hill and thrown into the sea. Not far from here is a village, the site of the massacre of thirty-seven thousand Christians who would not bow to the imperial edict, but preferred to die with the cross in their hands.

These are painful memories, but why recall them in Japan? Let us imitate our beloved mother, who has covered with consoling and beautiful green the harsh places—the sites of massacre and death—and forget the dark deeds of an early age, while we rejoice in the bright deeds of our own age, of the men who in our time have taken Japan out of the sepulchre, and given her room and a chance in the arena. There are statelier memories—memories of the daring navigators who forced the seas in heroic days. It was the dream of a northwest passage, of discovering a new road to the Indies—it was the influence which Japan and the East had thrown over the imaginations of men—that led to the series of enterprises in unknown lands and over unknown seas which culminated in the discovery of America. You see how closely our world is knit together, and that you cannot touch a spot which has not some chords, some memory, some associations, responsive to every other spot; and thus it is, strange to say, that Japan and America have so close a relation. In those days Nagasaki was a renowned city, and alone of cities in Japan she touched the outside world. When the warrior-king tumbled the missionaries and converts into the sea, and visited upon the followers of the cross untold misery, even the sacred, crowning misery of crucifixion, Nagasaki was still held as a foothold of the merchant. It was only a foothold. You can see the small, fan-shaped concession where the Dutch merchants were kept in seclusion, and whence their trade trickled into Japan. A flag floats over one of the bazaars, and by the arms of Holland, which it bears, you can trace out the memorable spot.

The "Richmond" steamed between the hills and came to an anchorage. It was the early morning, and over the water were shadows of cool, inviting green. Nagasaki, nestling on her hill-sides, looked cosy and beautiful; and it being our first glimpse of a Japanese town, we studied it through our glasses, studied every feature—the scenery, the picturesque attributes of the city, the terraced hills that rose beyond, every rood under cultivation; the quaint, curious houses; the multitudes of flags, which showed that the town knew of our coming and was preparing to do us honor. We noted also that the wharves were lined with a multitude, and that the available population were waiting to see the guest whom their nation honors, and who is known in common speech as the American Mikado.

THE PROGRESS OF CIVILIZATION.

Then the "Richmond" ran up the Japanese standard and fired twenty-one guns in honor of Japan. The forts answered the salute. Then the Japanese gun-boats and the forts displayed the American ensign, and fired a salute of twenty-one guns in honor of General Grant. Mr. W. P. Mangum, our consul, and his wife came on board.(1) In a short time the Japanese barge was seen coming, with Prince Dati and Mr. Yoshida and the Governor, all in the splendor of court uniforms. These officials were received with due honors, and escorted to the cabin. Prince Dati said that he had been commanded by the

478   CONVERSATIONS CONTINUED—ARRIVAL IN JAPAN.

Emperor to meet General Grant on his landing, to welcome him in the name of his Majesty, and to attend upon him as the Emperor's personal representative, so long as the General remained in Japan. The value of this compliment can be understood when you know that Prince Dati is one of the highest noblemen in Japan. He was one of the leading daimios, one of the old feudal barons who, before the revolution, ruled Japan, and had power of life and death in his own dominions. The old daimios were not only barons but heads of clans, like the clans of Scotland; and in the feudal days he could march an army into the field. When the revolution came Dati accepted it, not sullenly and seeking retirement, like Satsuma and other princes, but as the best thing for the country. He gave his adhesion to the Emperor, and is now one of the great noblemen around the throne. The sending of a man of the rank of the Prince was the highest compliment that the Emperor could pay any guest. Mr. Yoshida is well known as the present Japanese Minister to the United States, a discreet and accomplished man, and among the rising statesmen in the empire. Having been accredited to America during the General's administration, and knowing the General, the government called him home so that he might attend General Grant and look after the reception. So when General Grant arrived he had the pleasure of meeting not only a distinguished representative of the Emperor, but an old personal friend.

At one o'clock on the 21st of June, General Grant, accompanied by Prince Dati, Mr. Yoshida, and the Governor, landed in Nagasaki. The Japanese man-of-war "Kango," commanded by Captain Ito, had been sent down to Nagasaki to welcome the General. The landing took place in the Japanese barge. From the time that General Grant came into the waters of Japan it was the intention of the government that he should be the nation's guest. As soon as the General stepped into the barge the Japanese vessels and the batteries on shore thundered out their welcome, the yards of the vessels were manned, and as the barge moved slowly along the crews of the ships in the harbor cheered. It was over a mile from the

THE LANDING.

"Richmond" to the shore. The landing-place had been arranged not in the foreign section nor the Dutch Concession, carrying out the intention of having the reception entirely Japanese. Lines of troops were formed, the steps were covered with red cloth, and every space and standing spot and coigne of vantage was covered with people. The General's boat touched the shore, and with Mrs. Grant on his arm, and followed by the Colonel, the Japanese officials, and the members of his party, he slowly walked up the platform, bowing to the multitude who made their obeisance in his honor. There is something strange in the grave decorum of an Oriental crowd—strange to us who remember the ringing cheer and the electric hurrah of Saxon lands. The principal citizens of Nagasaki came forward and

VILLAGE NEAR NAGASAKI.

480   *CONVERSATIONS CONTINUED—ARRIVAL IN JAPAN.*

were presented, and after a few minutes' pause our party stepped into jinrickshaws and were taken to our quarters.

The jinrickshaw is the common vehicle of Japan. It is built on the principle of a child's perambulator or an invalid's chair, except that it is much lighter. Two men go ahead and pull, and one behind pushes. But this is only on occasions of ceremony. One man is quite able to manage a jinrickshaw. Those used by the General had been sent down from Tokio from the palace. Our quarters in Nagasaki had been prepared in the Japanese town. A building used for a female normal school had been prepared. It was a half mile from the landing, and the whole road had been decorated with flags, American and Japanese entwined, with arches of green boughs and flowers. Both sides of the road were lined with people who bowed low to the General as he passed. On reaching our residence the Japanese officials of the town were all presented. Then came the foreign consuls in a body, who were presented by the American Consul, Mr. Mangum. After this came the officers of the Japanese vessels, all in uniform. Then came a delegation representing the foreign residents of all nationalities in Nagasaki, who presented an address. Mr. Bingham, the American Minister, came as far as Nagasaki to meet General Grant and go with him to Yokohama. (2) He brought us sad news of the pestilence ravaging the empire, which would limit our journey. Mr. Bingham was fresh from America, and it was pleasant not only to meet an old friend, but one who could tell us of the tides and currents of home affairs. On the evening of the 23d there was a dinner at the Government House, at which General Grant made a speech. This speech became a subject of so much controversy through the East that I print it in full. The Governor of Nagasaki, Utsumi Togatsu, made a speech proposing General Grant's health. This was delivered in Japanese. After the interpreter had made a translation, General Grant rose and said:

"YOUR EXCELLENCY AND GENTLEMEN: You have here to-night several Americans who have the talent of speech, and who could make an eloquent response to the address in which my health is proposed. I have no such gift,

ULYSSES S. GRANT

and I never lamented its absence more than now, when there is so much that I want to say about your country, your people, and your progress. I have not been an inattentive observer of that progress, and in America we have been favored with accounts of it from my distinguished friend whom you all know as the friend of Japan, and whom it was my privilege to send as minister—I mean Judge Bingham. The spirit which has actuated the mission of Judge Bingham—the spirit of sympathy, support, and conciliation—not only expressed my own sentiments, but those of America. America has much to gain in the East—no nation has greater interests ; but America has nothing to gain except what comes from the cheerful acquiescence of the Eastern people and insures them as much benefit as it does us. I should be ashamed of my country if its relations with other nations, and especially with these ancient and most interesting empires in the East, were based upon any other idea. We have rejoiced over your progress. We have watched you step by step. We have followed the unfolding of your old civilization and its absorbing the new. You have had our profound sympathy in that work, our sympathy in the troubles which came with it, and our friendship. I hope it may continue, that it may long continue. As I have said, America has great interests in the East. She is your next neighbor. She is more affected by the eastern populations than any other power. She can never be insensible to what is doing here. Whatever her influence may be, I am proud to think that it has always been exerted in behalf of justice and kindness. No nation needs from the outside powers justice and kindness more than Japan, because the work that has made such marvelous progress in the past few years is a work in which we are deeply concerned, in the success of which we see a new era in civilization and which we should encourage. I do not know, gentlemen, that I can say anything more than this in response to the kind words of the Governor. Judge Bingham can speak with much more eloquence and much more authority as our minister. But I could not allow the occasion to pass without saying how deeply I sympathized with Japan in her efforts to advance, and how much those efforts were appreciated in America. In that spirit I ask you to unite with me in a sentiment : 'The prosperity and the independence of Japan.'" (3)

At the close General Grant proposed the health of General Bingham, and spoke of the satisfaction he felt at meeting him in Japan. Mr. Yoshida, the Japanese Minister to the United States, also made a speech, paying a tribute to General Bingham's sincerity and friendliness. Judge Bingham responding, said that he had come to Nagasaki to be among the first to welcome General Grant to Japan, which he did in the name of his government. It had been his endeavor to faithfully discharge his duties in such a manner as would strengthen the friendship between the two countries and promote the commercial interests of both. He knew that in so acting he reflected the wishes of the illustrious man who is the guest of the empire, and the wishes also of the President and people of the United States.

TEA-GARDEN, NAGASAKI.

There was a visit to the government schools and an address to the scholars, a short conversational speech on the value of education. There was a visit to the Nagasaki Fair, which had been in progress during the summer, but was then closed. The Governor opened it for our inspection, and it was certainly a most creditable display of what Japan could do in art, industry, and science. The fair buildings were erected in the town park, a pleasure ground with unique old temples gray and mossy with age, and tea-houses where tea was brought in the tiniest of cups by demure wee maidens from six to seven, dressed in the ancient costumes of Japan, who came and knelt as they offered their tea. The town people were out in holiday attire to take the air and look out on the bay and stare at the General. After we had made our tour of the fair grounds the Governor asked the General and Mrs. Grant to plant memorial trees. The species planted by the General was the *Ficus religiosa*, while to Mrs. Grant was given the *Saurus camphora*. The Governor then said that Nagasaki had resolved to erect a monument in honor of General Grant's visit, that this memorial would be near the trees, and that if the General would only write an inscription it would be engraved on the stone in English and Japanese characters. The General wrote the inscription as follows :

"NAGASAKI, JAPAN, June 22, 1879.

"At the request of Governor Utsumi Togatsu, Mrs. Grant and I have each planted a tree in the Nagasaki Park. I hope that both trees may prosper, grow large, live long, and in their growth, prosperity, and long life be emblematic of the future of Japan.

'U. S. GRANT"

ULYSSES S. GRANT

ULYSSES S. GRANT

Notes on Chapter XL

Page numbers refer to pagination of facsimile document.

(1) p. 477 The American consul at Nagasaki was Willie P. Magnum. From a prominent North Carolina political family, Magnum had served as an officer in the Confederate Army, reaching the rank of brigadier general. See Kidder, *Of One Blood All Nations*, p. 197.

Prince Dati was Date Munenari , a prominent figure in Japan's international relations in the early Meiji period.

Yoshida Kiyonari became Japanese minister to the United States in 1874.

(2) p. 480 John Bingham, United States Minister to Japan, had been appointed by Grant and began his service in 1873. He had recently been back in the United States on home leave so was able to give Grant his impressions on the political events and trends taking place since Grant left on his world circling voyage. Bingham had been a congressman from Ohio and in that role distinguished himself as lone civilian prosecutor on the military tribunal of the Lincoln Assassins, floor manager in the House for the impeachment of President Andrew Johnson, and primary author of the 14th amendment to the Constitution. Bingham is referred to as Judge Bingham noting his service during the Civil War as Judge Advocate of the Military Department of the Susquehanna. See Gerard Magliocca, *American Founding Son*, the authoritative Bingham biography and Sam Kidder, *Of One Blood All Nations*, for treatment of Bingham's contributions as minister to Japan.

(3) p. 481 Grant's speech on arrival in Japan is an excellent statement of his vision of America's policy in East Asia.

A JAPANESE FAMILY AT DINNER.

CHAPTER XLI.

JAPAN.

DURING our visit to Nagasaki we took part in a famous dinner given in honor of General Grant, about which I propose to write at some length, because it is interesting as a picture of ancient life in Japan.

In my wanderings round the world I am more interested in what reminds me of the old times, of the men and the days that are gone, than of customs reminding me of what I saw in France. All that reminds you of the old times is passing away from Japan. Here and there you can find a bit that recalls the days when the daimios ruled, when the two-sworded warriors were on every highway, when the rivalry of clans was as fierce as was ever known in the highlands of Scotland or the plains of North America, when every gentleman was as ready to commit suicide in defense of his honor as a Texas swashbuckler to fight a duel. All of this is crumbling under the growth of modern ideas. The aim of Japanese statesmen is now to do things as they are done in London and Washington, and this impulse sweeps on in a resistless and swelling current. It is best that it should be so. God forbid that Japan should ever try to arrest or turn back the hands of her destiny. What was picturesque and quaint in the old time can be preserved in plays and romances. This century belongs to the real world, and Japan's incessant pressing forward, even if she crushes the old monuments, is in the interest of civilization.

It seemed good to the citizens of Nagasaki to give General Grant a dinner that was to be in itself a romance and a play. Instead of doing what is done every day, and rivaling the taste of Paris, it was resolved to entertain him in the style of the daimios, the feudal lords of Japan. The place selected for the fête was an old temple in the heart of the city, from whose doors you could look over the bay. Moreover, it was to be the work of the citizens of Nagasaki. The merchants would do it, and this in itself was a delicate thought; for in the East it is not often that we have any recognition of men as men and citizens. The awakening of the people of Japan to a perception of the truth that the men who form the groundwork of the State, and upon whose genius and industry it rests, are as important as heaven-born rulers, is one of the thought-provoking incidents of the later amusements in Japan. That is a voice it is not easy to still. It may speak with the wavering tones of childhood, but will gather strength and in time be heard. It was peculiarly gratifying to General Grant to meet the citizens of Japan, and they left nothing undone to do him honor. The company was not more than twenty, including General Grant and party, our Japanese hosts, Consul Mangum and family, and Consul Denny and family. The dinner was served on small tables, each guest having a table to himself. The merchants themselves waited on us, and with the merchants a swarm of attendants wearing the costumes of old Japan.

The bill of fare was almost a volume, and embraced over fifty courses. The wine was served in unglazed porcelain wine cups, on white wooden stands. The appetite was pampered in the beginning with dried fish, edible sea-weeds, and isinglass, in something of the Scandinavian style, except that the attempt did not take the form of brandy and raw fish. The first serious dish was composed of crane, sea-weed, moss, rice bread and potatoes, which we picked over in a curious way, as though we

CHILDREN DANCING.

were at an auction sale of remnants, anxious to rummage out a bargain. The soup, when it first came—for it came many times—was an honest soup of fish, like a delicate fish chowder. Then came strange dishes, as ragout, and as soup, in bewildering confusion. The first was called namasu, and embodied fish, clams, chestnuts, rock mushrooms, and ginger. Then, in various combinations, the following:—duck, truffles, turnips, dried bonito, melons, pressed salt, aromatic shrubs, snipe, eggplant, jelly, boiled rice, snapper, shrimp, potatoes, mushroom, cabbage, lassfish, orange flowers, powdered fish flavored with plum juice and walnuts, raw carp sliced, mashed fish, baked fish, isinglass, fish boiled with pickled beans, wine and rice again. This all came in the first course, and as a finale to the course there was a sweetmeat composed of white and red bean jelly-cake, and boiled black mushroom. With this came powdered tea, which had a green, monitory look, and suggested your earliest experiences in medicine. When the first pause came in the dinner a merchant advanced and read an address to General Grant. This was at the end of the first course—the ominous course that came to an end amid powdered tea and sweetmeats composed of white and red bean jelly-cake and boiled black mushrooms. After the address had been read we rose from our tables and sauntered about on the gravel-walk, and looked down on the bay and the enfolding hills, whose beauty became almost plaintive under the shadows of the setting sun.

One never tires of a scene like Nagasaki, as you see it in evening more especially, the day ending and nature sheltering for repose in the embraces of night. Everything is so ripe and rich and old. Time has done so much for the venerable town, and you feel as the shadows fall that for generations, for centuries, they have fallen upon just such a scene as we look down upon from the brow of our hill. The eddies of a new civilization are rushing in upon Nagasaki, and there are many signs that you have no trouble in searching out. That Nagasaki has undergone a vast change since the day when Dutch merchants were kept in a reservation more secluded than we have ever kept our Indians, when Xavier and his disciples threaded those narrow streets preaching the salvation that comes through the blood of Jesus, when Christians were driven at the point of the spear to yon beetling cliff and tumbled into the sea. These are momentous events in the history of Japan. They were merely incidents in the history of Nagasaki. The ancient town has lived on sleepily, embodying and absorbing the features of Eastern civilization, unchanged and unchanging, its beauty expressive because it is a beauty of its own, untinted by Europeans. We have old towns in the European world. We even speak as if we had a past in fresh America. But what impresses you in these aspects of Eastern development is their antiquity, before which the most ancient of our towns are but as yesterday. The spirit of ages breathes over Nagasaki, and you cease to think of chronology, and see only the deep, rich tones which time has given and which time alone can give.

A trailing line of mist rises from the town and slowly floats along the hill-side, veiling the beauty upon which you have been dwelling all the afternoon. The green becomes gray, and on the tops there are purple shadows, and the shining waters of the bay become opaque. The ships swing at anchor, and you can see above the trim masts and prim-set spars of the

A JAPANESE MOTHER.

"Richmond" the colors of America. The noble ship has sought a shelter near the further shore, and as you look a light ascends the rigging and gives token that those in command are setting the watches for the night. Nearer us, distinguishable by her white wheel-house, rides the "Ashuelot," while ships of other lands dot the bay. As you look a ball of fire shoots into the air and hangs pendent for a moment, and explodes into a mass of shooting, coruscating stars, and you know that our friends in the town are rejoicing over the presence of General Grant. From the other hills a flame breaks out and struggles a few moments, and becomes a steady asserting flame, and you know that this is a bonfire, and that the people have built it to show their joy. Other bonfires creep out of the blackness, for while you have been looking night has come, and reigns over hill and valley and sea, and green has become black. Lines of light streak the town, and you see various decorations in lanterns, forming quaint shapes. One shapes itself into the flag of America, another into the flag of Japan, another into a triangle, another into a Japanese word—the word in red lanterns, surrounded by a border of white lanterns—and Mr. Yoshida translates the word to mean a sentiment in honor of General Grant. These lights in curious forms shoot up in all parts of the town, and you know that Nagasaki is illuminated, and that while here in this venerable temple the merchants have assembled to give us entertainment, the inhabitants are answering their hospitality with blazing tokens of approval. As you look below on the streets around the temple you see the crowd bearing lanterns, chattering, wondering, looking on, taking what comfort they can out of the festival in honor of the stranger within their gates.

But while we could well spend our evening strolling over this graveled walk, and leaning over the quaint brick wall, and studying the varied and ever-changing scene that sweeps beneath us, we must not forget our entertainment. The servants have brought in the candles. Before each table is a pedestal on which a candle burns, and the old temple lights up with a new splendor. To add to this splendor the wall has been draped with heavy silks, embroidered with gold and silver, with quaint and curious legends of the history of Japan. These draperies lend a new richness to the room, and you admire the artistic taste which suggested them. The merchants enter again, bearing meats. Advancing to the center of the room, and to the General, they kneel and press their foreheads to the floor. With this demure courtesy the course begins. Other attendants enter, and place on each table the lacquer bowls and dishes. Instead of covering the tables with a variety of food, and tempting you with auxiliary dishes of watermelon seeds and almond kernels, as in China, the Japanese give you a small variety at a time. I am afraid, however, we have spoiled our dinner. Our amiable friend, Mr. Yoshida, warned us in the beginning not to be in a hurry, to restrain our curiosity, not to hurry our investigations into the science of a Japanese table, but to pick and nibble and wait—that there were

TRAVELING IN THE KAGO.

good things coming which we should not be beyond the condition of enjoying. What a comfort, for instance, a roll of bread would be and a glass of dry champagne! But there are no bread and no wine, and our only drink is the hot preparation from rice, with its sherry flavor, which is poured out of a teapot into shallow lacquer saucers, and which you sip not without relish, although it has no place in any beverage known to your experience. We are dining, however, in strict Japanese fashion, just as the old daimios did, and our hosts are too good artists to spoil a feast with champagne. Then it has been going on for hours, and when you have reached the fourth hour of a dinner, even a temperance dinner, with nothing more serious than a hot, insipid, sherry-like rice drink, you have passed beyond the critical and curious into the resigned condition. If we had only been governed by the minister, we might have enjoyed this soup, which comes first in the course, and as you lift the lacquered top you know to be hot and fragrant. It is a soup composed of carp and mushroom and aromatic shrub. Another dish is a prepared fish that looks like a confection of cocoa-nut, but which you see to be fish as you prod it with your chopsticks. This is composed of the red snapper fish, and is served in red and white alternate squares. It looks well, but you pass it by, as well as another dish that is more poetic at least, for it is a preparation of the skylark, wheat flour-cake, and gourd. One has a sense of the violation of proprieties in seeing the soaring lark snared from the clouds, the dew, and the morning sunshine, to flavor a cake of wheat. We treat the lark better at home, and we might pass this to the discredit of Japan, if we did not remember how much the lark contributed to feasts in the Palais Royal, and that the French were alike wanting in sentiment. We are not offended by the next soup, which comes hot and smoking, a soup of buckwheat and egg-plant. The egg-plant always seemed to be a vulgar, pretentious plant that might do for the trough, but was never intended for the dignity of the table. But for buckwheat the true American, who believes in the country, and whose patriotism has not been deadened by debates on army appropriation bills, has a tender, respectful feeling. Somehow it has no business upon a foreign table, and at a daimio's dinner you feel that it is one of your contributions to the happiness of the world, that you have given it as your unit in the sum of human entertainment. You think of glowing buckwheat fields over which bees are humming—of overladen tables in many an American home, crowned with a steaming mound of brown and crisp cakes, oozing with butter. You think of frost and winter and tingling breezes from the granite hills. It brings you October, and in this wandering round the world, disposed as one always should be to see sunshine wherever the sun shines, I have seen nothing to rival an American October. But buckwheat in a soup is unfitting, and allied with the egg-plant is a degradation, and no sense of curious inquiry can tolerate so grave a violation of the harmony of the table. You push your soup to the end of the table and nip off the end of a fresh cigar, and look out upon the town, over which the dominant universe has thrown the star-sprinkled mantle of night, and follow the lines of light that mark the welcome we are enjoying, and trace the ascending rockets as they shoot up from the hill-side to break into masses of dazzling fire and illuminate the heavens for a moment in a rhapsody of blue and scarlet and green and silver and gold.

If you have faith, you will enter bravely into the dish that your silk-draped attendant now places before you, and as he does bows to the level of the table and slides away. This is called oh-hira, and was composed, I am sure, by some ambitious daimio, who had given thought to the science of the table, and possessed an original genius. The base of this dish is panyu. Panyu is a sea-fish. The panyu in itself would be a dish, but in addition we have a fungus, the roots of the lily, and the stems of pumpkins. The fungus is delicate, and reminds you of mushroom, but the pumpkin, after you had fished it out and saw that it was a pumpkin, seemed forlorn and uncomfortable, conscious no doubt of a better destiny in its New England home than flavoring a mess of pottage. What one objects to in these dishes is the objection you have to frogs and snails. They lack dignity. And when we come to real American food, like the pumpkin and buckwheat, we expect to see it specially honored, and not thrown into a pot and boiled in mixed company. The lily roots seemed out of place. I could find no taste in them, and would have been content to have known them as turnips. But your romantic notions about the lily—the lines you have written in albums, the poetry and water-colors—are dispelled by its actual presence in a boiled state, suffused with arrow-root and horseradish. Here are the extremes of life—the arrow-root which soothes

AN HISTORICAL DINNER.

the growing palate, the horseradish which stimulates the declining tastes—and yet they are necessary to a proper appreciation of the lily and the pumpkin. The combination seems

THE TEMPLE OF ASAXA.

like a freak of the imagination, the elements are so antagonistic and incongruous. But the kettle levels all distinctions, and once that the bending lily and the golden pumpkin, with their pretentious associates, are thoroughly boiled, they are simply soup after all. It must have been a philosophical daimio who invented this dish, meaning, no doubt, to teach his guests the solemn lesson that there is no glory, no pomp, no ambition, neither sentiment, nor virtue, nor modesty, nor pride, that can escape in the fulfillment of time the destiny to which time dooms us all.

Music! In the ancient days, when a great daimio dined his friends, music came and brightened the feast. Somehow it seems to have been always thus, even from the beginning—in Assyria, in Persia, in ancient Jerusalem, in the Indian forests. I should like to see a prize essay written in plain English on the subject of music, that would tell you something of the influence upon life of this world of harmony—how it brightens and heightens existence; how its tones follow us from the lullaby that soothes the unconscious ears of infancy to the dirge which falls unheeded upon the unconscious ears of death. Wherever we touch these ancient civilizations music comes to do us honor. At Jeypore, where our host claimed a descent from the stars, the nautch girls danced as was their wont before the shrines of Buddha. In Siam the Prince called Celestial honored us with music and dancers burdened with gold-embroidered raiment. In China music always attended our visits to princes and viceroys. Have you read what Confucius says about music? He liked bells and drums and harpsichords. "When," he said, "affairs are not carried on to success, propriety and music will not flourish, and if that is not the case punishments will not be properly awarded." Even in this seat of an antique civilization music reigns, and although the harmony is jarring to our modern ears, and you feel the want of expression and poetry, it has expression and poetry. One of the most intelligent Brahmins I met in India told me that if I once came to appreciate the music of India I would not care for any other. There was no difficulty in assenting to such a proposition, because I can conceive nothing more difficult than to find harmony in these discordant sounds. While our hosts are passing around the strange dishes, a signal is made and the musicians enter. They are maidens, with fair, pale faces, and small, dark, serious eyes. You are pleased

ULYSSES S. GRANT

CENTRAL JAPAN.

to see that their teeth have not been blackened, as was the custom in past days, and is even now almost a prevalent custom among the lower classes. We are told that the maidens who have come to grace our feast are not of the common singing class, but the daughters of the merchants and leading citizens of Nagasaki. The first group is composed of three. They enter, sit down on the floor, and bow their heads in salutation. One of the instruments is shaped like a guitar, another is something between a banjo and a drum. They wear the costume of the country, the costume that was known before the new days came upon Japan. They have blue silk gowns, white collars, and heavily brocaded pearl-colored sashes. The principal instrument was long and narrow, shaped like a coffin lid, and sounding like a harpsichord. After they had played an overture another group entered—fourteen maidens similarly dressed, each carrying the small, banjo-like instrument, ranging themselves on a bench against the wall, the tapestry and silks suspended over them. Then the genius of the artist was apparent, and the rich depending tapestry, blended with the blue and white and pearl, and animated with the faces of the maidens, their music and their songs, made a picture of Japanese life which an artist might regard with envy. You saw then the delicate features of Japanese decoration which have bewitched our artist friends, and which the most adroit fingers in vain try to copy. When the musicians enter the song begins. It is an original composition. The theme is the glory of America and honor to General Grant. They sing of the joy that his coming has given to Japan; of the interest and the pride they take in his fame; of their friendship for their friends across the great sea. This is all sung in Japanese, and we follow the lines through the mediation of a Japanese friend who learned his English in America. This anthem was chanted in a low almost monotonous key, one singer leading in a kind of solo and the remainder coming in with a chorus. The song ended, twelve dancing maidens enter. They wore a crimson-like overgarment fashioned like pantaloons—a foot or so too long—so that when they walked it was with a dainty pace, lest they might trip and fall. The director of this group was constantly on his hands and knees, creeping around among the dancers keeping their drapery in order, not allowing it to bundle up and vex the play. These maidens carried bouquets of pink blossoms, artificially made, examples of the flora of Japan. They stepped through the dance at as slow a measure as in a minuet of Louis XIV. The movement of the dance was simple, the music a humming thrumming, as though the performers were tuning their instruments. After passing through a few measures the dancers slowly filed out, and were followed by another group, who came wearing masks—the mask in the form of a large doll's face—and bearing children's rattles and fans. The peculiarity of this dance was that time was kept by the movement of the fan—a graceful, expressive movement which only the Eastern people have learned to bestow on the fan. With them the fan becomes almost an organ of speech, and the eye is employed in its management at the expense of the admiration we are apt at home to bestow on other features of the amusement. The masks indicated that this was a humorous dance, and when it was

JAPANESE MUSICIANS.

over four special performers, who had unusual skill, came in with flowers and danced a pantomime. Then came four others, with costumes different—blue robes trimmed with gold—who carried long, thin wands, entwined in gold and red, from which dangled festoons of pink blossoms.

All this time the music hummed and thrummed. To vary the show we had an even more grotesque amusement. First came eight children, who could scarcely do more than toddle. They were dressed in white, embroidered in green and red, wearing purple caps formed like the Phrygian liberty cap, and dangling on the shoulders. They came into the temple inclosure and danced on the graveled walk, while two, wearing an imitation of a dragon's skin, went through a dance and various contortions, supposed to be a dragon at play. This reminded us of the pantomime elephant, where one performer plays the front and another the hind legs. In the case of our Japanese dragon the legs were obvious, and the performers seemed indisposed even to protect the illusion. It was explained that it was an ancient village dance, one of the oldest in Japan, and that on festive occasions, when the harvests are ripe, or when some legend or feat of heroism is to be commemorated, they assemble and dance it. It was a trifling, innocent dance, and you felt as you looked at it, and, indeed, at all the features of our most unique entertainment, that there was a good deal of nursery imagination in Japanese fêtes and games. A more striking feature was the decorations which came with the second course of our feast. First came servants, bearing two trees, one of the pine the other of the plum. The plum-tree was in full blossom. One of these was set on a small table in front of Mrs. Grant, the other in front of the General. Another decoration was a cherry-tree, surmounting a large basin, in which were living carp fish. The carp has an important position in the legends of Japan. It is the emblem of ambition and resolution. This quality was shown in another decoration, representing a waterfall, with carp climbing against the stream. The tendency of the carp to dash against rocks and climb waterfalls, which should indicate a low order of intellect and perverted judgment, is supposed to show the traits of the ambitious man. Perhaps the old philosophers saw a great deal of folly and weakness of mind in the fever of ambition, and these emblems may have had a moral lesson for those who sat at the daimio feasts. This habit of giving feasts a moral feature,

A COUNTRY ROAD.

of adding music for the imagination and legends for the mind, if such were the purpose, showed an approach to refined civilization in the ancient days. I am afraid, however, if we were to test our dinner by such speculations it would become whimsical, and lose that dignity which princes at least would be supposed to give to their feasts. You will note, however, as our dinner goes on it becomes bizarre and odd, and runs away with all well-ordered notions of what even a daimio's dinner should be. The soups disappear. You see we have only had seven distinct soups served at intervals, and so cunningly prepared that you are convinced that in the ancient days of Japanese splendor soup had a dignity which it has lost. One of the mournful attributes of our modern civilization is the position into which soup is fallen. It used to be the mainstay of a feast, the salvation of bad dinners, something always to be depended upon when all went to the bad. Now the soup has been abandoned to the United States, where we have the gumbo and the oyster, the clam and the terrapin, to justify the proud pre-eminence of America. I am afraid, however, from what I see of bills of fare at home at the great feasts, that the clam and the oyster are in abeyance; that the soups of America, our country's boast, and the birthright of every patriot—that the soups which bring you memories of New England beaches, and the surf that tumbles along the shores of the modest Chesapeake, and the sandy reaches of New Jersey, are following the fate of these soups of Japan, which you only see at these solemn daimio feasts, which are as much out of keeping with even the feasts of to-day as the manners and costumes of Martha Washington's drawing-room in a Newport drawing-room. With the departure of the soups our dinner becomes fantastic. Perhaps the old daimios knew that by the time their guests had eaten of seven soups, and twenty courses in addition, and drank of innumerable dishes of rice liquor, they were in a condition to require a daring flight of genius.

The music is in full flow, and the lights of the town grow brighter with the shades of darkening night, and some of the company have long since taken refuge from the dinner in cigars, and over the low brick wall and in the recesses of the temple grounds crowds begin to cluster and form; and below, at the foot of the steps, the crowd grows larger and larger, and you hear the buzz of the throng and the clinking of the lanterns of the chair-bearers—for the whole town was in festive mood—and high up in our open temple on our hill-side we have become a show for the town. Well, that is only a small return for the measureless hospitality we have enjoyed, and if we can gratify an innocent curiosity, let us think of so much pleasure given in our way through the world. It is such a relief to know that we have passed beyond any comprehension of our dinner, which we look at as so many conceptions and preparations—curious contrivances, which we study out as though they were riddles or problems adjusted for our entertainment. The dining quality vanished with that eccentric soup of bassfish and orange flowers. With the General it went much earlier. It must be said that for the General the table has few charms, and long before we began upon the skylarks and buckwheat degraded by the egg-plant, he for whom this feast is given had taken refuge in a cigar, and contented himself with looking upon the beauty of the town and bay and cliff, allowing the dinner to flow along. You will observe, if you have followed the narrative of our feast, that meat plays a small and fish a large part in a daimio's dinner—fish and the products of the forest and field. The red snapper has the place of honor, and although we have had the snapper in five different shapes, as a soup, as a ragout, flavored with cabbage, broiled with pickled beans, and hashed, here he comes again, baked, decorated with ribbons, with every scale in place, folded in a bamboo basket. Certainly we cannot be expected to eat any more of the snapper, and I fancy that in the ancient feasts the daimio intended that after his guests had partaken freely they could take a part of the luxury home and have a subsequent entertainment. Perhaps there were poor folk in those days who had place at the tables of the great, and were glad enough to have a fish or a dish of sweetmeats to carry home. This theory was confirmed by the fact that when we reached our quarters that night we found that the snapper in a basket with various other dishes had been brought after us and placed in our chambers.

Here are fried snappers—snappers again, this time fried with shrimps, eggs, egg-plants and mashed turnips. Then we have dishes, five in number, under the generic name of "shima-

AN HISTORICAL DINNER.

dai." I suppose shimadai means the crowning glory, the consummation of the feast. In these dishes the genius of the artist takes his most daring flight. The first achievement is a composition of mashed fish, panyu, bolone, jelly and chestnut, decorated with scenery of Fusiyama. A moment since I called your attention to the moral lessons conveyed at a certain stage of our dinner, where the folly of ambition was taught by a carp trying to fly up a stream. Here the sentiment of art is gratified. Your dinner becomes a panorama, and when you have

VISIT TO HIOGO.

gazed upon the scenery of Fusiyama until you are satisfied, the picture changes. Here we have a picture and a legend. This picture is of the old couple of Takasago—a Japanese domestic legend, that enters into all plays and feasts. The old couple of Takasago always bring contentment, peace, and a happy old age. They are household fairies, and are invoked just as we invoke Santa Claus in holiday times. Somehow the Japanese have improved upon our legend; for instead of giving us a frosty, red-faced Santa Claus, riding along the snow-banked house-tops, showering his treasures upon the just and the unjust—a foolish, incoherent old fellow, about whose antecedents we are misinformed, of whose manner of living we have no information, and who would, if he ever came into the hands of the police, find it difficult to explain the possession of so many articles—we have a poem that teaches the peace that comes with virtue, the sacredness of marriage, and the beauty of that life which so soon comes to an end. Burns gives you the whole story in "John Anderson, my Jo," but what we have in a song the Japanese have in a legend. So at our daimio feasts the legend comes, and all the lessons of a perfect life of content and virtue are brought before you. The old couple are represented under trees of palm, bamboo, and plum. Snow has fallen upon the trees. Around this legend there is a dish composed of shrimp, fish, potato, water potatoes, eggs, and seaweed. The next dish of the shimadai family is decorated with pine trees and cranes, and composed of varieties of fish. There is another decorated with plum trees, bamboo, and tortoise, also of fish, and another, more curious than all, decorated with peony flowers and what is called the shakio, but what looked like a doll with long red hair. This final species of the shimadai family was composed of mashed fish—a Japanese fish named kisu, shrimps, potatoes, rabbits, gold fish and ginger. After the shimadai we had a series called sashimi. This was composed of four dishes, and would have been the crowning glory of the feast if we had not failed in courage. But one of the features of the sashimi was that live fish should be brought in, sliced while alive, and served. We were not brave enough for that, and so we contented ourselves with looking at the fish leaping about in their decorated basins and seeing them carried away, no doubt to be sliced for less sentimental feeders behind the screens. As a final course we had pears prepared with horse-radish, a cake of wheat flour and powdered ice. The dinner came to an end after a struggle of six or seven hours, and as we drove home through the illuminated town, brilliant with lanterns and fireworks and arches and bonfires, it was felt that we had been honored by an entertainment such as we may never again expect to see.

Our days in Nagasaki were pleasant, but few. We saw all the institutions of the town, the courts of law, the schools, the dock-yard—and every hour of our stay was marked by considerate and gracious hospitality. We passed six nights in Nagasaki, and every night there was an illumination with bonfires on the hills and fireworks, the people vieing with the government in doing honor to the General. All day long the crowds never wearied at hanging around the gates of the Normal School Building in which General Grant lived, watching for him. Our final hours were spent at an entertainment at the house of Mr. Mangum, the consul. The General re-embarked on the "Richmond" in a heavy rain, on the afternoon of the 26th of June. We at once went out to sea, the "Ashuelot," and the Japanese man-of-war keeping us company. Prince Dati remained on board his own vessel, while Mr. Yoshida and General Bingham accompanied General Grant to the "Richmond." In the evening, as we sailed out of Nagasaki harbor, the rain was falling and gloomy clouds darkened the sky. In the morning the sun was out, the green hills smiled upon us, and around us was the beauty of the Inland Sea of Japan. There for five days we sailed over a sea famous for its beauty and its romance, away from the world of telegraphs and journalism, on every side of us pictures of an ancient and picturesque civilization; passing from sea to sea, not as hurried merchantmen, with mails to carry and goods to sell, but cruising on a man-of-war, going easily and stopping as they list. There is very little that I can tell of a journey like this, except to lament that we could not catch up and carry away some of the glory with which nature surrounded us.

During the day we spent our time on deck. There were attempts at reading and writing, episodes of talk, and no end of smoke. One day seemed to repeat itself, like yesterday, for instance, the last day of June. As the sun went down, the sea, which had been a blue whispering ripple all day long, became as smooth as glass. The "Ashuelot" had been tugging on in our rear, near enough for us to distinguish our friends on the deck. Signals had been exchanging, signals necessary to the management of the ships, signals of courteous inquiry between Mrs. Grant and the ladies on board. All day long we had passed a succession of hills, valleys, islands covered with green, island rocks standing like sentinels over the channels of trade. In the formation of the hills you observe the preponderance of the conglomerate rock. Sometimes a ragged, cowl-like rock leaped up from among its comelier neighbors; and the jagged sides gave intimation of the immemorial ages when volcanic fires covered the land. Even nature, which with loving considerate hand has covered the rocks with verdure, and bidden the valleys to smile, and called forth flowers and grass and budding forest trees—even nature has not been able to extinguish the tokens of the fiery ages. Sometimes even the Inland Sea becomes restive and unruly, and heavy waves surge against these shores, but our trip is especially favored. All day we have only the suspicion of a breeze, just enough to corrugate the waters. As the evening falls, we come within a mile of a village. Rumors that cholera prevails

MAIL COURIER.

along the coast prevent our landing. So all that we can do is to study the village through our glasses—the temple on the side of the hill, the mass of tiled cottages, the fishing boats which come out toward us laden with curious villagers, not to barter, but only to go around and around us and see. Civilization has not penetrated these inland seas. All the people know of the outside world whose power is in ships, are the steamships carrying mails and merchandise that occasionally pass without pausing. We are on a man-of-war not concerned with commerce or the cares of trade, drifting along, taking the course that pleases us, shooting into one bay and another, seeking only the beauty of nature, and how to get on not in too great a hurry. We can visit spots where foreign ships never go. We had counted a great deal upon these opportunities, but the rumor of cholera met us at Nagasaki, and our Japanese friends who have us in charge as the representative of the Mikado forbid us to land. This prohibition extends to all the ships, and all communication with the shore, and is a disappointment, because we had counted on our opportunities of visiting out of the way places. After all, the life you see in Nagasaki in a great measure mirrors the life you bring. But the prohibition is so severe that the boats from the shore are warned to keep at a distance from the ship, and Mr. Yoshida proposes the dissemination of carbolic acid over the ship as a disinfectant.

In the evening General Grant gave a dinner party, one of a series of dinners in which the General meant to include all the officers of the two ships of war, from the captains down to the cadet midshipman. It is the General's only way of returning the gentle and considerate kindness he has received from all the naval officers of whatever grade. The dinner was served in the main cabin, General Grant presiding, with Captain Benham as *vis-à-vis*. Mrs. Grant sat on the right of the captain. Judge Bingham, the American Minister to Japan, and Mr. Yoshida, the Japanese Minister to America were also present. At the close, the General, lifting his glass and without rising said, "I drink to the American navy, and hope that it may never meet a foe except to be victorious over it." This was the only sentiment, unless I add a sentiment of the most radical character added in an undertone by Mrs. Grant, that she hoped they would all soon become admirals. Mrs. Grant's good wish was accepted in the best spirit by all present without introducing those burning questions of rank, pay, grade, and seniority which would be sure to arise in the event of its consideration by Congress. Then we all came on deck, and looked out on the calm sea, and the fleecy clouds overhead that made a mockery of covering the stars, and the lights that marked the outline of the town. The Japanese vessel was dressed from stem to stern with a rainbow decoration of lanterns, showing forth a dark red light. The spars were dressed, and the graceful vessel looked like some lurid phantom ship that had suddenly appeared on these weird, unknown seas. The brown night and the black hills made a fine background for the ship, giving the red lines of the illumination a deeper tint. Fireworks were displayed, and every few moments for an hour or two, we had ravishing masses of light, flaming, bursting, and dying. Then from the shores came cheering—peals of cheering—an unusual phenomenon in these sober Eastern lands, where the emotions are always suppressed. This cheering, far away and faint, was so homelike, and so unusual that it came upon us like a sound from home. Then our friends of the "Ashuelot" burned lights that changed from red to green and purple and other tints in an almost miraculous manner, and although a poor display compared with the Japanese, added another beauty to the night and brought renewed cheers from the shore. The "Richmond" had no lights to burn, and no fireworks, and our contribution to the evening was the band. So the band was lowered into a boat, and rowed toward the Japanese vessel, and around it, playing the Japanese air in honor of the empire, and other airs. Among them was Auld Lang Syne, which I venture to say was never heard to better advantage than as it came back to us softly borne by the evening winds over the sea of Japan. Music is a good deal like prayer and meditation and the sacred offices. We must be in the proper frame of mind to invoke it. And so we sat until the attentive bells told us that midnight was coming, and not without regret we left the revelation of beauty which the night had brought.

These were our evening amusements as we sailed on the sea of Japan. We only sail by day, and at night anchor. By day we sit on the deck and look at the scenery. For hours and hours we look at the unchanging beauty. Sometimes we come near to the shore, so near that we can almost throw a stone to the beach. We note clusters of houses that in America would be respectable villages, dotted about over the landscape in the radius of two or three hundred acres. One is accustomed to see wide spaces for cultivation around villages. But in Japan you see a half dozen villages all apart, distinct, evidently separate communes, and then comes a long reach of country with only groves and verdure. Children come running down to the shores, and give us a wondering welcome. We come to a bluff, ascended by stone steps to a terrace where

OUT FOR A RIDE.

there is a stone house, its white walls shining in the sun. From the terrace floats the flag of Japan, and we know that a guard of some kind keeps watch over the empire. The hills, which have been green and radiant, begin to look bare and show whitish brown blotches that tell of barrenness, and finally sink away in a succession of decreasing foot hills, and are lost in the sea. The land suddenly breaks away, and the land we have been skirting so closely proves to be a promontory, and we have to look for a moment steadily through the glasses before we can determine whether the line that bounds the horizon is a line of clouds or the land. Both shores break away, and we are in the middle of a sea many miles wide, the white sails of inland coasting vessels dotting the horizon. Fleets of boats—stumpy, clumsy boats—with sharp, angular prows, in groups of two or three, are in the service of fishermen searching the sea for food. These boats are all propelled by a long and supple bamboo pole swinging at the stern. The boatmen, in scanty blue raiment, with wide overlapping hats as large as the head of a flour-barrel, propel the boat by wobbling the pole from side to side. One cannot help thinking, as he sees this primitive method of seamanship, that there is little use of science or improved machinery at sea, and that Providence is the best sailor after all. I question if the most skillful seaman that ever left the Naval Academy could do as well with these lumbering crafts as the unlearned boatmen who have lived on these waters as their fathers have done for centuries. The currents are capricious and strong, and the officers on the bridge keep a keen lookout, and orders are constantly passing to the man at the wheel. Sometimes an uncouth, unwieldy junk, yielding to curiosity, comes sidling up so close to our prow as to cause a little anxiety. Then the orders are quick and sharp, and we rush to the side to see what the fate of the junk will be, and in a few moments our anxiety passes, as we almost graze the junk and go on our way. At the entrance of the sea there are two forts, one on either shore. One is an old fort, without guns, covered with grass; the other, a new one, with white, well-cemented walls. Beautiful as the sea is to idle voyagers on a calm, sunny, summer Sabbath afternoon, there is treachery in these currents, and rocks are hidden, and we are shown the red outlines of a buoy where an English steamer struck a rock and went down. But the sea has many such admonitions. Science and skill and the most perfect discipline fail you in the presence of these ambuscades, of the sudden winds, of the seas and currents. Nor does habit deaden experience. The best sailors I have known, the men who have the most experience, are always on their guard. No one can tell what an hour may bring forth, and the Eastern seas especially are noted for the ruin they have caused. All goes well with us, however, and the grim stories of disaster which mark the mariner's career only add a zest to our voyage through the sea of Japan.

The cloud which hangs over our trip thus far is the cholera. Mr. Yoshida has been telegraphing along the coast to know of the progress of this sinister disease. While at anchor we have a dispatch from Hiogo announcing that there had been a large number of deaths since the beginning of the month, that many were dying in the neighboring city of Osaka—the Venice of Japan, as it is called—and that landing was impossible.[1] I am afraid if our Japanese friends had not been peremptory and anxious on the cholera question, that our party would have landed. The naval people were disposed to treat the question lightly, one of our ward-room friends remarking that he had had the yellow fever twice, and would not object to a little cholera by way of change. But we were the guests of Japan, we were under the charge of the Emperor's representatives, and they were persistent on the point of our not landing.

We arrived at Hiogo about five o'clock in the afternoon. All the day we had been slowly steaming over a summer sea, the three vessels in company, our Japanese escort leading, and behind, near enough for us to distinguish our friends on the quarter deck through a telescope, was the "Ashuelot." We came to anchor about two miles from shore—nearer would have been dangerous. It was rather a satire on the fears of our friends, that no quarantine existed, that the port was full of shipping, and that mails came to us from the mail-boat at anchor, which was going ahead to Yokohama. The Consul-General, Stahel, came out to pay his respects to General Grant.(2) He confirmed the reports about the epidemic, which might be cholera or might not, but was certainly of the cholera family, coming rapidly and doing its will in a short time. None of the foreign settlement had suffered, and the authorities were doing what they could to stay the disease with carbolic acid and other disinfectants. The governor also came on board, a courteous Japanese official in blazing uniform resembling the court dress of an English official at a queen's drawing-room. He expressed his regret that he could not entertain us, but hoped that we might come again, overland from Tokio, as there was a palace prepared for our reception. Captain Benham issued an order forbidding any communication with the shore, so we swung at anchor watching the town and the glorious scenery which surrounded it. There could not be a more attractive site for a town. All along the shore the hills rise and break and fall, reaching their highest altitude at

A PEDDLER.

Hiogo. From base to summit they were covered with green. Instead of stately slopes and rugged rocks, the sides of the hills seemed to ripple and dimple, curving and bending into the oddest fancies until they broke against the sky. Above the summits was another summit of white clouds, the whiteness of an incandescent heat, which we took for snow until we knew that we had not come to the snow-tops. The hills slope toward the shore, and on the slope Hiogo is built. We studied it through our glasses and picked out the European bits and traced the concession.

General Grant tried to make our quarantine as pleasant as possible by giving a dinner to Prince Dati and the members of the Japanese deputation, Judge Bingham, Mr. and Mrs. Denny, Captain Johnson of the "Ashuelot," and a number of the officers of the "Richmond." After dinner, while we were gathered on deck, a steam launch came from the shore having a committee. Under the orders of the captain they were not allowed on board, and so the leader delivered an address in Japanese, at a high pitch of voice, in which he expressed the regret of the people that the General could not land, and hoped he would return again. The General listened to the address, leaning against the taffrail of the poop-deck. Mr. Yoshida translated it, as well as the response of the General, which was to the effect that he appreciated the kindness of the people in their desire to do him honor, and regretted the cause which prevented his landing. Then the committee in the launch went back. Although the General could not land, the town had made preparations to celebrate his coming. All the vessels in the harbor were dressed, and as the sun went down, the lights of rockets and lanterns began to appear. Some of these decorations were very fine, and when darkness came, the town seemed to be a glowing mass of fire. The general effect of the lanterns and the fireworks which arose in the air, and broke into a spray of colored flame, outdazzling in brilliancy the lustre of the constellations, the brown rolling hills, the shadows upon the water, the ships burning signals, and the music of our band, all combined to make Hiogo quite a fairy picture. The sea was smooth with scarcely a murmur, and for two or three hours the display continued.

So passed another of our midsummer nights on the sea of Japan. From what we heard and saw of Hiogo it was a great disappointment not to be able to visit the town. General Stahel told us of all that had been done by the people, and especially by the foreign residents, who are few in number, but had united in a hearty desire to make our visit as pleasant and instructive as possible. This desire of all classes of foreign nationalities, wherever we have met them in Asiatic settlements, to do honor to General Grant, and through him to America, is one of the most pleasant experiences of the trip. Those who dream about the federation of man which Mr. Tennyson sings, or the commonwealth of nations which M. Hugo invokes, will see in the sympathy and good feeling which pervades the citizens of all nations on the coasts of Asia a harbinger of the good time. Pleasant also to those who believe in the Eastern nations, and labor for the opening of the Chinese and Japanese ports to our commerce and our civilization, is the eagerness with which Chinese and Japanese vie with the Europeans in their desire to do honor to an ex-President of the United States. That is the contribution which General Grant's journey around the world makes to the politics of the East. However the General may desire to make this journey personal, however much he may shrink from the honors, the ceremony, the pageantry, however earnestly he may waive any claim to other consideration than that which a private gentleman should receive in his journeys, the authorities insist upon regarding the visit as official, as the coming of a ruler, as an embassy of the highest rank. China invoked his good offices as mediator between Japan and herself in the Loochoo question. (3)Japan is anxious for his good offices to secure the revision of the treaties which cripple her revenues in the interest of British trade. General Grant, while never giving indication of any power to affect one way or the other these important questions, appreciates the honor paid him, and has used his influence to impress upon the statesmen and rulers of these people the fact

HIOGO.

that their true interest lies in the fullest and freest intercourse with the younger nations; that they have nothing to fear from European civilization; that the good things we have given to the world are good for Japanese and Chinamen, as well as for Britons and Americans; that international law will secure them as many rights as other nations enjoy; that they will not always appeal in vain to the sympathy and justice of the aggressive war-making powers; and that profitable development will only

JAPANESE FIREMEN.

come when their own people are educated so as to appreciate and extend the lessons of Western civilization.

Whatever may be the effect of this advice, it is worthy of note that the General has lost no opportunity of giving it. He has given it to men who have gone out of their way to do him honor, and to ask his advice and aid. I allude to the fact because it would be a mistake to suppose that we are merely an idle party, sailing over summer seas, our days given to the wonderful scenery with which the All-beneficent Hand has decked these shores, our nights to the universe, the constellations, the serene whispering sea, music and fireworks, talk and song. If I have dwelt in these writings upon the lighter and brighter aspects of our journey, it is because I am glad to escape from serious themes, from politics and statesmanship, and gather up in a feeble, wandering way the impressions of nature. You sit on the deck, as I am sitting now, a steel breech-loading three-inch rifle gun for a table. The movement of the boat makes writing difficult, for the hand trembles, and the pen bobs over the paper as though I were tattooing, not writing. The General sits on the rear of the deck with Mr. Bingham and Mr. Yoshida, the Japanese minister, with a map unrolled, marking out our course and noting the prominent points of the scenery. Captain Benham is on the bridge, Mr. Sperry bends over the charts, Lieut.-Commander Clarke walks slowly up and down, waiting for the moment when, taking the trumpet from Mr. Stevens, the officer of the watch, he will bring the ship to anchor. "Three bells!" It is half-past one, and we are slowly moving into the bay of Sumida, where we are to anchor. A trim orderly comes tripping up the steps with the captain's compliments and the news that Fusiyama is in sight. Fusiyama is one of the glories of the mountain world, with its lofty peak, wrapped in eternal snow, over fourteen thousand feet high, occasionally sending out fire and smoke, making the earth tremble, and admonishing men of the awful and terrible glory embosomed in its rocky sides. We all go to the taffrail, and although clouds are clustered in the heavens, in time we trace the outlines of the mountain towering far into the inaccessible skies. Its beauty and its grandeur are veiled, and we dwell upon the green, dimpled hills, and the rolling plains. The sea becomes a lighter blue. Our Japanese convoy stops. A signal is made to the "Ashuelot" to slacken speed. Mrs. Grant, leaning on the arm of one of the officers, saunters up and down the deck enjoying the blended beauty of hill and sea. The loud word of command echoes along the deck. Sailors bustle about and make the boats ready for lowering. "Stand by the port-anchor!" and the boatswain's whistle answers the command. The bell rings admonition to go slowly, to back, to stand still. "Let go the port-anchor!" The chain rumbles over the side. The anchor plunges into the sea, and the noble vessel slowly swings around in a hissing sea, under the shadow of the mountain.

I thought of Naples as we swung at anchor in Sumida Bay, Naples perhaps coming to my mind because of Fusiyama, the famous volcano—one of the mountain beauties of the globe, which hid herself in the clouds, and only looked at us now and then through the coy and sheltering mist. Fusiyama is a noble mountain, and although thirty miles away, looked as near as Vesuvius from Naples. Then I thought of Longfellow's dream-picture of Japan, in which he draws an outline of Fusiyama, and as I was fortunate enough to find the lines in one of the naval officers' rooms, I quote them:

> "Cradled and rocked in Eastern seas,
> The islands of the Japanese
> Beneath me lie. O'er lake and plain
> The stork, the heron, and the crane
> Through the clear realms of azure drift;
> And on the hill-side I can see
> The villages of Iwari,
> Whose thronged and flaming workshops lift
> Their twisted columns of smoke on high—
> Cloud-cloisters that in ruins lie,
> With sunshine streaming through each rift,
> And broken arches of blue sky.
>
> "All the bright flowers that fill the land,
> Ripples of waves on rock or sand,
> The snow on Fusiyama's cone,
> The midnight heaven so thickly sown
> With constellations of bright stars,
> The leaves that rustle, the reeds that make
> A whisper by each stream and lake,
> The saffron dawn, the sunset red,
> Are painted on these lovely jars;
> Again the sky-lark sings, again
> The stork, the heron, and the crane
> Float through the azure overhead,
> The counterfeit and counterpart
> Of nature reproduced in art.'(4)

The bay of Sumida is not open to the outside world, and we are only here because we are the guests of the Emperor. Under the treaties there are specified ports open to trade, and in others vessels are forbidden to enter except under stress of weather. The Japanese would be glad to open any port in their kingdom, if the foreign powers would abate some of the hard conditions imposed upon them at the point of the bayonet. On this there will, one hopes, soon be an understanding honor-

A VILLAGE ON THE COAST.

able to Japan, and useful to the commercial world. But we are especially privileged in being allowed to come to a closed port, because we see Japan untouched by the foreigner. We have a glimpse of the land as it must have been before the deluge. The coming of these men-of-war was a startling circumstance, and the whole town, men, women, and children, were soon out in boats and barges and junks to see us. Captain Benham gave orders that they should be allowed to come on board fifty at a time and go through the ship. It would be a treat, he thought, and they would remember our flag, and when next it came into their port, remember the kindness that had been shown them. This seemed to be a wise and benevolent diplomacy, and was in no ways abused. Old men and old women, mothers with children strapped on their shoulders or tugging at their breasts, fishermen, all classes in fact, with clothes and without clothes, came streaming over the side to look and wonder, and marvel at the great glowering guns.

The governor of the province called, and invited us to visit him in his capital town, an old-fashioned town about six miles in the interior. We landed and spent a few minutes looking at the catch of fish made by the fishermen, and noted a species with fins colored like the wings of a butterfly. We visited a tea house and saw the tea in its various processes of curing. There were maidens with nimble fingers who sorted out the good from the bad, and earned in that labor ten cents a day. Mr. Bingham, Captain Benham, and several officers of the "Ashuelot" and "Richmond" increased our number, and when finally about ten in the morning we set out for a visit to Shiguoka, we had quite a procession of jinrickshaws. The whole town was out, and every house displayed the Japanese flag. Schools dismissed, and the scholars formed in line, their teachers at their head, and bowed low as we passed. The roads were fairly good, much better than I have seen in the suburbs of New York, and our perambulators spun along at a good pace. When we left the town we passed under shady trees, and stretches of low rice fields, almost under water, and fields of tea. Policemen, dapper little fellows in white uniforms with small staffs, were stationed at regular points to keep order. But the policeman seemed quite out of place in smiling, happy, amiable Japan. The people were in the best of humor, and rumors of our coming evidently had preceded us, for all along the road we found people watching and waiting to welcome the General with a smile and a bow. About noon we reached the town, and bowled along merrily over streets which had rarely if ever seen the foot of a European. As a pure Japanese town, without a tint of European civilization, it was most interesting. The streets were clean and narrow, the people in

518   *JAPAN.*

Japanese costumes. The houses were tidy, and the stores teemed with articles for sale. We saw no beggary, no misery, no poverty, only a bright contented people who loved the sunshine. We drove on, up one street and down another, a roundabout way, I am sure, so that we should see the town and the

WRITING UNDER DIFFICULTIES.

town see us, until we came to a park and a temple. I observe in these Eastern nations, and especially in Japan, that places of worship and of recreation are together, so that the faithful may perform their devotions and have a good time. Here we sat and took tea. The carving on the temple was two centuries old, but looked fresh and new. The floors were covered with clean white matting, and the screens were decorated with birds of gay plumage. While the tea was served there was music, and after the music bonbons. Priests in white and brown flowing garments, active young men not apparently suffering from an ascetic life, came and bowed to the General. Day fireworks were set off—a curious contrivance in pyrotechny which makes a cloud in the sky and shoots out fans and ribbons and trinkets. One of these fans took fire, and while burning lodged on the wood-work of the temple, and for a moment it seemed as if we were to have an additional and unexpected pageant. But the priests and policemen scrambled up the carved pillars and put out the fire. At the doors of the temple were offerings of white flowers.

The presence of the General in the town was made the occasion for a fête-day, and the people enjoyed the fireworks and the music. Then we were taken to breakfast, a Japanese breakfast of multitudinous and curious dishes, and after breakfast we rode home. We passed on our way the walls surrounding the home of the dethroned Tycoon. That once-dreaded monarch is now a pensioner, and lives a life of seclusion and study. The drive back was picturesque and pleasant, in all respects most interesting as our first unruffled glimpse of Japan. The roads were smooth, the streams were covered with round stone bridges, and there were brooks with clear running water. We stopped at a tea-house to allow our jinrickshaw men to cool themselves and drink, and saw heaps of the green tea-leaves ready to be cured. On our return to the village we found the whole town waiting for us, and as we rolled down to the beach, the people came flying and tramping after. During the night we kept on in a slow, easy pace, and in the morning at ten we saw the hills of Yokohama, and heard the guns of the "Monongahela"—Admiral Patterson's flagship—thunder out their welcome to General Grant.

ULYSSES S. GRANT

ULYSSES S. GRANT

Notes on Chapter XLI
Page numbers refer to pagination of facsimile document.

(1) p. 509   Hiogo is Kobe. American respect for Japanese quarantine measures contrasted with other western powers and was a factor in the good feeling of the local population towards the visiting Americans.

(2) p. 510   Consul Stahel had served in the Union Army during the Civil War and was awarded the Medal of Honor for his bravery at the battle of Piedmont in 1864. He was later named by Secretary of State Evarts to a commission to study and find remedies for corruption in the diplomatic service. (see also footnote 5 and photo in Seward section, Chapter 10)

(3) p. 512   At the time of Grant's visit, China and Japan contested control of the Loochoo Island chain or Okinawa as it is known in Japan. Grant's involvement unfortunately did not lead to a settlement.

(4) p. 515   The passage of the poem that Young quotes and which he says he found in a naval officer's room is from Henry Wadsworth Longfellow's "Keramos," first published in *Harper*'s in 1877, then the next year in a Longfellow anthology. The poem is a poetic journey around the globe, especially to well-known pottery making sites, from Delft in Holland to the Mediterranean, Egypt, India, China and Japan. The turning of the potter's wheel, the turning of the earth, are images that fit the optimistic mood of American world travellers of the 1870s as another passage from "Keramos" makes explicit:

Turn, turn, my wheel! The human race,
Of every tongue, of every place,
  Caucasian, Coptic, or Malay,
All that inhabit this great earth,
Whatever be their rank or worth,
Are kindred and allied by birth,
  And made of the same clay.

THE HARBOR OF YOKOHAMA.

CHAPTER XLII.

JAPAN.

GENERAL GRANT'S landing in Yokohama, which took place on the 3d of July, as a mere pageant, was in itself a glorious sight. Yokohama has a beautiful harbor, and the lines of the city can be traced along the green background. The day was clear and warm—a home July day tempered with ocean winds. There were men-of-war of various nations in the harbor, and as the exact hour of the General's coming was known, everybody was on the lookout. At ten o'clock our Japanese convoy passed ahead and entered the harbor. At half-past ten the "Richmond" steamed slowly in, followed by the "Ashuelot." As soon as the "Monongahela" made out our flag, and especially the flag at the fore, which denoted the General's presence, her guns rolled out a salute. For a half hour the bay rang with the roar of cannon and was clouded with smoke. The "Richmond" fired a salute to the flag of Japan. The Japanese and the French and Russian vessels fired gun after gun. Then came official visits—Admiral Patterson and staff, the admirals and commanding officers of other fleets, Consul-general Van Buren, and officers of the Japanese navy, blazing in uniform. The officers of the "Richmond" were all in full uniform, and for an hour the deck of the flag-ship was a blaze of color and decoration.[1] General Grant received the various dignitaries on the deck as they arrived. It was arranged that General Grant's landing was to take place precisely at noon. The foreign residents were anxious that the ceremony should be on what is called the foreign concession, but the Japanese authorities preferred that it should be on their own territory. At noon the imperial barge and the steam launch came alongside the "Richmond." General Grant, accompanied by Mrs. Grant, his son, Prince Dati, Judge Bingham, Mr. Yoshida, and the naval officers specially detailed to accompany him, passed over the side and went on the barge. As soon as General Grant entered the barge, the "Richmond" manned yards and fired a salute. In an instant, as if by magic, the Japanese, the French, and the Russians manned yards and fired salutes. The German ship hoisted the imperial standard, and the English vessel dressed ship. Amid the roar of cannon and the waving of flags the General's boat slowly moved to the shore. As he passed each of the saluting ships the General took off his hat and bowed, while the guards presented arms and the bands played the American national air. The scene was wonderfully grand—the roar of the cannon, the clouds of smoke wandering off over the waters; the stately, noble vessels streaming with flags; the yards manned with seamen; the guards on deck; the officers in full uniform gathered on the quarter-deck to salute the General as he passed; the music and the cheers which came from the Japanese and the merchant ships; the crowds that clustered on the wharves; the city; and over all a clear, mild, July day, with grateful breezes ruffling the sea.

522　　　　　　*JAPAN.*

As the General's barge slowly came to the Admiralty wharf, there in waiting were the princes, ministers, and the high officials of the empire of Japan. As the General stepped out of the boat the Japanese band played the American national air, and Mr. Iwakura, Second Prime Minister, advanced and shook hands with him.(2) General Grant had known Mr. Iwakura in America, when he visited our country at the head of the Japanese embassy. The greeting, therefore, was that of

THE ARRIVAL AT YOKOHAMA.

old friends. There were also Ito, Inomoto, and Tereshima, also members of the Cabinet, two princes of the imperial family, and a retinue of officials.(3) Mr. Yoshida presented the General and party to the Japanese, and a few moments were spent in conversation. Day fireworks were set off at the moment of the landing—representations of the American and Japanese flags entwined. That, however, is the legend that greets you at every door-sill—the two flags entwined. The General and party, accompanied by the ministers and officials and the naval officers, drove to the railway station. There was a special train in waiting, and at a quarter past one the party started for Tokio.

Our ride to Tokio was a little less than an hour, over a smooth road, and through a pleasant, well-cultivated, and apparently prosperous country. Our train being special made no stoppage; but I observed as we passed the stations that they were clean and neat, and that the people had assembled to wave flags and bow as we whirled past.(4) About two o'clock our train entered the station at Tokio. A large crowd was in waiting, mainly the merchants and principal citizens. As the General descended from the train a committee of the citizens advanced and asked to read an address. At the close of the address General Grant was led to the private carriage of the Emperor. Among those who greeted him was his Excellency J. Pope Hennessy, British Governor of Hong-Kong, who said that he came as a British subject, to be among those who welcomed General Grant to Japan. (5)

The General's carriage drove slowly, surrounded by cavalry, through lines of infantry presenting arms, through a dense mass of people, under an arch of flowers and evergreens, until, amid the flourish of trumpets and the beating of drums, he descended at the house that had been prepared for his reception —the Emperor's summer palace of Enriokwan.(6) The Japanese, with almost a French refinement of courtesy, were anxious that General Grant should not have any special honors paid to him in Japan until he had seen the Emperor. They were also desirous that the meeting with the Emperor should take place on the Fourth of July. Their imaginations had been impressed with the poetry of the idea of the reception of one who had been the head of the American nation on the anniversary of American Independence. Accordingly it was arranged that at two o'clock on the afternoon of the Fourth of July the audience with the Emperor should take place. The day was very warm, although in our palace on the sea we had whatever breeze might have been wandering over the Pacific. General Grant invited some of his naval friends to accompany him, and in answer to this invitation we had Rear Admiral Patterson,

ULYSSES S. GRANT

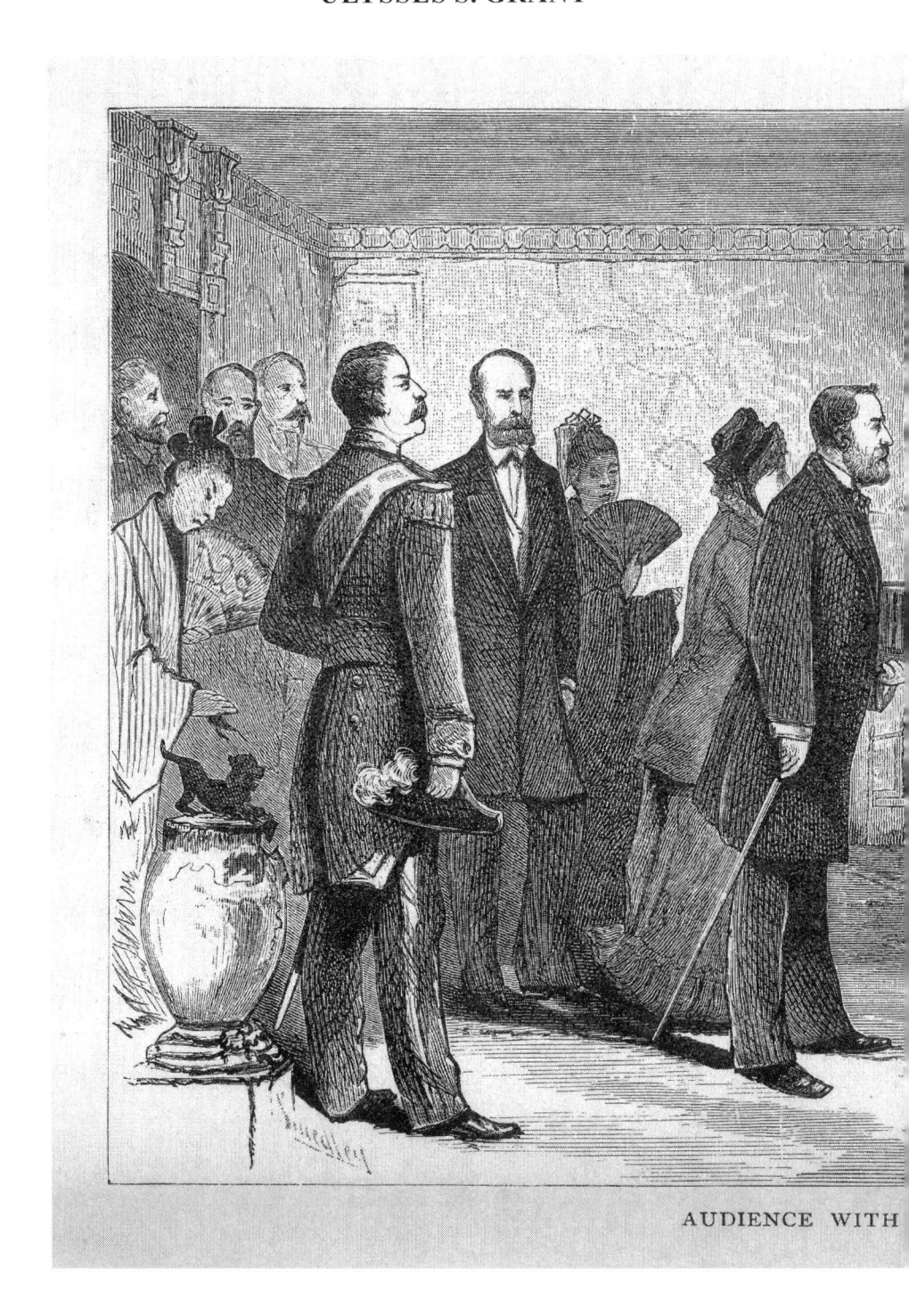

AUDIENCE WITH

ULYSSES S. GRANT

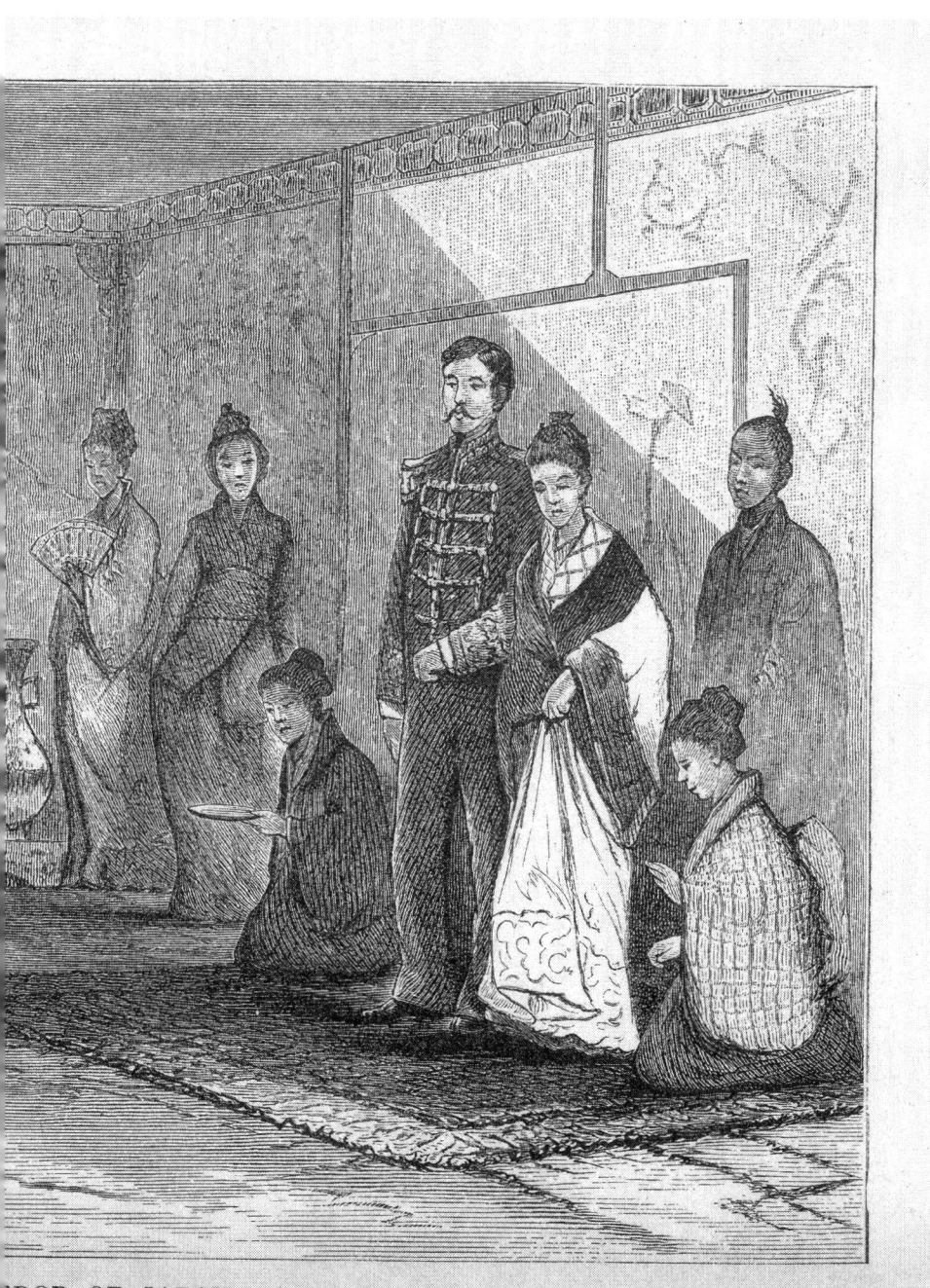

EROR OF JAPAN.

attended by Pay Inspector Thornton and Lieutenant Davenport of his staff; Captain Benham commanding the "Richmond;" Captain Fitzhugh, commanding the "Monongahela;" Commander Johnson, commanding the "Ashuelot;" Lieutenant Springer, and Lieutenant Kellogg. At half-past one Mr. Bingham, our Minister, arrived, and our party immediately drove to the palace. The home of the Emperor was a long distance from the home of the General. The old palace was destroyed by fire, and Japan has had so many things to do that she has not built a new one. The road to the palace was through the section of Tokio where the old daimios lived when they ruled Japan as feudal lords, and made their occasional visits to the capital. There seems to have been a good deal of Highland freedom in the manners of the old princes. Their town-houses were really fortifications. A space was inclosed with walls, and against these walls chambers were built—rude chambers, like winter quarters for an army. In these winter quarters lived the retainers, the swordsmen and soldiers. In the center of the inclosure was the home of the lord himself, who lived in the midst of his people, like a general in camp, anxious to fight somebody, and disappointed if he returned to his home without a fight. A lord with hot-tempered followers, who had come from the restraints and amenities of home to have a good time at the capital and give the boys a chance to distinguish themselves and see the world, would not be a welcome neighbor. And as there were a great many such lords, and each had his army and his town fortress, the daimio quarter became an important part of the capital. Some of the houses were more imposing than the palace—notably the house of the Prince of Satsuma. There was an imposing gate, elaborately buttressed and strengthened, that looked quite Gothic in its rude splendor. These daimio houses have been taken by the government for schools, for public offices, for various useful purposes. The daimios no longer come with armies and build camps and terrorize over their neighbors and rivals.

We drove through the daimios' quarter and through the gates of the city. The first impression of Tokio is that it is a city of walls and canals. The walls are crude and solid, protected by moats. In the days of pikemen and sword-bearers there could not have been a more effective defense. Even now it would require an effort for even a German army to enter through these walls. They go back many generations;

THE MIKADO'S GROUNDS.

I do not know how many. In these lands nothing is worth recording that is not a thousand years old, and my impression is that the walls of Tokio have grown up with the growth of the city, the necessities of defense, and the knowledge of the people in attack and defense. We passed under the walls of an inclosure which was called the castle. Here we are told the Emperor will build his new palace. We crossed another bridge—I think there were a dozen altogether in the course of the drive—and came to a modest arched gateway, which did not look nearly as imposing as the entrance to the palace formerly occupied by the great Prince Satsuma. Soldiers were drawn up, and the band played "Hail Columbia." Our carriages drove on past one or two modest buildings and drew up in front of another modest building, on the steps of which the Minister Iwakura was standing. The General and party descended, and were cordially welcomed and escorted up a narrow stairway into an anteroom. When you have seen most of the available palaces in the world, from the glorious home of Aurungzebe to the depressing, mighty cloister of the Escurial, you are sure to have preconceived notions of what a palace should be, and to expect something unique and grand in the home of the long-hidden and sacred Majesty of Japan. The home of the Emperor was as simple as that of a country gentleman at home. We have many country gentlemen with felicitous investments in petroleum and silver who would disdain the home of a prince who claims direct descent from heaven, and whose line extends far beyond the Christian era. What marked the house was its simplicity and taste; qualities for which my palace education had not prepared me. You look for splendor, for the grand—at least the grandiose—for some royal whim like the holy palace near the Escurial, which cost millions, or like Versailles, whose cost is among the eternal mysteries. Here we are in a suite of plain rooms, the ceilings of wood, the walls decorated with natural scenery—the furniture sufficient but not crowded—and exquisite in style and finish. There is no pretense of architectural emotion. The rooms are large, airy, with a sense of summer about them which grows stronger as you look out of the window and down the avenues of trees. We are told that the grounds are spacious and fine, even for Japan, and that his Majesty, who rarely goes outside of his palace grounds, takes what recreation he needs within the walls.

The palace is a low building, one story in height. They do not build high walls in Japan, especially in Tokio, on account of the earthquakes. We enter a room where all the Ministers are assembled. The Japanese Cabinet is a famous body, and tested by the laws of physiognomy would compare with that of any Cabinet I have seen. The Prime Minister is a striking character. He is small, slender, with an almost girl-like figure, delicate, clean-cut, winning features, a face that might be that of a boy of twenty or a man of fifty. The Prime Minister reminded me of Alexander H. Stephens in his frail, slender frame, but it bloomed with health and lacked the

STREET IN YOKOHAMA.

sad, pathetic lines which tell of the years of suffering which Stephens has endured. The other Ministers looked like strong, able men. Iwakura has a striking face, with lines showing firmness and decision, and you saw the scar which marked the attempt of the assassin to cut him down and slay him, as Okubo, the greatest of Japanese statesmen, was slain not many months ago.(7) That assassination made as deep an impression in Japan as the killing of Lincoln did in America. We saw the spot where the murder was done on our way to the palace, and my Japanese friend who pointed it out spoke in low tones of sorrow and affection, and said the crime there committed had been an irreparable loss to Japan. A lord in waiting, with a heavily-braided uniform, comes softly in, and, making a signal, leads the way. The General and Mrs. Grant, escorted by General Bingham, and followed by the remainder of our party, entered. The General and the Minister were in evening dress. The naval officers were in full uniform, Colonel Grant wearing the uniform of lieutenant-colonel. We walked along a short passage and entered another room, at the farther end of which were standing the Emperor and the Empress. Two ladies in waiting were near them, in a sitting, what appeared to be a crouching, attitude. Two other princesses were standing. These were the only occupants of the room. Our party slowly advanced, the Japanese making a profound obeisance, bending the head almost to a right angle with the body. The royal princes formed in line near the Emperor, along with the princesses. The Emperor stood quite motionless, apparently unobservant or unconscious of the homage that was paid him. He is a young man, with a slender figure, taller than the average Japanese, and of about the middle height according to our ideas. He has a striking face, with a mouth and lips that remind you something of the traditional mouth of the Hapsburg family. The forehead is full and narrow, the hair and the light mustache and beard intensely black. The color of the hair darkens what otherwise might pass for a swarthy countenance at home. The face expressed no feeling whatever, and but for the dark, glowing eye, which was bent full upon the General, you might have taken the imperial group for statues. The Empress, at his side, wore the Japanese costume, rich and plain. Her face was very white, and her form slender and almost childlike. Her hair was combed plainly and braided with a gold arrow. The Emperor and Empress have agreeable faces, the Emperor especially showing firmness and kindness. The solemn etiquette that pervaded the audience chamber was peculiar, and might appear strange to those familiar with the stately but cordial manners of a European court. But one must remember that the Emperor holds so high and so sacred a place in the traditions, the religion, and the political system of Japan that even the ceremony of to-day is so far in advance of anything of the kind ever known in Japan that it might be called a revolution.

His Imperial Majesty, for instance, as our group was formed, advanced and shook hands with General Grant. This seems

THE HAMAGARTEN.

a trivial thing to write down, but such a thing was never before known in the history of Japanese majesty. Many of these details may appear small, but we are in the presence of an old and romantic civilization, slowly giving way to the fierce, feverish pressure of European ideas, and you can only note the change in those incidents which would be unnoticed in other lands.

The incident of the Emperor of Japan advancing toward General Grant and shaking hands becomes a historic event of consequence, and as such I note it. The manner of the Emperor was constrained, almost awkward, the manner of a man doing a thing for the first time, and trying to do it as well as possible. After he had shaken hands with the General, he returned to his place, and stood with his hand resting on his sword, looking on at the brilliant, embroidered, gilded company as though unconscious of their presence. Mr. Bingham advanced and bowed, and received just the faintest nod in recognition. The other members of the party were each presented by the minister, and each one, standing about a dozen feet from the Emperor, stood and bowed. Then the General and Mrs. Grant were presented to the princesses, each party bowing to the other in silence. The Emperor then made a signal to one of the attendants, Mr. Ishibashi, who advanced. The Emperor spoke to him for a few moments in a low tone, Mr. Ishibashi standing with bowed head. When the Emperor had finished, Mr. Ishibashi advanced to the General, and said he was commanded by his Majesty to read him the following address:

"Your name has been known to us for a long time, and we are highly gratified to see you. While holding the high office of President of the United States you extended toward our countrymen especial kindness and courtesy. When our ambassador, Iwakura, visited the United States, he received the greatest kindness from you. The kindness thus shown by you has always been remembered by us. In your travels around the world you have reached this country, and our people of all classes feel gratified and happy to receive you. We trust that during your sojourn in our country you may find much to enjoy. It gives me sincere pleasure to receive you, and we are especially gratified that we have been able to do so on the anniversary of American independence. We congratulate you, also, on the occasion."

This address was read in English. At its close General Grant said:

"Your Majesty: I am very grateful for the welcome you accord me here to-day, and for the great kindness with which I have been received, ever since I came to Japan, by your government and your people. I recognize in this a feeling of friendship toward my country. I can assure you that this feeling is reciprocated by the United States; that our people, without regard to party, take the deepest interest in all that concerns Japan, and have the warmest wishes for her welfare. I am happy to be able to express that sentiment. America is your next neighbor, and will always give Japan sympathy and support in her efforts to advance. I again thank your Majesty for your hospitality, and wish you a long and happy reign, and for your people prosperity and independence."

At the conclusion of this address, which was *extempore*, Mr. Ishibashi translated it to his Majesty. Then the Empress made a sign and said a few words. Mr. Ishibashi came to the side of Mrs. Grant and said the Empress had commanded him to translate the following address:

"I congratulate you upon your safe arrival after your long journey. I presume you have seen very many interesting places. I fear you will find many things uncomfortable here, because the customs of the country are so different from other countries. I hope you will prolong your stay in Japan, and that the present warm days may occasion you no inconvenience."

Mrs. Grant, pausing a moment, said in a low, conversational tone of voice, with animation and feeling:

"I thank you very much. I have visited many countries and have seen many beautiful places, but I have seen none so beautiful or so charming as Japan."

All day, during the Fourth of July, visitors poured in on the General. The reception of so many distinguished statesmen and officials reminded one of state occasions at the White House. Princes of the imperial family, princesses, the members of the cabinet and citizens and high officials, naval officers, ministers and consuls, all came; and carriages were constantly coming and going. In the evening there was a party at one of the summer gardens, given by the American residents in honor of the Fourth of July. The General arrived at half-past eight, and was presented to the American residents by Mr. Bingham, the minister. At the close of the presentation, Mr. Bingham made a brief but singularly eloquent address. Judge Van Buren made a patriotic and ringing speech, after which there were fireworks and feasting, and, after the General and Mrs.

Grant retired, there was dancing. It was far on toward morning before the members of the American colony in Tokio grew weary of celebrating the anniversary.

The morning of the 7th of July was set apart by the Emperor for a review of the troops. Japan has made important advances in the military art. One of the effects of the revolution which brought the Mikado out of his retirement as spiritual chief of the nation, and proclaimed him the absolute temporal sovereign, was the employment of foreign officers to drill and instruct the troops, teach them European tactics, and organize an army. It is a question whether a revolution which brings a nation out of a condition of dormant peace in which Japan existed for so many centuries—so far as the outer world is concerned—into line with the great military nations, is a step in the path of progress. But an army in Japan was necessary to support the central power, suppress the daimios' clans, whose strifes kept the land in a fever, and insure some degree of respect from the outside world. It is the painful fact in this glorious nineteenth century, which has done so

WORSHIPING THE MIKADO'S PHOTOGRAPH.

much to elevate and strengthen, and so on, that no advancement is sure without gunpowder. The glorious march of our civilization has been through battle smoke, and when Japan threw off the repose and dream-life of centuries, and came into the wakeful, vigilant, active world, she saw that she must arm, just as China begins to see that she must arm. The military side of Japanese civilization does not interest me, and I went to the review with a feeling that I was to see an incongruous thing, something that did not belong to Japan, that was out of place amid so much beauty and art. The Japanese themselves think so, but Europe is here with a mailed hand, and Japan must mail her own or be crushed in the grasp.

The Emperor of Japan is fond of his army, and was more anxious to show it to General Grant than any other institution in the Empire. Great preparations had been made to have it in readiness, and all Tokio was out to see the pageant. The review of the army by the Emperor in itself is an event that causes a sensation. But the review of the army by the Emperor and the General was an event which had no precedent in Japanese history. The hour for the review was nine, and at half-past eight the clatter of horsemen and the sound of bugles were heard in the palace grounds. In a few moments the Emperor's state carriage drove up, the drivers in scarlet livery and the panels decorated with the imperial flower, the chrysanthemum. General Grant entered, accompanied by Prince Dati, the cavalry formed a hollow square, and our procession moved on to the field at a slow pace. A drive of twenty minutes brought us to the parade ground, a large open plain, the soldiers in line, and behind the soldiers a dense mass of people—men, women, and children. As the General's procession slowly turned into the parade ground a group of Japanese officers rode up and saluted, the band played "Hail Columbia," and the soldiers presented arms. Two tents had been arranged for the reception of the guests. In the larger of the two we found assembled officers of state, representatives of foreign powers, and Governor Hennessy, all in bright, glowing uniforms. The smaller tent was for the Emperor. When the General dismounted, he was met by the Minister of War and escorted into the smaller tent. In a few minutes the trumpets gave token that the Emperor was coming, and the band played the Japanese national air. His Majesty was in a state carriage, surrounded with horsemen and accompanied by one of his cabinet. As the Emperor drove up to the tent, General Grant advanced to the carriage steps and shook hands with him, and they entered and remained a few minutes in conversation.

At the close of the review, General Grant and party drove off the ground in state, and were taken to the Shila palace. This palace is near the sea, and as the grounds are beautiful and attractive, it was thought best that the breakfast to be given to General Grant by his Majesty should take place here. The Emperor received the General and party in a large, plainly furnished room, and led the way to another room where the table was set. The decorations of the table were sumptuous and royal. General Grant sat on one side of the Emperor, whose place was in the center. The Emperor conversed a great deal with General Grant through Mr. Yoshida, and also Governor Hennessy. His Majesty expressed a desire to have a private and friendly conference with the General, which it was arranged should take place after the General's return from Nikko. The feast lasted for a couple of hours, and the view from the table was charming. Beneath the window was a lake, and the banks were bordered with grass and trees. Cool winds came from the sea, and, although in the heart of a great capital, we were as secluded as in a forest.

General Grant's home in Tokio—Enriokwan—was only a few minutes' ride from the railway station. This palace was one of the homes of the Tycoon. (8)It now belongs to the Emperor. If your ideas of palaces are European, or even American, you will be disappointed with Enriokwan. One somehow associates a palace with state, splendor, a profusion of color and decoration, with upholstery and marble. There is nothing of this in Enriokwan. You approach the grounds over a dusty road that runs by the side of a canal. You cross a bridge and enter a low gateway, and going a few paces enter another gateway. Here is a guard-house, with soldiers on guard and lolling about on benches waiting for the bugle to summon them to offices of ceremony. There is a good deal of ceremony in Enriokwan, with the constant coming and going of great people, and no sound is more familiar than the sound of the bugle. You pass the guard-house and go down a pebbled way to a low, one-story building, with wings. This is the

TOKIO.

palace of Enriokwan. Over the door is the chrysanthemum. Enriokwan is an island. On one side is a canal and embanked walls, on the other side the ocean. Although in an ancient and populous city, surrounded by a busy metropolis, you feel as you pass into Enriokwan that you are as secure and as secluded as in a fortress. The grounds are large, and remarkable for the beauty and finish of the landscape gardening. In the art of gardening Japan excels the world, and I have seen no more attractive specimen than the grounds of Enriokwan. Roads, flower-beds, lakes, bridges, artificial mounds, creeks overhung with sedgy overgrowths, lawns, boats, bowers over which vines are trailing, summer-houses, all combine to give comfort to Enriokwan. If you sit on this veranda, under the columns where the General sits every evening, you look out upon a ripe and perfect landscape dowered with green. If you walk into the grounds a few minutes, you pass a gate—an inner gate, which is locked at night—and come to a lake, on the banks of which is a Japanese summer-house. The lake is artificial and fed from the sea. You cross a bridge and come to another summer-house. Here are two boats tied up, with the imperial chrysanthemum emblazoned on their bows. These are the private boats of the Emperor, and if you care for a pull you can row across and lose yourself in one of the creeks. You ascend a grassy mound, however, not more than forty feet high. Steps are cut in the side of the mound, and when you reach the summit you see beneath you the waves and before you the ocean. The sea at this point forms a bay. When the tides are down and the waves are calm you see fishermen wading about seeking shells and shell-fish. When the tides are up, the boats sail near the shore.

What impresses you as you look at Enriokwan from the summit of your mound is its complete seclusion. The Tycoons, when they came to rest and breathe a summer air tempered by the sea, evidently wished to be away from the world, and here they could lead a sheltered life. It is a place for contemplation and repose. You can walk about in the grounds until you are weary, and if you take pleasure in grasses and shrubbery and wonderful old trees, gnarled and bending under the burden of immemorial years, every step will be full of interest. You can climb your mound and commence with the sea—the ships going and coming, the fishermen on the beach, the waves that sweep on and on. If you want to fish, you will find the poetry of fishing in Enriokwan, for servants float about you and bait your hook and guard what you catch, and you have no work or trouble or worms to finger, no scales to pick from your hands. If you care to read or write, you can find seclusion in one of the summer-houses. If it is evening, after dinner, you can come and smoke or wander around under the trees and look at the effect of the moonlight on the sea or the lake. Whatever you do, or wherever you go, you have over you the sense of protection. Our hosts are so kind that we cannot leave the palace without an escort. You stroll off with a naval friend from one of the ships to show the grounds, or hear the last gossip from the hospitable wardrooms of the "Ashuelot" or "Richmond." Behind you come a couple of servants, who seem to rise out of the ground as it were. They come unbidden, and carry trays bearing water and wine, or cigars. If you go into one of the summer-houses they stand on guard, and if you go on the lake they await your return. The sense of being always under observation was at first oppressive. You felt that you were giving trouble. You did not want to have the responsibility of dragging other people after you. But the custom belongs to Enriokwan, and in time you become used to it and unconscious of your retinues.

You wonder at the number of servants about you—servants for everything. There, for instance, is a gardener working over a tree. The tree is one of the dwarf species that you see in Japan—one of the eccentricities of landscape gardening—and this gardener files and clips and adorns his tree as carefully as a lapidary burnishing a gem. "There has been work enough done on that tree," said the General, "since I have been here, to raise all the food a small family would require during the winter." Labor, the General thinks, is too good a thing to be misapplied, and when the result of the labor is a plum-tree that you could put on your dinner-table, he is apt to regard it as misapplied. Here are a dozen men in blue cotton dress working at a lawn. I suppose in a week they would do as much as a handy Yankee boy could achieve in a morning with a lawn-mower. Your Japanese workman sits down over his meadow, or his flower-bed, or his bit of road, as though it were a web of silk that he was embroidering. Other men in blue are fishing. The waters of the lake come in with the tide, and the fish that come do not return, and much of our food is found here.

The sprinkling of the lawns and of the roads is always a serious task, and employs quite an army of servants for the best part of the afternoon. One of the necessities of palace life is that you have ten times as many servants about you as you want, and work must be found to keep them busy. The

A JAPANESE VILLAGE.

summer-houses by the lake in the grounds at Enriokwan are worthy of study. Japan has taught the world the beauty of clean, fine-grained natural wood, and the fallacy of glass and paint. I am writing these lines in one of these houses—the first you meet as you come to the lake. Nothing could be more simple and at the same time more tasteful. It is one room, with grooves for a partition should you wish to make it two rooms. The floor is covered with a fine, closely-woven mat of bamboo strips. Over the mat is thrown a rug, in which black and brown predominate. The walls looking out to the lake are a series of frames that can be taken out—lattice-work of small squares, covered with paper. The ceiling is plain unvarnished wood. There are a few shelves, with vases, blue and white pottery, containing growing plants and flowers. There are two tables, and their only furniture a large box of gilded lacquer for stationery, and a smaller one containing cigars. These boxes are of exquisite workmanship, and the gold chrysanthemum indicates the imperial ownership. I have described this house in detail because it is a type of all the houses that I have seen in the palace grounds, not only at Enriokwan but elsewhere in Japan. It shows taste and economy. Everything about it is wholesome and clean, the workmanship true and minute, with no tawdry appliances to distract or offend the eye.

The weather was such that going out during the day was a discomfort—warm, torrid, baking weather. During the day there are ceremonies, calls from Japanese and foreign officials, papers to read, visits to make. If the evening is free the General has a dinner party—sometimes small, sometimes large. To-night it will be the royal princes, to-morrow the Prime Ministers, on other evenings other Japanese of rank and station. Sometimes we have Admiral Patterson or officers from the fleet. Sometimes Mr. Bingham and his family. Governor Hennessy, the British Governor of Hong-Kong, has been a frequent visitor, and no man was more welcome to the General. General Grant was the guest of the Governor during his residence in Hong-Kong, and formed a high opinion of his genius and character. Prince Dati, Mr. Yoshida, and some other Japanese officials live at Enriokwan and form a part of our family. They represent the Emperor, and remain with the General to serve him and make his stay as pleasant as possible. Nothing could be more considerate or courteous than the kindness of our Japanese friends. Sometimes we have merchants from the bazaars with all kinds of curious and useful things to sell. Sometimes a fancy for curiosities takes possession of some of the party, and the result is an afternoon's prowl about the shops in Tokio, and the purchase of a sword or a spear or a bow and arrows. The bazaars of Tokio teem with beautiful works of art, and the temptation to go back laden with achievements in porcelain and lacquer is too great to be resisted, unless your will is under the control of material influences too sordid to be dwelt upon. Sometimes we have special and unique excitements, such as was vouchsafed to us a few evenings since. Our party was at dinner—an informal dinner—with no guests except our Japanese friends and Governor Hennessy. While dining there was a slight thunder-storm, which gave some life to the baked and burning atmosphere. Suddenly we heard an unusual noise—a noise like the rattling of plates in a pantry. The lanterns vibrated, and there was a tremulous movement of the water and wine in our glasses. I do not think we should have regarded it as anything else than an effect of the thunder-storm, but for Governor Hennessy. "That," he said, "is an earthquake." While he spoke the phenomenon was repeated, and we plainly distinguished the shock. So, altogether, nothing could be more quiet than our days in Enriokwan. We read and wrote and walked about the grounds, and sat up very late at night on the veranda, talking about home, about the East, and our travels in Japan. Japan itself grew upon us more and more. The opportunities for studying the country, its policy, the aims of its rulers, its government, and its diplomacy, have been very great.

In this palace there took place one of the most important events in the modern history of Japan—a long personal interview between General Grant and the Emperor. The circumstance that an ex-President of the United States should converse with the chief of a friendly nation is not in itself an important event. But when you consider the position of the Emperor among his subjects, the traditions of his house and his throne, you will see the value of this meeting, and the revolution it makes in the history of Japan. The imperial family is, in descent, the most ancient in the world. It goes back in direct line to 660 years before Christ. For more than twenty-five centuries this line has continued unbroken, and the present sovereign is the 123d of his line. The position of Mikado has always been unique in Japan. For centuries the emperors lived in seclusion at Kiyoto. The Mikado was a holy being. No one was allowed to look upon his face. He had no family name, because his dynasty being unending he needed none. During his life he was revered as a god. When he died he was translated into the celestial presence. Within ten years it

STREET IN TOKIO.

was not proper that even his sacred name should be spoken.

That is now permitted, but even now you cannot buy a photograph of the Mikado.

The Emperor had sent word to General Grant that he desired to see him informally, and the General answered that he was entirely at the pleasure of his Majesty. Many little courtesies had been exchanged between the Empress and Mrs. Grant, and the Emperor and his ministers kept a constant watch over the General's comfort. The day fixed for the imperial interview was unusually warm. At half-past two in the afternoon, as we were sitting on the veranda, a messenger came to say that his Majesty had arrived, and was awaiting the General in the little summer-house on the banks of the lake, which I have described. The General, accompanied by Colonel Grant, Prince Dati, Mr. Yoshida, and the writer, left the palace and proceeded to the summer-house. We passed under the trees and toward the bridge. The imperial carriage had been hauled up under the shade of the trees and the horses taken out. The guards, attendants, and cavalrymen who had accompanied the sovereign were all seeking the shelter of the grove. We crossed the bridge and entered the summer-house. Preparations had been made for the Emperor, but they were very simple. Porcelain flower-pots, with flowers and ferns and shrubbery, were scattered about the room. One or two screens had been introduced. In the center of the room was a table, with chairs around it. Behind one of the screens was another table, near the window, which looked into the lake. As the General entered, the Prime Minister and the Minister of the Imperial Household advanced and welcomed him. Then, after a pause, we passed behind the screen and were in the presence of the Emperor. His Majesty was standing before the table in undress uniform, wearing only the ribbon of a Japanese order. General Grant advanced, and the Emperor shook hands with him. To the rest of the party he simply bowed. Mr. Yoshida acted as interpreter. The Emperor said:

"I have heard of many of the things you have said to my ministers in reference to Japan. You have seen the country and the people. I am anxious to speak with you on these subjects, and am sorry I have not had an opportunity earlier."

General Grant said he was entirely at the service of the Emperor, and was glad indeed to see him and thank his Majesty for all the kindness he had received in Japan. He might say that no one outside of Japan had a higher interest in the country or a more sincere friendship for its people.

A question was asked which brought up the subject now paramount in political discussions in Japan—the granting of an assembly and legislative functions to the people.

ULYSSES S. GRANT

AN INFORMAL CONVERSATION WITH THE EMPEROR.

General Grant said that this question seemed to be the only one about which there was much feeling in Japan, the only one he had observed. It was a question to be considered with great care. No one could doubt that governments became stronger and nations more prosperous as they became representative of the people. This was also true of monarchies, and no monarchs were as strong as those who depended upon a parliament. No one could doubt that a legislative system would be an advantage to Japan, but the question of when and how to grant it would require careful consideration. That needed a clearer knowledge of the country than he had time to acquire. It should be remembered that rights of this kind—rights of suffrage and representation—once given could not be withdrawn. They should be given gradually. An elective assembly, to meet in Tokio, and discuss all questions with the Ministry might be an advantage. Such an assembly should not have legislative power at the outset. This seemed to the General to be the first step. The rest would come as a result of the admirable system of education which he saw in Japan.

An expression of gratification at the treaty between Japan and the United States, which gave Japan the right to manage her own commerce, led to a conversation about foreign policy in Asia. "Nothing," said the General, "has been of more interest to me than the study of the growth of European and foreign influence in Asia. When I was in India I saw what England had done with that empire. I think the British rule is for the advantage of the Indian people. I do not see what could take the place of British power but anarchy. There were some things to regret, perhaps, but a great deal to admire in the manner in which India was governed. But since I left India I have seen things that made my blood boil, in the way the European powers attempt to degrade the Asiatic nations. I would not believe such a policy possible. It seems to have no other aim than the extinction of the independence of the Asiatic nations. On that subject I feel strongly, and in all that I have written to friends at home I have spoken strongly. I feel so about Japan and China. It seems incredible that rights which at home we regard as essential to our independence and to our national existence, which no European nation, no matter how small, would surrender, are denied to China and Japan. Among these rights there is none so important as the right to control commerce. A nation's life may often depend upon her commerce, and she is entitled to all the profit that can come out of it. Japan especially seems to me in a position where the control of her commerce would enable her statesmen to relieve the people of one great burden—the land-tax. The effect of so great a tax is to impoverish the people and limit agriculture. When the farmer must give a half of his crop for taxes he is not apt to raise more than will keep him alive. If the land-tax could be lessened, I have no doubt that agriculture would increase in Japan, and the increase would make the people richer, make them buy and consume more, and thus in the end benefit commerce as well. It seems to me that if the commerce of Japan were made to yield its proportion of the revenue, as the commerce of England and France and the United States, this tax could be lessened. I am glad the American government made the treaty. I hope other powers will assent to it. But whether or not, I think I know the American people well enough to say that they have, without distinction of party, the

NIGHT.

warmest wishes for the independence of Japan. We have great interests in the Pacific, but we have none that are inconsistent with the independence of these nations."

Another subject which arose in the course of the conversation was national indebtedness. General Grant said that there was nothing which Japan should avoid more strenuously than incurring debts to European nations. So long as the government borrowed from its own people it was well. But loans from foreign powers were always attended with danger and humiliation. Japan could not go into a European money market and make a loan that would be of an advantage to her. The experience of Egypt was a lesson. Egypt was allowed to borrow right and left, to incur an enormous debt. The result is that Egypt has been made a dependency of her creditors. Turkey owed much of her trouble to the same cause. A country like Japan has all the money she wants for her own affairs, and any attempt to bring her into indebtedness to foreign powers would only be to lead her into the abyss into which Egypt has fallen.

The General spoke to the Emperor on this question with great earnestness. When he had concluded he said there was another matter about which he had an equal concern. When he was in China he had been requested by the Prince Regent and the Viceroy of Tientsin to use his good offices with the Japanese government on the question of Loochoo. The matter was one about which he would rather not have troubled himself, as it belonged to diplomacy and governments, and he was not a diplomatist and not in government. At the same time he could not ignore a request made in the interest of peace. The General said he had read with great care and had heard with attention all the arguments on the Loochoo question from the Chinese and Japanese sides. As to the merits of the controversy, it would be hardly becoming in him to express an opinion. He recognized the difficulties that surrounded Japan. But China evidently felt hurt and sore. She felt that she had not received the consideration due to her. It seemed to the General that his Majesty should strive to remove that feeling, even if in doing so it was necessary to make sacrifices. The General was thoroughly satisfied that China and Japan should make such sacrifices as would settle all questions between them, and become friends and allies, without consultation with foreign powers. He had urged this upon the Chinese government, and he was glad to have the opportunity of saying the same to the Emperor. China and Japan are now the only two countries left in the East capable, through their resources, of becoming great, that are even partially independent of European dictation and laws. The General wished to see them both advance to entire independence, with the power to maintain it. Japan is rapidly approaching such a position, and China had the ability and the intelligence to do the same thing.

The Prime Minister said that Japan felt the most friendly feelings toward China, and valued the friendship of that nation very highly, and would do what she could, without yielding her dignity, to preserve the best relations.

General Grant said he could not speak too earnestly to the Emperor on this subject, because he felt earnestly. He knew of nothing that would give him greater pleasure than to be able to leave Japan, as he would in a very short time, feeling that between China and Japan there was entire friendship. Other counsels would be given to his Majesty, because there were powerful influences in the East fanning trouble between China and Japan. One could not fail to see these influences, and the General said he was profoundly convinced that any concession to them that would bring about war would bring unspeakable calamities to China and Japan. Such a war would bring in foreign nations, who would end it to suit themselves. The history of European diplomacy in the East was unmistakable on that point. What China and Japan should do is to come together without foreign intervention, talk over Loochoo and other subjects, and come to a complete and friendly understanding. They should do it between themselves, as no foreign power can do them any good.

General Grant spoke to his Majesty about the pleasure he

had received from studying the educational institutions in Japan. He was surprised and pleased at the standing of these schools. He did not think there was a better school in the world than the Tokio school of engineering. He was glad to see the interest given to the study of English. He approved of bringing forward the young Japanese as teachers. In time Japan would be able to do without foreign teachers ; but changes should not be made too rapidly. It would be a pity to lose the services of the men who had created these schools. The men in the service of the Japanese government seemed to be, as far as he could learn, able and efficient.

I have given you the essential points of a conversation that lasted for two hours. General Grant said he would leave Japan with the warmest feelings of friendship toward the Emperor and the people. He would never cease to feel a deep interest in their fortunes. He thanked the Emperor for his princely hospitality. Taking his leave, the General and party strolled back to the palace, and his Majesty drove away to his own home in a distant part of the city.

MORNING

The march in Japanese civilization, or rather in the approach of Japan to European civilization, is seen in the contrast between this interview and the reception of Mr. Seward when he came to Japan in October, 1870. Mr. Seward came in the early days of the revolution, and saw the Emperor in the color and blaze of the ancient days. In those days there were no social relations between the Japanese and the Europeans, and I suppose a negro would have been as welcome to a Southern ball, before the war, as a Japanese gentleman to an American ball in Yokohama. The same Emperor is on the throne who received Mr. Seward, and in his cabinet are many statesmen who were then his ministers. Mr. Ishibashi, who escorted Mr. Seward to the imperial presence, is the same gentleman who has been in attendance upon General Grant, and who has acted as interpreter on the occasion of the official visits. There was no railway in those days, and Mr. Seward came by boat, through a driving rain and swelling sea, from Yokohama to Tokio. Mr. Seward was the first foreigner of distinction who had been received by the Emperor, and special pains were taken to do it, according to the words of Mr. Ishibashi, "not in the customary official manner, but in a private audience, as an expression of personal respect and friendship." The scene of this audience was in the Great Castle, the home of the Tycoons. The castle has been destroyed, and the grounds are a marvel of gardening. These grounds are surrounded by a moat and a series of walls which may be ranked among the wonders of the world. It seems a pity that a scene of so rare culture and beauty, which might add so much to the comfort of the people of this teeming capital as a public garden, should be sealed up. There is a project to build a palace for the Emperor on the site of the old castle. This I suppose will be done some day. Thus far the Emperor has prevented it, loath to incur the expense and satisfied with his home as it is.

Mr. Seward was received in the gardens of the castle, and met by several of the ministers. He was served with tea-cakes, cigars, and confectionery. After waiting half an hour, it was announced that the Emperor would receive Mr. Seward. The ministers joined the Emperor, and Mr. Seward, accompanied by the Foreign Minister and our friend Ishibashi, followed. "They came," says Mr. Seward in describing the interview, "to a high shaded knoll, conversing by the way. The Minister and Ishibashi now stopped, and, making low genuflections, announced in subdued and almost whispering tones that his Majesty was to be in a summer-house directly behind this hill. After this no word was spoken." They came to the summer-house and entered, and "looking directly forward saw only Ishibashi, surrounded by a crowd of official persons, all crouched on the floor. Having reached the exact center of the room, Mr. Seward was requested to turn to the right." "In this position he directly confronted the Mikado, who was sitting on a throne raised on a dais ten feet above the floor." "The Mikado was dressed in a voluminous robe of reddish-brown brocade, which covered his whole person." "What with the elevation of the dais, and the height of his elongated cap, the Emperor's person, though in a sitting posture, seemed to stretch from the floor to the ceiling. His appearance in that flowing costume, surrounded by a mass of ministers and courtiers, enveloped in variegated and equally redundant silken folds, resting on the floor, reminded Mr. Seward of some of the efforts in mythology to represent a deity sitting in the clouds." "He held a scepter in his right hand, and at his left side wore one richly-ornamented straight sword." The interview began by the Prime Minister kneeling, and the Emperor raising his scepter. A manuscript was presented to his Majesty containing the speech of welcome. The Emperor touched it with his scepter and it was read. All that the Emperor did was to sit on his throne, draped in brocade, look at Mr. Seward, and touch with his scepter the speech that was made in his name. Strange as this reserve and mystery may sound now, when contrasted with the manner of General Grant's reception by the same sovereign and the same statesmen, it was at the time a stupendous advance and made a profound impression. The audience in its minutest details had been arranged between the Japanese Cabinet and the American Minister. Mr. Seward commended the Japanese for their ease and reserve. "Japan," he said, commenting on his own reception, "has especial reasons for prudence. The empire is a solitary planet, that has remained stationary for centuries, until now it is suddenly brought into contact with constellations which, while they shed a dazzling light, continually threaten destructive collisions."

Another evidence of the progress of Japan may be understood when we recall the changes which have taken place even during the time of Mr. Bingham. I have seen an allusion to them in a speech made by his predecessor in the mission. Mr. DeLong has passed away, and although there was some strife during his period of service, I found many in Japan anxious to pay a cordial respect to his memory. When Mr. DeLong came

OUR LIFE AT ENRIOKWAN.

as Minister, the authorities at first refused to allow him to see the Emperor. He would have an audience. The sovereign would see him, but he would be behind screens, and could not be seen. Mr. DeLong declined to present his letter of credentials unless he saw the Emperor and delivered it into the imperial hands. Finally an audience was granted. The Emperor received the Minister in the old castle. "On entering it," said Mr. DeLong, "I threaded through corridors to an extent unknown, to the sound of the most weird and dismal music that ever saluted the ears of man; and when finally I reached the audience chamber, I found the whole building filled with courtiers abasing themselves on the ground, with their hands upon their swords, his Majesty sitting on a throne, backed by a perfect arsenal of weapons immediately within his reach, and his sword-bearer having his sword about three inches out of his sheath." On the occasion of this visit Mr. DeLong was escorted to the castle by perhaps five hundred troops, and the corners of the streets were protected by ropes to keep back the thronging multitude. Four years later, when Mr. DeLong went to present his letters of recall and present Mr. Bingham, there was no escort, no ropes, the people pursued their calling, and the Emperor received him "standing on the same level as ourselves, dressed in a uniform like that of a hussar in foreign service, with cocked hat and plume." In the time of Mr. DeLong the government, under the advice of Mr. Iwakura, then as now a high state officer, had resolved to persecute all Japanese who were Christians. The same minister reversed the decree, and no man can now be punished in Japan for professing the religion of Jesus Christ.

ULYSSES S. GRANT

Notes on Chapter XLII
Page numbers refer to pagination of facsimile document.

(1) p. 521 Thomas Van Buren of New Jersey had been the American representative to the 1873 Vienna World's Fair. After leaving that position because of a financial scandal, he was selected as consul-general in Yokohama. During his decade in Yokohama he had repeated run-ins with Minister John Bingham. See; Kidder, *Of One Blood*. Thomas Van Buren's father was a cousin of President Martin Van Buren.

(2) p. 522 Iwakura Tomomi led Japan's major mission to the United States and Europe in 1871-73. Japan's first major diplomatic mission in the Meiji era, the Iwakura Mission aimed to convince the western powers to end the unequal treaties that granted treaty ports, zones not subject to Japanese legal jurisdiction, to the western powers. The treaties also restricted the Meiji government's ability to control its international trade. While unsuccessful in this effort, the mission was a watershed moment in Japan's progress toward joining the emerging international diplomatic order as an equal. On March 4, 1872, Iwakura had met Grant at the White House.

(3) p. 522 Ito Hirobumi was among a handful of Japan's most prominent Meiji era political leaders. He had studied in England before the Meiji Restoration, accompanied Iwakura on the mission to the United States and Europe and had become Minister of Home Affairs the year before Grant's visit. He was assassinated by a Korean nationalist in Manchuria in 1909.

(4) p. 523 Charles Longfellow had been present when the line from Yokohama to Tokyo was opened by the Emperor in 1872.

(5) p. 523 J. Pope-Hennessy, British Governor of Hong Kong, had met with President Grant when he visited Hong Kong. Pope-Hennessy disagreed with British Minister to Japan Sir Harry Parkes over the issue of the unequal treaties. Pope-Hennessy wanted prompt revision of Britain's unequal treaties with Japan while Sir Harry favored retention of the existing system.

(6) P. 523 Enriokwan or Enryokan. Also noted in Seward section. In 1870 the Meiji government took possession of Hamagoten, a residential compound and garden site used by the Tokugawa Shogun's family. A palace on the compound, Enryokan, was used as a guest house for important visitors. The Enryokan no longer stands and the compound grounds are now a park, Hamarikyu Gardens.

ULYSSES S. GRANT

(7) p. 527 Okubo Toshimichi had participated in the Iwakura Mission and upon return took the position of Minister of Home Affairs. He is credited with asserting central Meiji government control over competing, often violent opposition during this key period of institutional, political, and social change. He was assassinated in 1878.

(8) p. 534 As mentioned earlier, Seward and his party had also stayed at Enriokwan. See notes in the Seward and Longfellow sections. Longfellow mentions having attended a dinner there.

ULYSSES S. GRANT

A STREET IN NIKKO.

CHAPTER XLIII.

JAPAN.

ON the morning of the 17th of July General Grant and party, accompanied by Prince Dati, Mr. Yoshida, and Mr. Tateno, left Tokio for a visit to the shrine and temple of Nikko. It was expected that we would visit Kiyoto, Osaka, Kobe, and other points famous in Japanese history, but the prevalence of the cholera made this impossible. General Grant rode in the imperial carriage, but the remainder of our party preferred jinrickshaws. The day was warm, and it was pleasant to escape from the close and parched streets of Tokio into the fields. As we came to the little villages policemen were assembled, wearing blue coats, white

BETWEEN DECKS ON THE STEAMSHIP TOKIO.

pantaloons, and white caps trimmed with yellow. Under the trees were groups of old and young, women and children, who had been waiting for hours in the sun to see the General pass-Japan is the paradise of children. It was pleasant, as we came from village to village, to see the whole population assembled, to see the little thatched houses decorated with American flags, and the school children drawn up in line, to go bounding along over the well-made roads, our jinrickshaw-men as merry as crickets. The aspect of the people changes as you go into the interior of Japan, and you catch glimpses of the old manners and customs. The clothes question, which makes an unpleasant impression upon Europeans, when they first arrive, is one to which you soon become accustomed. The lower classes of the Japanese wear the slightest possible clothing, and sometimes even this is overlooked. But you become accustomed to the nudities in time, and think no more of the undraped forms that crowd under the trees to look at you than of the cattle who browse in the fields. The jinrickshaw-men show great endurance, and some of them are able to go forty or fifty miles a day. On the evening of our first day's journey we found we had made twenty-eight miles. We remained all night at a little village, at the house of the governor. Next morning at half-past five we crossed the river and kept on our journey. At noon we came to a small tea-house, and the weather was so warm that we rested for two or three hours. In the evening we reached a village where the soldiers were drawn up in line to meet us, and the whole town was gathered in front of the tea-house which had been set apart for our reception. There was a review of the troops, the General inspecting and going through the barracks. During our stay in this village the population spent their time on the opposite side of the street watching our movements, and enjoying a tremendous sensation when they detected Colonel Grant in the act of tying his cravat. There was a garden in the rear of the house where rocks and trees were arranged with a striking effect. In the evening General Grant and Prince Dati tried to walk about the town, but the people assembled in force, and the mob that followed them so continued to grow that they were obliged to give it up and come home. The next morning at eight we continued our way, but as we were now ascending a hill the trip became slow and severe. At noon we came to the town of Imaichi, which was decorated with lanterns and flags, and where we took tea. At four o'clock we reached Nikko, and all the town was out to give us welcome. We left our jinrickshaws and took kagoes, a sort of hammock in which you are borne on the shoulders of men. Crossing a bridge we were carried up the heights to the temple, and found ourselves at home in the quarters of the priests. Here

IN THE GARDEN, NIKKO.

we lived for ten days, enjoying the mountain scenery, visiting the waterfalls, strolling about the temple, looking at the tombs and monuments, especially the shrine of Iyeyas, one of the great names of Japan, whose tomb makes Nikko a sacred spot in Japan.(1)

IYEYAS—THE LAWGIVER.

The legacy of Iyeyas is one of the most interesting phases of the ancient customs in Japan. Iyeyas was the great chief and lawgiver, successor to Takio-Samo, the hero of Japan. He flourished about the time of William III. of England. When he died he was deified, and his ashes now rest in the temple of Nikko, within a stone's throw of the temple where General Grant resided during his residence at Nikko. The legacy of Iyeyas is cherished as one of the sacred treasures of the empire, and can only be seen by the eyes of noblemen. It is really a code of laws, contained in sections or chapters, a hundred in all. Those who had followed Iyeyas and shared his fortunes in the days of his adversity, were singled out for special honor, themselves and their descendants, who, no matter in what they might offend, unless in actual treason, should not lose their estates. The people are the foundation of the empire. To assist the people is to give peace to the empire. "Let my posterity," says Iyeyas, "hold fast to this principle. Any one turning his back upon it is no descendant of mine." Respect was shown for conservative principles in the enactment that even a faulty regulation should not be amended if it had been allowed to remain in force for fifty years. In making appointments for the government of towns only those should be taken who had an ancient lineage: refugees and adventurers should not be appointed, and especially to collect taxes. The method of rewards was minutely described. Names and titles could be granted even after death, as was really done in the case of Okubo, after his assassination. There were ten forms of punishment for crimes. Branding or tattooing, splitting the nose, banishment, transportation, strangulation, imprisonment, decapitation and exposure of the head, crucifixion and transfixion, burning, and so on. It was forbidden to tie criminals' legs to two oxen and drive them in different directions, or to boil a condemned man in oil. Capital punishment, however, was not to be hastily imposed, and the science of successful government was in showing due deference on the part of a ruler to his vassals. Hawking, fishing, and hunting with the spear were commended as useful sports. Although singing and music were not the calling of the soldiers, yet they relieved depression, and were delightful recreations in time of peace. "Let there be a careful attention to parents, and let them be followed when long gone." "Eighteen times have I escaped with my life"—from hand-to-hand encounters in battle; "therefore have I founded eighteen sandal-grove temples." All manner of religion was tolerated except "the false and corrupt school of Roman Catholicism." As religious disputes had been

A JAPANESE THEATER.

the bane of the empire they should be discountenanced. Confucianism was recognized as teaching the only principles by which an empire could be governed. Doctors were not to be allowed large estates, lest they straightway become indolent in their profession. All wandering mendicants, "such as male sorcerers, female diviners, hermits, blind people, beggars and tanners," were put under special regulations. Persons wounding others with weapons should be punished according to the nature and extent of the wounds. It was a capital offense to murder by stratagem or after premeditation, or to poison for selfish purposes, or wound others while robbing a house. The Samauri, or bearers of two swords, were a privileged class, and placed above the others. No farmer, workman, or merchant should be rude to a Samauri, and if a Samauri chose to cut down a fellow who had been rude to him he was not to be interrupted.

Iyeyas, in his laws, especially commended marriage as the supreme relation. No one should live alone after sixteen years of age. All mankind recognize marriage as the first law of nature. "A family of good descent should be chosen to marry into; for when a line of descendants is prolonged the foreheads of ancestors expand." Childless men were enjoined to adopt children to insure succession to the family estate. The estate of a person dying without male heirs, born or adopted, was forfeited to the state. An infant at the point of death might prolong his race by adopting one who was older than himself. Daimios were not to be too long in the government of the same territory, lest they become oppressors of the people. If a married woman of the lower classes committed adultery, the husband could put his wife and her accomplice to death. But if he slew one and not the other, then he was guilty of murder. Men and women of the military class were expected to know better than to commit the sin of adultery. If they did, they were to be severely and promptly punished. The duty of avenging a wrong to master or father was a high duty, but to take such revenge without notice was to act like the wolves. When one had such a wrong to avenge he should give notice to the criminal court, and then, unless a riot ensued, he was permitted to carry out his purpose unmolested. If a vassal murdered his lord, his immediate companions, relatives, and even those most distantly connected with him, should be cut off, and "mowed to atoms, root and fiber. The guilt of a vassal who raises his hand against his master, even though he does not assassinate him, is the same." In this code of laws concubinage was permitted. An emperor could have twelve, a prince eight, and officers of high grade five concubines. A Samauri could have two, all others only one. In these families the wife was as far above the concubine as the lord was above his vassal. He who neglected his true wife for a mistress was a silly and ignorant man, and disturbed the most important relation of life. Such men were without fidelity and sincerity. "It is," said Iyeyas, "a righteous and world-recognized rule, that a true husband takes care of outside business, while a true wife manages the affairs of the house. When a wife occupies herself with outside affairs, her husband loses his business, and it is a pre-evidence of the ruin of the house; it is as when a hen is afflicted with a propensity to crow at morn—an affliction of which every Samauri should beware. This is an assistance to the knowledge of mankind."

In conclusion, says the lawgiver, "In all questions of policy cherish precedents, and do not give exclusive attention to small or large matters; let this be the rule of your conduct." "Let my posterity thoroughly practice with their bodies what I here declare. They are not permitted to be looked upon save by the great noblemen. In them I have exposed and laid bare the limited reflections of my heart. Let not future generations be induced to ridicule me as having the heart of a venerable old grandmother. I bequeath this record to posterity."

Life at Nikko was a pleasant episode in General Grant's visit to Japan, because it took him out of the rush and roar of Tokio life and ceremony and parade. It was at Nikko that General Grant met the representatives of the Japanese government who came to speak to him officially of the difficulty between China and Japan on the Loochoo question. This conference, which may some day have historical value, took place on the 22d of July. General Grant had intimated to the Japanese government, on his arrival in Tokio, that he had received a communication from the Chinese government which he would like to present officially to the Japanese cabinet, if he could do so without appearing to interfere in their concerns. The Emperor sent Mr. Ito, Minister of the Interior, and General Saigo, the Minister of War, to receive the statement. Mr. Ito presented the case of Japan at length, contending that Japan's rights of sovereignty over Loochoo were immemorial, and going over the whole question. When Ito had finished, General Grant said that he had been anxious to have this conversation with the Japanese government, because it enabled him to fulfill a promise he had made to Prince Kung and the Viceroy, Li Hung Chang. He had read the Chinese case and studied it. He had heard with great interest the case of Japan. As to the merits of the controversy he had no opinion to express. There were many points, the General said, in

GENERAL GRANT AND PRINCE DATI IN THE STREETS OF TOKIO.

both cases, which were historical and could only be determined by research. His entire interest arose from his kind feeling toward both Japan and China, in whose continued prosperity America and the entire world were interested. Japan, the General said, had done wonders in the past few years. She was, in point of war materials, army and navy, stronger than China. Against Japan, China, he might say, was defenseless, and it was impossible for China to injure Japan. Consequently, Japan could look at the question from a high point of view. At the same time, China was a country of wonderful resources, and although he had seen nothing there to equal the progress of Japan, there had nevertheless been great progress.

General Grant continued by saying that there were other reasons why Japan should, if possible, have a complete and amicable understanding with China. The only powers who would derive any benefit from a war would be foreign powers. The policy of some of the European powers was to reduce Japan and China into the dependence which had been forced upon other nations. He had seen indications of this policy during his travels in the East which made his blood boil. He saw it in Siam and China and Japan. In Siam the king was unable, as he had told the General, to protect his people from opium. In China opium had been forced upon the people. That was as great a crime against civilization as slavery. In Japan, only the other day, he saw the Germans deliberately violate a Japanese quarantine by sending down a German gun-boat and taking a German merchantman out of quarantine. No European power would dare to do such a thing in the United States. But it illustrates European policy in the East. If war should ensue between China and Japan, European powers would end it in their own way and to their own advantage, and to the disadvantage of the two nations. "Your weakness and your quarrels are their opportunity," said the General. "Such a question as Loochoo offers a tempting opportunity for the interference of unfriendly diplomacy." Minister Ito said that these were all grave considerations; but Japan, standing on her immemorial rights, had simply carried out an act of sovereign power over her own dominions. General Grant answered that he could not see how Japan, having gone so far, could recede. But there might be a way to meet the susceptibilities of China, and at the same time not infringe any of the rights of Japan. The conversation then took a range that I do not feel at liberty to embrace, as propositions and suggestions were made which it would be premature to disclose, and which, in fact, would have no value until they were considered and adopted by the cabinets of Japan and China. The Japanese ministers showed the most conciliatory spirit. General Saigo did not speak English, but Mr. Ito and Mr. Yoshida both conversed fluently in that tongue. The subject of the Formosan expedition, which General Saigo commanded, came up, and was discussed for some time.

The afternoon was warm and the clouds swept over the mountains, and it was pleasant to watch the sun's rays toying around the stately cedars that clothed the mountain sides, lighting up the green summits, and losing themselves in the clouds and the mist. But this land of the mountains is also a land of rain, and suddenly the black clouds came over the ridges and we had a rattling summer thunder-storm. When the talk ran out and the rain ceased, Minister Ito said that what had been communicated by General Grant would be submitted to the cabinet and be considered very carefully. He had no idea what the cabinet would decide. He would probably have occasion to speak with General Grant again on the subject. But on behalf of the government of Japan he desired to express their thanks and their gratitude to General Grant for

TEMPLE OF THE FIRST SOIGON.

having presented this question, and for his efforts to continue between Japan and China relations of peace, based upon the honor and independence of both nations. Japan had no desire but peace, and no feeling toward China but a desire to preserve the friendship which had existed so long. (2)

Many were the entertainments given to us in Nikko by the people. One especially I remember, when the whole town came in procession carrying banners and trophies. It was understood that we were to have a public reception by the people, and that it would take place at the temple. So we strolled over to the temple steps, and the priests gave us chairs. The first performance was theatrical. A stage was erected in front of the temple. When the curtain arose three actors made their appearance, one male and two females. The male was dressed in elaborately embroidered robes, which trailed under his feet, of red and gold, with an under robe of light blue, embroidered with flowers. One of the women was dressed in a gown of crimson pantaloons, with a green sash, and the other in purple and deep blue. The man walked across the stage and danced slowly. His face was covered with powder, his changeless and solemn features giving him an expression of solemn gravity. The faces of the women were almost as white as the clowns in our shows. Sometimes they knelt, keeping time to the music with their knees, sometimes there was a merry measure of the tambourine, which was used as the Spaniards do the castanets. What you observed was the serious intensity of every act of the performance. One of the performances which amused the people was that of a man who, with a fan, tried to catch two butterflies which a crouching supernumerary dangled from a stick. All this was done with a graceful and lively movement to the music, which never ceased to play. Then came two children in scarlet gowns, with butterfly wings, who skipped about like romping children, while the women waved their fans, as though directing their motions. Then came three other children, wearing wigs of brown, white, and black hair. I did not discover any special point in the performance, which was pantomime and dancing. The curtain rose again and we had a little comedy. The scene discovered a maiden sitting on a bench, a priest crouched at her side reading from a scroll, which he carried in his bosom, some verses of poetry. After reading, the priest relapsed into a condition of repose. Then came two women, with a serious expression on their faces, looking as though they were about to cry. They slowly danced around the stage. After they had danced a few minutes with fans, there was a long conversation developing the plot of the play. I was told that the two women were supposed to be jealous of each other about the priest. What became of their emotions was a mystery, for after dancing for a few minutes the curtain fell. At the close of the performance the citizens marched in procession past the General, beating gongs and carrying small booths, some of which were elaborately carved and ornamented. These booths, which look something like shrines, are greatly prized by the people, and are brought out on great occasions only. They were decorated with Japanese and American flags, and each detachment of people came with a special booth, and while they passed in front of the stage played a deafening fanfaronade on their drums. When night came lanterns added to the beauty of the scene. Then came suddenly heavy peals of thunder and lightning, like rifle-shots, and the whole procession dissolved in the rain. But the rain was only temporary, and later in the evening the jugglers came to the temple grounds and insisted upon performing their tricks before the General after he had dined. There was nothing specially interesting in the jugglery excepting the singular dexterity with which the actors threw around plates and umbrellas and balanced fans in the air.

Nothing could be more pleasant than our life at Nikko, and it was not without regret that on the morning of the 28th of July we took leave of our kind friends the custodians of the temple. The priests came with us to the end of the town, and the General thanked them for their courtesy. There was a thin, falling mist, as we took up our journey to the valley and the sea-shore. At the foot of the hill the children from the school were ranged in order, and bowed a grave farewell as we were carried past them dangling in our kagoes. There also were the chief men of the town, who bowed their heads in token of courtesy and farewell. On reaching the town we took jinrickshaws and started on a run. The roads were heavy with the rain, and we were weary with the day's journey, when, in the evening, we drew up in front of a tea-house. Here also there was a visit to the barracks, and there would have been a parade but for a thunder-storm. Next morning we went to Kanagana, to see the silk-works, and the next day we continued on our way, and stopped for the night at a frowsy, dirty village. The governor came to wait upon us, and we spent the evening conversing with him. On the 31st of July, tired and worn with travel, we returned to our pleasant quarters at Enriokwan.

No event in the visit of General Grant to Japan excited more attention than the public festival at Uyeno, on the 25th of August. This event may be regarded as the culminating incident in the General's visit. There was much to attract, more to interest, perhaps, in other fêtes and ceremonies. Nothing, for instance, could be more stately than our progress through the Inland Sea, with a vessel of war to carry our flag, and two additional vessels, one of the Japanese, the other of our own navy, to keep us company. One cannot hope to see again so much beauty as was there unfolded. All things combined to favor that incomparable journey. Nature in a romantic mood composed that wonderful blending of hill and slope—of mountain-crag, meadow, and sea—of terraced garden-summits, of snow-clad volcano heights losing themselves in the clouds. The sea itself welcomed us with a smile, and never ceased to smile while we rested on her bosom. Nor did we hurry through after the manner of travelers who go in company of the mails. At night we found rest, and every night was adorned with an illumination and a fête. In looking back over our Japanese reception, the journey through the Inland Sea transcends all the rest, and was well worth a journey around the world to enjoy.

There were features in the Uyeno fête, however, that lifted it out of the range of mere festivals and gave it a political significance. When I come to write about our visit to Japan, I am oppressed with a sense of my inability to do justice to the hospitality of our friends. I am conscious of having said little in the way of direct acknowledgment of the efforts of our hosts to entertain us. I have avoided the subject because it

MEETING THE EMPEROR IN THE SUMMER-HOUSE.

seemed that no words of mine could express an acknowledgment of a kindness so courteous, so thoughtful, so princely, so imperial. From the hour that General Grant came under the green, sheltering hills of Nagasaki, and heard the thunder of the guns which welcomed him to Japan, down to the present, when we are saying farewell, and spreading our sails for California—nothing has been wanting that Emperor or citizen could desire to show honor to our country, our flag, and our ex-President. We have been in the fullest sense the guests of the nation, and it is hard to say now whether we have been received with the more cordiality by the rulers or the ruled. It would be ungracious to make any distinction, and I am far from doing so. In the case of the Emperor and the high officers of the state, there have no doubt been political reasons why the good feeling of Japan toward America should be shown to a representative American. But in many of its phases the intercourse of the Mikado with the General has been an event in the history of Japan. You cannot imagine, without ascending into the regions of mythology, and recalling what the poets have dreamed of the gods of Mount Olympus, the position in which the Mikado is held in Japan. The office is the highest known development of the royal quality. Other sovereigns reign because of the divine right, the grace of God. The Mikado reigns because he is divine—not alone because his office is sacred, but that he is sacred himself, destined when he passes away to become one of the immortal gods. In all the changes that have befallen Japan the reverence that surrounds the throne has never abated. When the tycoons reigned, holding the sword and the purse—absolute masters of Japan—a word from the secluded monarch of Kiyoto, who had never seen the sun shine beyond the walls of his castle, was sufficient to undo them. At his bidding the Tycoon resigned an empire. When the Emperor commanded, the feudal princes—men of ancient lineage, of rank and wealth, sovereigns over their own clans—surrendered rank, honor, heritage, and emolument. In obedience to his will the chivalry of Japan, the soldiers and gentlemen, gave up their swords and feudal rank, which had been in their families for generations. The priests, the noblemen, the army, all obeyed his command because they regarded it as a command from Heaven. Even the people, conservative as the Oriental mind naturally is, and proud of the traditions of an ancient civilization, changed in a day, and never questioned the change, because it was the will of the Emperor. No internal commotion or external pressure has affected the legend that makes holy the imperial person. The revolutions have never been against the Mikado, only against his officers, while the treaties made with the Tycoons never had any value in the eyes of the Japanese until they had been confirmed by the sacred will.

The Mikado has never failed in courtesy to the princes of other royal families who have visited him. But while he treated English, Russian, and German princes as princes, he has treated General Grant as a friend. The honors have been such that would have been given to the head of a nation. But it is in other ways that the Mikado showed his esteem. The conversation of which I have given a narrative may have seemed an ordinary and perhaps an indifferent affair. But when you consider it was the Mikado, and that never before had he allowed any such intercourse with an alien, you will see the importance of the incident in the history of Japan. While the Mikado has departed from the traditions of centuries to do honor to his guest, the people have on their part shown a strange interest in General Grant. The people in Japan have never had a pleasant position. One of the features of the Oriental civilizations, picturesque and quaint as we find them, is that development runs to the top. The throne, the nobility, the military classes, are magnified at the expense of the people. Such an institution as the people was not known in ancient Japan, except to labor, pay taxes, and contribute to the comfort and glory of the feudal lords. In our western civilizations the merchant has a high place. We honor those who excel in handicraft. We have a sentiment for those who till the soil. But in Japan it was almost a degradation to be a farmer, an artisan, or a merchant, especially a merchant. To work in leather was to rank with mendicants. When Mr. Seward was in Japan he was desirous of presenting to the Mikado, at the time of his own audience, the merchant with whom he lived at Yokohama, an honorable and worthy gentleman. But it was impossible. The Mikado had never spoken to a merchant, no one of the degraded merchant class had ever looked upon his sacred face. I question if these classes had before the revolution a much higher place than the slaves in the Southern States

THE FALLS OF HONG-TOKI.

before the war. They certainly had not, so far as the samauri were concerned. In the South even a slave had under the laws a certain protection from his master. In Japan, if a samauri felt that a farmer, a merchant, or an artisan had been rude to him, he could cut him down. One of the features of the revolution has been the awakening of the people, and this awakening has received a strange impulse from the presence of General Grant. Since the revolution there have been cases of men of rank going into business, and of professional men, and others who had been in trade, taking high office. A member of the present cabinet was formerly a physician, which is as great a change in the social relations of Japan as it was in the United States for a negro to sit as a senator by the side of the man who once owned him as a slave.

The people have taken a novel interest in General Grant. In some respects this is the feature of our visit most worthy of consideration. The future of Japan of course depends much more upon the freedom, the education, and the independence of the people than upon any other agency. And while the courtesy of princes and gentlemen is worthy of note, and has been marked with princely grace, the part taken by the people is memorable. Several reasons have contributed to this. Ever since the revolution the people have taken an interest in affairs. They have newspapers, and although the press is under a severe curb, still there is room for free thought and independent criticism. They send their sons to the best schools—to Europe and America. They have debating clubs, where they assemble and discuss every kind of theme. They run to new and strange doctrines. "I am afraid," said one distinguished but conservative authority in Japan, "I am afraid of these new ideas. It is not a good sign, those young men rushing to debating clubs. They imbibe democratic and skeptical tendencies. There never was much religion in Japan, but everybody is now running to atheism. It is all Mill and Darwin and Spencer. The Japanese mind is not strong enough to take what is good and reject what is bad in that teaching." Professor Morse, of Harvard, one of those able and devoted young professors of science who have done so much in Japan, and who is now closing a period of brilliant service as a teacher of science, told me that there was no part of his work that was more interesting than his lectures to Japanese students—to young men of all ranks, from the highest to the lowest—on the doctrines of evolution. (3) Then the Japanese, all classes of them, are a warlike and brave people, fond of the parade and circumstance of war, and loving a hero. The military side of General Grant's career has taken hold of their imagination, and the street literature of the day is devoted to the achievements of the General and the Northern armies. You find these written in pamphlets, in broadsides, in penny tracts. You find rude engravings of the General in the shop-windows. Sometimes these pictures are in a heroic stage of color, and although I am not familiar with the Japanese text, I am sure, from looking over the illustrations in the pictorial lives of the General, that he has achieved tremendous feats in war. Most of these engravings depict the General as a military athlete doing marvelous things with his sword. This, however, is how history becomes mythology; and in looking over these rude designs you see the operation of the doctrine of evolution, how fact is gradually blended into romance and poetry. Sometimes this takes an unfortunate turn, as was the case the other day in Yokohama. The cholera was prevailing, and the authorities were sending the people to the hospital. This measure was unpopular, for, somehow, all the world over, human nature has a prejudice against the hospital. The people became panic-stricken. If they went to the hospital they would surely die, and when they died their livers would be taken out and sold to General Grant, or Iwakura, or Sanjo, for a thousand dollars apiece, as talismans. This was one of the rumors that was in the air during our visit, and it shows the hold that General Grant had taken upon the imagination of the people, down to the lowest and most ignorant classes.

There were several methods proposed of doing popular honor to the General. There was the play at the Shintomiga Theater, where the incidents of the life of the General were performed as a drama, and as having occurred in the earlier days of the history of Japan. There was the fête at Yokohama, as well as the reception at the Engineering College. These were brilliant incidents, but all was to be crowned by a public festival in the park. The citizens took it up and managed it in their own way. The government had nothing to do with it. The people subscribed money to defray expenses. The money came in so freely that the subscriptions were closed, and I heard of folks complaining because they had not been allowed to pay money. It was arranged that the Emperor should attend, and that the event should be one of unusual splendor. The cholera came, and it was feared that the gathering of such a multitude, in a time of pestilence, would extend the epidemic, and so it was postponed. It was interesting to witness the preparations by the people for the fête. Beginning at the gates of Enriokwan, and continuing along the canal to the main street, and out along this street as far as the public park, it was one line of lanterns and flags. Special bamboo frames had been erected from which the lanterns could swing, and wherever the streets came to a crossing, or there were bridges, there were special trophies of flags and banners and lanterns. These lanterns were of various designs, some red, some blue, some white, some

JAPANESE LADIES.

variegated, some with the flag of Japan—the majority with the flag of Japan on one side, and on the other the flag of the United States—the banner of the stars blended with the banner of the sun. The announcement that the cholera would interfere with the festival gave great uneasiness, and the papers showed the disappointment of the people. So, after many debates, and in the hope that the cholera would abate, it was resolved to postpone the popular fête until during the last days of the General's visit. The date was fixed for the 25th of August.

It was a day of general festivity and rejoicing. Tokio fluttered with flags. People came in from the country, and as I strolled out in the morning, I noted curious groups, wandering about seeing the sights. All work was given up, and the city had that holiday look which you note at home in our own towns on a festival day. The Japanese love a festival. They rejoice in the sunshine, in the trees, in doing nothing. The pleasure-loving side of their character is what first attracts you. In this you are constantly reminded of the French. They are like the French in their gayety, good-humor, courtesy, and love of pleasure; like the French, too, as history shows, in their power of forming daring resolves, and doing terrible deeds. The day was very warm, but the people did not seem to mind the weather, going about in the lightest clothing. In the matter of clothing, your impression as you look at a Japanese crowd is, that Japan is an empire of thirty-five millions of people, and fifty thousand pairs of pantaloons. Travel in the East soon deadens any emotions you may have on the question of clothes, and what you note in a Japanese crowd is the lightness and gayety of the people, the smiling faces, the fun-loving eyes. Moreover, you note the good order, the perfect order, the courtesy, the kind feeling. I have come to the conclusion that the mob is a product of our Western civilization. I have never seen a crowd, a multitude, until I came to China and Japan. But here I have not seen a mob. You look out upon such masses of human beings as our sparse countries could not show. You look upon what you could call without extravagance a sea of faces. But it is the sea when the sun shines upon it, and the light plays over the waters, and the waves ebb and flow with genial, friendly welcome. The good-humor and the patience of the crowd seemed to have no end. General Grant and party left Enriokwan at two o'clock. The hour and the route and every step in the programme had been considered,

THE FISH MARKET AT TOKIO.

and set down in a programme, and we found ourselves going through the day as though we were in a drama, and everything had been written down for us and for everybody else by a careful prompter. General Grant's party on the occasion was a large one. As the fête was partly in his honor, and all the people were out to see, and his progress was to be in state, it was thought that the presence of the naval officers would be a compliment to the citizens, and add to the interest of the day. Accordingly the General invited Admiral Patterson, Captain Benham, and the leading officers of the American ships to join him at the palace, take luncheon, and go with him to the park. At the hour named our company started from Enriokwan, and what with our Japanese escort, and our friends from the navy in their uniforms of blue and gold, it was quite a procession. The party rode in the Emperor's state carriages, preceded and surrounded by cavalry, and going at a slow pace, so that the crowd could see the General. I should say that the distance from Enriokwan to Uyeno was three miles, and every step of the way was through a crowd. Every house was decorated with flags and lanterns. The people, as the General's carriage came near, would rush to the windows and look in, but there was perfect order and courtesy.

As we approached the park the crowd grew denser and denser. The streets at certain points were covered with arches of evergreens and flags and lanterns, with inscriptions in Japanese. When we came to the park a line of infantry was drawn up, and as the General's carriage slowly turned in, the soldiers presented arms, and a Japanese band played "Hail Columbia." We drove on until we came to a certain part of the gardens, where we halted. Here a committee was in waiting, and the General was informed that, as a memento of his visit, it was hoped that he and Mrs. Grant would each plant a tree. This was done, and already the stone monuments were erected which signified the event in an inscription in English and Japanese. (4)

This ceremony over, we re-entered our carriages and drove to the pavilion prepared for the General. This pavilion was a small Japanese house swathed in American flags. Here we were joined by Mr. Bingham and family, and several American friends. Just beyond us was a canopy reserved for the foreign ministers, where we met Sir Harry Parkes, the Chinese minister, and other members of the diplomatic body.(5) Shortly after General Grant arrived the sound of guns and the music of the band playing the Japanese national air announced that the Emperor was on his way.

When the Emperor arrived on the ground he gave a special audience to General Grant and his party. Then advancing into a large pavilion, he received the foreign ministers and the naval officers who were present. Sir Harry Parkes, the British Minister, made a few remarks to his Majesty on behalf of the diplomatic corps. This ceremony passed, the Emperor took his seat in a high amphitheater, General Grant sitting on his right, the ministers of the cabinet surrounding him. Here he remained for an hour, while there were various sports and amusements, mainly feats of horsemanship. When his Majesty retired, the General, accompanied by the cabinet, dined, and when the sun went down were escorted back to their pavilion. After the fireworks, which were unusually beautiful, the General and party drove home. I recall this drive as among the most extraordinary phases of our Japanese visit. For miles the General's carriage slowly moved through a multitude that might have been computed by the hundreds of thousands, the trees and houses dangling with lamps and lanterns, the road spanned with arches of light, the night clear and mild, all forming a scene the like of which I had never witnessed, and which I can never hope to see again. It was the culmination of the General's visit to Japan, the highest honor that could be paid to him by the Japanese government and people.

ULYSSES S. GRANT

ULYSSES S. GRANT

Notes on Chapter XLIII
Page numbers refer to pagination of facsimile document.

(1) p. 554 Iyeyas is Tokugawa Ieyasu (1543-1616), founder of the Tokugawa Shogunate.

(2) p. 561 See Kidder, *Of One Blood All Nations*, chapter 5. In 1873 there was tension between China and Japan over possession of the Loochoo or Okinawa island chain, when a Japanese force organized by Saigo Takamori launched a military invasion of Taiwan. Several American military advisors were involved on the Japanese side.

(3) p. 570 Edward Sylvester Morse was a Harvard zoologist and naturalist. He was hired by the Meiji government as an instructor. His discovery and excavation of ancient shell middens near Tokyo Bay was an important event that brought contemporary archaeology to Japan. He is also credited with introducing Darwin's theory of evolution to Japan.

(4) p. 574 The stone monument and the trees planted by President and Mrs. Grant still stand in Ueno Park in Tokyo, near the park's side entrance to the zoo.

(5) p. 574 As dean of the diplomatic corps, British Minister Sir Harry Parkes had pride of place at the event. The position of dean is accorded to the longest serving foreign chief of mission in the host country.

STREET IN TOKIO.

CHAPTER XLIV.

JAPAN.

GENERAL GRANT made a short visit to Hakone to see the beautiful scenery that surrounds Fusiyama. On his return he prepared to leave Japan. We had already stayed longer in the country than we had intended, but life was pleasant in Tokio, and every day seemed to open a new scene of beauty and interest, and we felt ourselves yielding to the fascinations of this winning civilization. The hospitality of our hosts seemed to show no sign of weariness. We became attached to our palace home of Enriokwan, and began to feel acquainted with the rooms, the curious figures on the walls, the odd freaks in the way of gardening, the rustic bridges, the quaint and clean little summer-houses, where we could sit in the afternoon and feel the breezes from the sea. The weather kept unusually warm, and with the heat came the pestilence, and, although in Enriokwan we were not conscious of its presence, and felt safe under the sheltering influence of the ocean, yet it saddened the community and seemed to rest upon the capital like a cloud, and we sorrowed with our friends. There were trips to Yokohama, where our naval ships were at anchor; and Yokohama itself was well worth seeing, as an evidence of what the European had done in making a trading camp on the shores of Asia. For, after all, these Eastern European cities are but trading camps, and remind you in many ways of the shifting towns in Kansas and Nebraska during the growing, railway days. Now that the time was coming when we were to leave Japan there were discussions as to where and when we should go.

When it was finally determined to return, it was surprising to see how much we had to do. There was the gathering together of the odds and ends of a long journey—the bundling up for home. Sticks from Malacca, fragments of gauze from Delhi, brasswork from Benares, bits of crockery from Pekin—what you call your "things"—assume a consequence that their importance does not justify. When I started on my journey around the world one of the pleasures that I set apart for myself was that I would not buy anything; that I should not burden my mind with curiosities, nor allow any of the porcelain or ivory manias to afflict me. There seemed to be among my friends so much useful energy gone to waste on crockery and bronze that I resolved to make a merit of my own self-denial, and bring back from the East only a flush of radiant memories. But no virtue, however robust, can stand the temptations of Canton and Yokohama, and I found myself taking an interest in "things" like other people, and going into silk shops, and fumbling the light and airy stuffs which the genius of the East has fashioned for woman's adornment, and studying out the beauty of a saucer or a vase. And although I clung to my resolution valiantly, "things" began to accumulate, and the great question of our latter days in Japan was what should we do with them, and, moreover, what would the Collector at the California Custom-House do with them? I never knew that there was so much to interest you in the revenue laws until I began to look up the duties on a bit of "old blue." If any of my readers do not know what "old blue" means, I would advise them never to learn. I happened at times, while in Tokio, to be the companion of an honored friend who has mastered

IMAICHI.

the "curio" question; who knew bronze and ivory, silk and clay and iron, and whose amusement was to run away from the hospitalities of his Japanese hosts, and lose himself in a suburb of Tokio, and prowl from shop to shop. "You see," he would say, "by doing this we get away from the range of the globe-trotters, who ruin the market and give the people false ideas as to prices and degrade the taste of the sellers. Here we are in old Japan, and I never pay more than one dollar for anything." These were interesting expeditions.

General Grant has thrown a good deal of suspicion upon one's enthusiasm for the antique by circumstantial narratives of a certain factory which flourishes in Newark, New Jersey, whose owners declare large dividends—a factory devoted to the manufacture of curios, where they make antique and modern works of art, especially old blue and hawthorn blue and blue after the rain, and mark them with the mark of the Ming dynasty. But I believe in my vase. I certainly believe in the reverent and friendly spirit that sent it to my table; and although if I were buying "old blue" from my own unaided experience I would not give a large sum for such a vase, I know that it is the result of my ignorance, and that I really have a treasure, something that the Chinese artisan labored over with loving hand in the days of the Mings, before the Tartar came to harden and desolate his land, and I idealize it in various ways, and think myself into the belief that it has a poetic beauty of its own. And this leads me back to the revenue laws, and to wonder whether Mr. Merritt will put the poetic value upon the vase, or assess it at my own estimate of its worth. As I was saying, I never knew how much there was to interest you in the revenue laws until I began to look over my "things," and wonder what they will cost in New York. As to taking them to California, no one would dream of it. You hear terrible stories of the California Custom-House; how the officers rummage your trunks and break your vases, and make you pay a double valuation, and have no respect for your word, or even your oath; and how one independent American, with a temper easily heated, took a Satsuma vase, a lovely work that cost him five hundred dollars, and dashed it to pieces before the eyes of the excisemen rather than be taxed for more than its value. I am afraid this is not a true story, but hope it is, as I like to read of anything original or eccentric, and you hear so many stories of revenue exactions that you become a free-trader. You think about your "things" and talk about them so much that they assume princely proportions, and you begin to feel like a collector, that you have exhausted the bazaars of the East and that you have rare possessions, and not, as happens to me, only a few odds and ends that have, as it were, trickled in upon you as you wandered along, and will have no value when they reach home but the value of the memories that surround them.

After mature deliberation and taking everybody's advice—and on this subject everybody is anxious to advise you—I concluded to send my "things" home, by the way of the Suez Canal, direct to New York, and to go to California in light marching order, and when the excisemen came down upon me for curios, show them only my clothes and a few volumes of useful information. Somehow, even after the question had been settled and was out of your mind, there was an irresistible fascination in talking about your "things." I suppose the real reason was that the talk about the "things" led in an indirect way to a talk about home, and that we were all of us just a little homesick, more than we would care to admit. I have observed that people are apt to treat homesickness as they would a love affair. They like to talk about such emotions in other people, but not in themselves. Take our naval friends, for instance, who have been on this station for some time. You never saw so much fortitude! "Home"—away with such a sentiment—it is not home but "duty" which animates a sailor, and since duty commits them to the Asiatic coast, why, of course! But I observed, all the same, when the mail day drew near, and it was time for the steamers to come in from the seas, that a strange interest took possession of our naval friends, and you heard only prayers for good weather and impatience at the slow, lingering hours. Our naval friends are the most patient of men. Weather, climate, pestilence—it makes very little difference whether the winds blow high or blow low, so that the mails come in. I fancied that we talked about our "things," because it led to talk about home and what people would say, and how affairs had changed in our absence. We are none of us willing to confess to a homesick feeling except the Colonel, who has been avowedly homesick ever since we left Singapore, and has announced that his travels are at an end, except over the road that leads by the shortest and most direct route to General Sheridan's head-quarters in Chicago. I am sure that not all the "old blue" made, either in China under the Ming dynasty or in General Grant's Newark curio manufactory, would keep our gallant comrade over another steamer from the performance of his duties at the head-quarters of the Military Division of the Missouri. As we are all going home together it makes little difference, and I only allude to the Colonel's military enthusiasm because I like to see such a

A JAPANESE BED.

spirit among the young officers in our army, and to hold it up for public notice and commendation.

Our last days in Japan were crowded with incidents of a personal and public character. I use the word personal to describe events that did not find their way into the newspapers nor belong to public receptions. There were constant visits to the General from members of the cabinet—from Mr. Iwakura, especially, who came to talk about public affairs. There were conferences on the Loochoo question, when General Grant used his best efforts to bring China and Japan to a good understanding. What the effect of these conversations will be, history alone can tell, but I may add that the counsel which the General has given in conversations with Mr. Iwakura and the Ministry he has also given in writing, and very earnestly, to Prince Kung and Li Hung Chang. Since hearing both sides of the Loochoo question—the Japanese case and the Chinese case—General Grant has felt himself in a position to speak with more precision than when, in China, he heard only the Chinese story. Other questions arose—questions connected with the industrial and agricultural advancement of Japan. The General pointed out to his Japanese friends the large area of fertile land awaiting cultivation, and how much might be added to the wealth and revenues of the country if the people were induced to develop the whole territory. This led to a discussion of the land tax, so heavy a burden to the people, and which the government is compelled to impose for revenue. If, instead of taxes on land the authorities could levy a tariff for revenue—such a tariff as we see in Germany and France—then the tax on land could be abated. This led up to the revision of the treaties, the absorbing question in Japanese politics, and which is no further advanced than it was when Mr. Iwakura went to the treaty powers on his mission many years ago. The General has always given the same advice on the treaty question. One of the odd phases of the English policy in the East is, that while England allows her own colonies to do as they please in tariffs, to have free-trade or protection, she insists that Japan and China shall arrange their imposts and tariffs solely with the view of helping English trade. In other words, Japan, an independent power, is under a duress that Canada or Australia would never accept. This anomalous condition of affairs will exist so long as the treaty remains, and England has never shown an inclination to consent to any abrogation of her paramount rights under the treaty. General Grant's advice has been that Japan should make a statement of her case to the world. She should show the circumstances under which this treaty was made—how her ignorance was used to put her in an unfortunate and humiliating position. She should recall her own extraordinary progress in accepting and absorbing the modern civilization; that in doing this she has opened her empire to modern enterprise, and shown the best evidence of her desire to be friendly with the world. She should recount the disadvantages under which this treaty places her—not alone moral, but material, crippling and limiting her resources. She should announce that the treaty was at an end, but that she was prepared to sign the most favorable conventions that could be devised, provided the treaty powers recognized her sovereign, independent rights. She should at the same time proclaim her tariff, open her ports and the interior of her country, welcome foreign capital, foreign immigration, foreign labor, and assert her sovereignty. The objection to this in the minds of the Japanese is that fleets may come, and the English may bombard Tokio as they did Simonoseki. "If there is one thing more certain than another," reasoned the General, "it is that England is in no humor to make war upon Japan for a tariff. I do not believe that under any circumstances Lord Beaconsfield would consent to such an enterprise. He has had two wars, neither of which have commended themselves to the English people. An Englishman does not value the glory that comes from Afghan and Zulu campaigns. To add to these a demonstration against Japan, because she had resolved to submit no longer to a condition bordering on slavery, would arouse against Lord Beaconsfield a feeling at home that would cost him his government. Just now," the General advised, "is the best time. Lord Beaconsfield must soon go to the people. His Parliament is coming to an end, and even if he had adventurous spirits in his cabinet or in the diplomatic service disposed to push Japan, he would be compelled to control them. Japan has a great many friends in England who are even now making her cause their own, and who would support her when she was right. More than all, there is a widespread desire for justice and fair play in England, to which the Eastern nations, and especially Japan, need never appeal in vain. Japan has peculiar claims upon the sympathy and respect of mankind, and if she would assert her sovereign rights she would find that her cause met the approval of mankind."

Time will show how far this clear and firm advice will be accepted by the Japanese. While a good deal of politics was talked in these last days between the General and the rulers of Japan, there were other and more pleasant occupations. Attached to the palace was a billiard-room, and here every morning would come tradesmen from the bazaars of Tokio, with cloths and armor and swords and all manner of curious things to sell or to show. The hour after breakfast was our hour of temptation. "This," said the emotional young lady, as she moved away from the piano while Moore was singing one of his love-songs, "this is not for the good of my soul." I used to think of this story when I went into the billiard-room after breakfast to see the fresh invoices from the bazaars. What a world of art and of beauty and of taste has been created by the genius of Japan!

AFTER "OLD BLUE."

Here is a scroll of silk on which the artist, with a few daring lines, has drawn a history or a poem. Here is a morsel of bronze not much larger than a dollar. It was formerly a sword ornament, and looks like a trifle until you closely examine it and see the fine touches—a sunrise, a volcano, a flight of storks in the air, sea or stream, all told on the smallest space, with touches of silver or gold. Sometimes we had collections of toys and dolls, for Japan is the paradise of children, and in nothing does the genius of the people assert itself with more sincerity than in devising pleasures for the little people. There is something tangible in Japanese toys. The monkeys have real hair, and you can wool the dogs about and worry the cats without seeing them unravel over the nursery floor. And the dolls! You take an assortment of dolls at home, and they seem to have been cast in the same mold. They look alike, they have no expression—the faces are dead, dull, flabby; it will be a mercy if they have noses or ears; and the only way the boys can be told from the girls is by the way the hair is parted. But what can you expect from a mighty people thinking of canals and railways? The genius of America does not run to dolls, but to manifest destiny and bonanza mines. The Japanese artist makes a doll as though he loved it, and when he is through with the toy it is not alone a toy, but a story, or it may be a poem; something to come home to the baby heart, to have joys and sorrows, to be loved with the passionate love of innocence and childhood. Those were, indeed, our hours of temptation, those after-breakfast hours in the billiard-room at Enriokwan, especially in the matter of swords. There is no place in the world where you can buy such beautiful swords as in Japan. Until within the last few years every gentleman's retainer carried two swords—a long and a short one. These weapons were the mark of his rank—his badge of gentle life. He took pride in his swords, and aimed to have them of the keenest temper and most exquisite adornment. But in the hour of change came a decree forbidding the wearing of the swords, suppressing the two-sworded men, the samauri, as they are called, as a class. So all that was left for the abolished samauri was to carry their swords to the bazaars and turn them into rice and fish. Consequently the bazaars are now overstocked with swords and spears of the finest workmanship, with scabbards of lacquer and bronze, ingeniously worked in silver and gold. I have looked at innumerable specimens and never found two alike. Each separate weapon seemed to be the expression of an idea, and you never cease to marvel at the endless variety and sweep of the decorative art.

You felt also, if you bought one of the swords, that you were investing in the antiquity and chivalry of Japan. The two-sworded men are now as other people, and wear plain clothes, and work for their living, and use civil language, which was not always their custom when Sir Rutherford Alcock flourished. And yet, now that nothing is left of the poor samauri but their swords, which litter the bazaars, and over which you haggle and chaffer, trying to cheapen the weapon that for generations, perhaps, was the heirloom and the pride of a gentleman's family—now that the samauri no longer infest the streets, to worry British Ministers and foreign merchants—I am disposed to think kindly of them, and not feel as harshly as Sir Rutherford's narrative would justify me in doing. "It is rather a pity," said Sir Harry Parkes, the British Minister, one day to the writer, "that the samauri were abolished. They included in their ranks men of culture and valor. They were the middle class—or one might say the martial class—and were a kind of backbone to the social system. Some of the old samauri now hold high places. I do not think they did any harm, and the country would have been stronger with them." I quote this indulgent opinion of the British Minister in justice to the memory of the samauri, and rather as an offset to the unfavorable impression given of their character by Sir Harry's predecessor. Mr. Seward was in Japan when the samauri class were in power, and at the crisis of the revolution which was to destroy their power; and he noted that while there was abroad a warlike, turbulent body of men, he did not see one act of rudeness nor hear one word of ill-temper. I take it one never feels more generous toward his friends, more disposed to do them justice and see the real virtues in their character, than when he is attending a bankruptcy or executor's sale of their effects, and possessing himself of their household gods for about one-fourth their value. It awakens the hidden springs of benevolence in your nature, and as I marvel at the finish of these samauri swords I think of all the kind things possible about the poor, shorn gentlemen who once bore them. One advantage about the sword market in Japan is that swords are cheaper than they will ever be again, and they make capital presents. That is one of the problems of travel—to find something unique and valuable that you can buy cheap. What a pity it is that you cannot make presents on the principle that England governs India—by prestige. When some Maharajah gives the Prince of Wales a diamond aigrette for his wife, the Prince knows he cannot give diamonds in return. So the Maharajah is declared to be a loyal and deserving prince, and has two guns added to his salute. The Prince has the diamonds and the Maharajah the guns, and both are satisfied, the Indian more especially. Now, if a traveler could only give his friends his good intentions, and have them accepted at their par value, what a relief it would be, and what trouble it would save you in wondering how so-and-so would be pleased with this or that; and what heart-burnings would be avoided when the various idols of your existence came in after days to compare your offerings and sit in judgment upon your affection.

But while we had our hours of temptation in the billiard-room, and struggles with conscience—the extent of which, I am afraid, so far as some of us are concerned, will never be known until the time cometh when all things must appear—we had hours of instruction. Our hosts were ever thinking of some new employment for each new day. We grew tired in time of the public institutions, which are a good deal the same the world over, and after we had recovered from our wonder at seeing in Japan schools and workshops like those we left behind us, they had no more interest than schools and workshops generally. The heat of the weather made going about oppressive, and even the sea lost its freshness; and when the tides went down and the breeze was from the land the effect of the water was to increase the heat. Our interest in earthquakes was always fresh, and whenever the atmosphere assumed certain conditions our Japanese friends would tell us that we might expect a shock. In Japan the earthquake is as common a phenomenon as a thunder-storm at home in midsummer, although

ULYSSES S. GRANT

THE ARRIVA

ULYSSES S. GRANT

FRANCISCO.

there are no laws that govern its approach. I have told you of one experienced when we were all at dinner, and when we owed it to Governor Hennessy that we discovered there had been an earthquake. On that day it had rained, and all that I remember specially was that in walking about the grounds before dinner the air seemed to be heavy and the sea was sluggish. A few mornings before we left Enriokwan there was another experience. Our hosts had sent us some workers in pottery, to show us the skill of the Japanese in a department of art in which they have no superiors. One of the famous potters had expressed a desire to show the General his work. After breakfast we found the artisans arranged in the large drawing-room. There was the chief worker, a solemn, middle-aged person, who wore spectacles. He was dressed in his gala apparel, and when we came into the room went down on his face in Japanese style. There were three assistants. One worked the wheel. Another baked the clay. A third made himself generally useful. The chief of the party was a painter. We saw all the processes of the manufacture, the inert lump of clay going around and around, and shaping itself under the true, nimble fingers of the workmen into cups and vases and

A JAPANESE BEAUTY.

bowls. There is something fascinating in the labors of the wheel, the work is so thoroughly the artisan's own; for when he begins he has only a lump of mud, and when he ends his creation may be the envy of a throne-room. It seems almost like a Providence—this taking the dust of the valley and creating it—for the work is creation, and we are reminded of Providence in remembering that when the Creator of all fashioned his supreme work it was made of clay. The decoration of the clay was interesting, requiring a quick, firm stroke. We were requested to write something on the clay before it went into the furnace. General Grant gave his autograph and the rest of us inscriptions, written as well as we could write with a soft, yielding brush. After the inscriptions had been written, the cups were washed in a white substance and hurried into the furnace. When they came out, the fire had evaporated the coating and turned into a gloss the tints of our writing, and the painter's colors had changed, and our inscriptions were fastened in deep and lasting brown.

It was while we were watching the potters over their clay, and in conversation with a Japanese citizen, who spoke English and came as interpreter, about the progress of this special industry in Tokio, that we heard a noise as though the joists and wooden work of the house were being twisted, or as if some one were walking on the floor above with a heavy step. But there was no second floor in Enriokwan, and I suppose the incident would have passed without notice if our Japanese friend had not said, "There is an earthquake." While he spoke we paused, and again heard the wrenching of the joists and the jingling of the glass in the swinging chandelier. This was all that we noted. We walked out on the porch and looked at the foliage and toward the sea, but although observation and imagination were attuned, we saw nothing but an unusual deadness in the air, which we might have seen on Broadway on a midsummer day. These were our only earthquake experiences in Japan. I have noted them because an earthquake is always an interesting subject, and because I was impressed with the indifference shown by our Japanese friends toward this supreme and awful manifestation of the power of nature. This comes from the fact that earthquakes are rarely severe in Japan. History tells of a fearful disaster, even here, in imperial Tokio, not many years since. In conversing with some of our naval friends who had been in the West Indies and seen our tropical American earthquakes, I discovered that they did not share the indifference of the Japanese toward the earthquake. They felt toward it as experienced mariners toward the sea—the more they saw of its power the more they held it in awe. I was told that the prudent thing to do, when you hear the tremor of the earthquake, is to rush out into the open, and there remain until the second shock spends its force. The shocks of the earthquake come in twos, and generally give you warning. The houses in Japan, however, seem to have been built for the fire and the earthquake. They are put together in a loose, elastic manner, of light woods, so as to stand a great deal of shaking. Even if they fell they would not do much harm. As to fires, the custom is to have in each block of houses one small fireproof building, whither, in case of need, all in the neighborhood can hurry with their special treasures. If Tokio were to burn, what you would see would be a wilderness of ruins, with fireproof buildings at regular stations, containing the essential wealth of the town. If a resident can afford it he has his own special fire-proof building. But this is a luxury only enjoyed by the rich.

There were dinners and *fêtes*, and many quiet, pleasant parties during our last days at Enriokwan. The British Minister, Sir Harry Parkes, proposed an entertainment, but we were about to sail, and every night and every day we were engaged, and the General was compelled to decline Sir Harry's hospitality. There was a luncheon with Mr. House, the editor of the Tokio *Times*, in a pretty little house near the American Legation, looking out on the sea. [1] I had known House years ago, more years I am afraid than I care to remember, when he was among the most brilliant of a noted group of young men, who were then making their way in the world, through the attractive but not always fruitful fields of journalism. I was glad

LAST DAYS IN TOKIO.

to see him again, and although Time had laid his hand upon him, as I fear it had upon both of us, and there was the suggestion of care and labor in his features, it had not dimmed the buoyancy, the grace, and the genius that made him, in our early New York times, attractive and envied among men. House, even in those days—it was before the rebellion, Heaven help us! ages and ages ago!—felt a singular interest in Japan. He became familiar with the embassy, the Tycoon's embassy,

A MOUNTAIN INN.

in 1860, and his interest in Japan deepened, but everybody was surprised when they heard that he had left a career of promise and renown to seek his love in the far East. Since then House has given himself to Japan with a spirit that I might call the missionary spirit of self-abnegation. He has fought her battles. He has defended her name. He has endeavored to win her a place among the nations. He has accepted contumely and misrepresentation in her cause, for I found—how quickly you find it out!—that if you take sides with the Eastern nations in this far East you bring upon you the rancor of the foreigners. You are as much an outlaw as Wendell Phillips in anti-slavery days was an outlaw in Beacon Street. You are not respectable. You are against the interests of your own country. You are anxious to see Japan close up again, and the foreigners driven into the sea. You are bribed, bought, corrupted. You are possessed of the devil. But House has held his place and made his fight, and still makes it with all the brilliancy of old days, and his name is a power in Japan. I have ventured upon this allusion to his career because I happen to know a great deal about it, and I am glad to honor, especially in my own craft, what seems to be a lofty and self-denying spirit. And certainly nothing but that self-denial which love alone can inspire, would have induced House to surrender the career he was enjoying when I knew him in New York, to bury himself in Japan.

Among the most pleasing incidents of our last days in Tokio was a dinner with Sanjo, the Prime Minister, who entertained us in Parisian style, everything being as we would have found it on the Champs Elysées—the perfection of French decoration in the appointments of the house, and of French taste in the appointments of the table. Mr. Mori, who was formerly Japanese Minister to the United States, and is now Vice-Minister for Foreign Affairs, and one of the strong and rising men in the empire, gave a dinner and a reception. Here the General met most of the men noted in literary and scientific pursuits. Mr. Terashima, the Foreign Minister, also gave a dinner, which was Parisian in its appointments. Mr. Yoshida entertained a portion of our party—the General not being able to attend—in Japanese style. Among the guests were Saigo, Ito, and Kawamura, of the cabinet, and our good friends and daily companions Tateno and Ishibashi, of the Emperor's household, who had been sent by his Majesty to attend upon the General and give him the advantage of their knowledge of English. We had had a stately Japanese dinner in Nagasaki, when we were entertained after the manner of the old daimios, but with Mr. Yoshida we dined as we would have dined with any Japanese gentleman of distinction if we had been asked to his house in a social way. Mr. Yoshida lives some distance from Enriokwan, in one of a group of houses built on a ridge overlooking the sea, on the road toward Yokohama. There are grounds where the master of the house indulges a fancy for gardening, a fancy which in no place do you see so perfect as in Japan, for the gardener in Japan is a poet. He loves his trees and shrubs and flowers, and brings about results in his treatment of them that show new possibilities and a new power of expression in nature.

Mr. Yoshida had a few lanterns among his trees, but beyond this modest bit of decoration—just a touch of color to light up the caverns of the night—there was no display. Dinner was served in Japanese style. Our host wore Japanese costume, and the room in which we dined was open on three sides and looked out on the gardens. When you enter a Japanese house you are expected to take off your shoes. This is not alone a mark of courtesy, but of cleanliness. The floors are spotless, and covered with a fine matting which would crack under the grinding edges of your European shoes. We took off our shoes and stretched ourselves on the floor, and partook of our food from small tables a few inches high. The tables were of lacquer and the dishes were mainly of lacquer. There is no plan, no form, in a Japanese dinner—it is simply to dine with comfort. Of the quality of the food I have not confidence enough in my judgment to give an opinion. Dining has always appeared to me one of the misfortunes that came with Adam's fall, and I have never been able to think of it with enthusiasm. I know that this is a painful confession, the display of ignorance and want of taste, but it cannot be helped. I gave myself seriously to my dinner, because I am fond of Mr. Yoshida, and wanted to pay him the compliment of enjoying his gracious and refined hospitality. Then I thought that it would be something that I might want to write about. But the dinner was beyond me. I cannot say that I disliked it, and I liked it about as well as nineteen out of twenty of the dinners you have in New York. It was picturesque and pleasing, and in all its appointments so unlike anything in our close and compact way of living that you felt somehow that you were having a good time; you felt like laughing, and if you gave way to your impulse it would have been to roll about on the floor in the delight and abandon of boyhood. If you did not want to eat you could smoke, and if not to smoke, to drink—and there was drinking, smoking, and eating all the time. Your attendants were maidens, comely and fair, who knelt in the middle of the floor and watched you with unmoving features, fanning you and noiselessly slipping

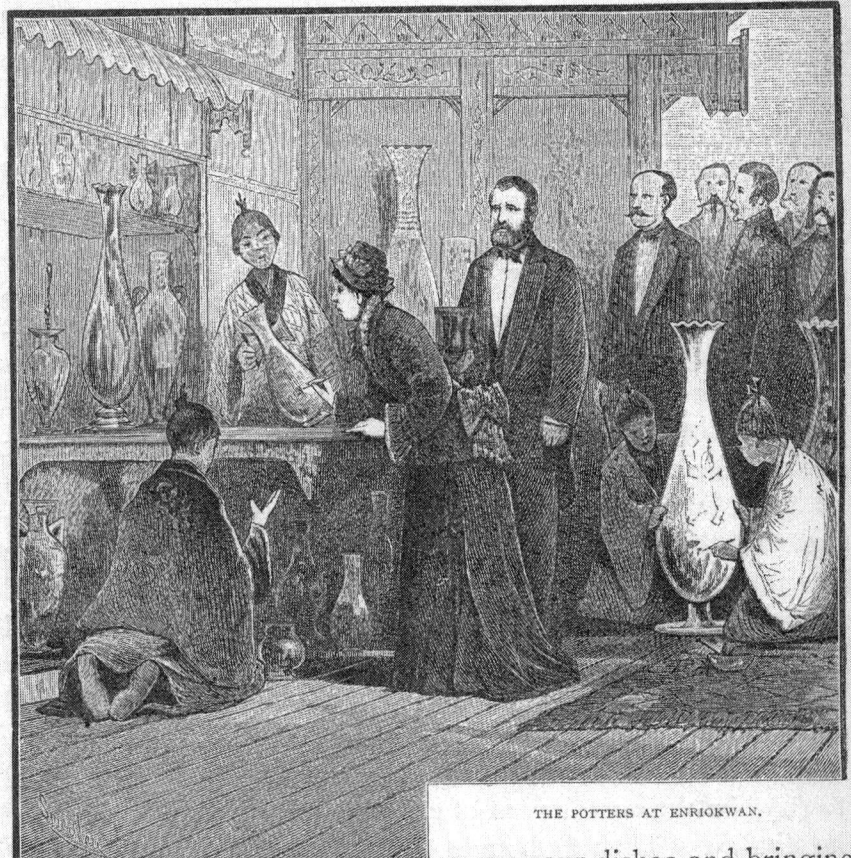

THE POTTERS AT ENRIOKWAN.

away your dishes and bringing new ones. They were so modest, so graceful, that you became unconscious of their presence. They became, as it were, one of the decorations of the dinner. They watched the guests and followed their wishes, as far as comfort was concerned. Beyond that I saw no word or glance of recognition. At home your servants are personages with all the attributes of human nature, and sometimes in a form so aggravated that they become a serious care, and you dine under fear, in the presence of some oppressive responsibility. But our maidens might have been sprites, they were so far from us, and at the same time their grace and quickness made the mechanism of our dinner smooth and noiseless.

I have been trying to think of something concerning this dinner that would be regarded as useful information. I am conscious of the absence of that quality in all that I have written about Japan. I would give the world if I could only tell you how some of the soups were made and how the ragouts were seasoned. But if I had been told I never would have remembered, and would have certainly written it wrong, and so I am compelled to fall back upon my impressions. My main impression was that we were having a good time, that we were amusing ourselves, playing, romping—not dining. I have never been upon the stage, but I can fancy that if I had taken part in a comedy I should have had the same sensations with which I enjoyed Mr. Yoshida's dinner—that I was having a merry time and giving others a merry time. To chat and listen, to lie prone on the floor and see the red lanterns among the trees; to see the universe beyond, the calm and infinite stars; to run into light and airy talk about music and books and songs and folk-lore; to hear our friends tell us of the martial songs of Japan, and chant for us some of their stirring strains; to try and tell them something of our own martial songs, what our soldier boys sang during the war; to note the energy and conscientious desire to please and give instruction with which Colonel Grant sang "John Brown," and "Sherman's March through Georgia," and "Johnny Comes Marching Home"— these are the impressions I recall.(2) Neither the Colonel nor myself know anything about the words or music of these songs, nor about music in general, and would have given a large part of our fortunes if, for that evening at least, we had had any musical faculty. But what could we do? Our friends were curious on the subject, and there was no way of changing the theme, and we told all we knew—who John Brown was, and what Sherman marched for, and who Johnny was supposed to be.

There was a line in the Sherman song—something about the soldiers marching off with the turkey gobblers—which amused our friends, although it was difficult to explain to them the exact meaning of the word "gobblers." The Colonel's singing was mainly in heroic measure, and his tunes seemed to run into the same key; but our friends were interested. In this fashion the evening passed on. A good deal of the pleasure, no doubt, came from the fact that we were all friends, good friends, anxious to please and to be in each other's society. That would add grace to a dinner of pottage and herbs; and when at last the inevitable hour came it was late before we accepted it, and when our carriage drove up to take us home we took our leave of our host and of our Japanese friends with regret, and the feeling that we had enjoyed our evening as much as any we had spent in Japan.

BRONZE IDOL, HAKONE.

Another dinner worth noting, for it was the last expression of Japanese hospitality, was the entertainment given to General Grant by Prince Dati. Since we came to Japan Prince Dati has been always with us. The Prince is about sixty years of age. Under the old régime he was a daimio, or feudal lord, of ancient family, who had the power of life and death over his retainers. When the change came, and the power of the lords was absorbed by the Mikado, and many of their rights and emoluments taken away, most of the daimios went into retirement. Some came to Tokio, others remained at their country homes. The great princes, like Satsuma, have ever since only given the government a sullen, reserved obedience. You do not feel them in State affairs. You do not see them. The authorities do not have the prestige of their influence and authority. They are names in Japan, possible centers of rebellion; while the forces of the State are in the hands of men who, a few years ago, were their armor-bearers and samauri. The daimios appear to accept the revolution and give allegiance to the present government of the Mikado, but their acceptance is not hearty. Some of them, however, regard the revolution as an incident that could not be helped, as the triumph of the Mikado over the Tycoon, and altogether a benefit to the nation. Among these is Prince Dati. His position in Japan is something like that of one of the old-fashioned Tory country lords in England after the Hanoverian accession. His office in the State is personal to the Emperor. We have all become much attached to Prince Dati, and it seems appropriate that our last festival in Japan should be as the guest of one who has been with us in daily companionship. The Prince had intended to entertain us in his principal town-house, the one nearest Enriokwan, but the cholera broke out in the vicinity, and the Prince invited us to another of his houses in the suburbs of Tokio. We went by water, embarking from the sea-wall in front of Enriokwan. We turned into the river, passing the commodious grounds of the American Legation, its flag weather-worn and shorn; passing the European settlement, which looked a little like a well-to-do Connecticut town, noting the little missionary churches surmounted by the cross; and on for an hour or so past tea-houses and ships and under bridges, and watching the shadows descend over the city. It is hard to realize that Tokio is a city—one of the greatest cities of the world. It looks like a series of villages, with bits of green and open spaces and inclosed grounds breaking up the continuity of the town. There is no special character to Tokio, no one trait to seize upon and remember, except that the aspect is that of repose. The banks of the river are low and sedgy, at some points a marsh. When we came to the house of the Prince we found that he had built a causeway of bamboo through the marsh out into the river. His house was decorated with lanterns. As we walked along the cause-

FALLS NEAR HAKONE.

way all the neighborhood seemed to be out in a dense crowd, waiting to see the General. Our evening with the Prince was very pleasant. He lives in palatial style. He has many children, and children's children have come to bless his declining years. He took an apparent pride in presenting us to the various members of his family. Our dinner was served partly in European, partly in Japanese style. There were chairs, a table, knives, forks, napkins, bread, and champagne. This was European. There were chopsticks, sea-weed jellies, raw fish, soups of fish and salvi. This was Japanese. There was as a surprise a special compliment to our nation—a surprise that came in the middle of the feast—a dish of baked pork and beans, which would have done honor to Boston. Who inspired this dish and who composed it are mysteries. It came into our dinner in a friendly way, and was so well meant, and implied such an earnest desire to please on the part of the host, that it became idyllic, and conveyed a meaning that I venture to say was never expressed by a dish of pork and beans since the "Mayflower" came to our shores. The dinner over we sat on the porch and looked out on the river. In the courtyard there were jugglers who performed tricks notable for dexterity, such as making a fan go around the edge of an umbrella, and keeping a bevy of balls in the air, on the wing, like birds.

Our last Japanese entertainment was that of Prince Dati. But there were others from Americans. Admiral Patterson gave a dinner on board his flagship, the "Richmond," at which were present officers from our various ships, the Japanese Admiral, the Minister, and the Consul-General. The dinner was served on deck, and our naval friends gave us another idea of the architectural triumphs possible in a skillful management of flags. The dinner was quite a family affair, for the officers had been our shipmates and we knew all their nicknames, and the Admiral had won our friendship and respect by his patience, his care, his courtesy, his untiring efforts to make General Grant's visit to Japan as pleasant as possible. When the rain began to fall, and to ooze through the bunting and drip over the food, it added to the heartiness of the dinner, for a little discomfort like that was a small matter, and only showed how much we were at home, and that we were resolved to enjoy ourselves, no matter what the winds or waves might say. When Consul-General Van Buren came he brought with him rumors of a typhoon that was coming up the coast, and might break on us at any moment and carry us all out to sea. This gave a new zest to our dinner, but the typhoon broke on Tokio, turning aside from our feast, and when we returned on shore at midnight the rain was over and the sea was smooth. There was a garden party at the Consulate, brilliant and thronged, said by the Yokohama press to be the most successful fête of the kind ever given in the foreign settlement. The Consular building in Yokohama is a capacious and stately edifice, standing in the center of a large square. The building and the grounds were illuminated with lanterns—festoons of lanterns dangling from the windows and the balconies—running in lines to the gate, and swaying aloft to the cross-trees of the flagstaff. A special tent had been erected on the lawn, and the band from the "Richmond" was present. The evening was clear and beautiful, and everybody came, the representatives of the foreign colony, of the consular and diplomatic bodies, of the local government, officers of our navy with Admiral Patterson at the head, members of the cabinet, and high officials of the Japanese government. There was dancing, and during the supper, which took place in the tent, there was a speech from Consul-General Van Buren, in honor of General Grant, in which he alluded to the approaching departure of the General for home, and wishing him and the rest of the party a prosperous and successful voyage. To this General Grant made a brief response, and the entertainment went on far beyond midnight and into the morning hours.

On Saturday General Grant took his leave of the Emperor. An audience of leave is always a solemn ceremony, and the court of Japan pays due respect to splendor and state. A farewell to the Mikado meant more in the eyes of General Grant than if it had been the ordinary leave-taking of a monarch who had shown him hospitality. He had received attentions from the sovereign and people such as had never before been given. He had been honored not alone in his own person, but as the representative of his country. His visit had this political significance, that the Japanese government intended by the honors they paid him to show the value they gave to American friendship. In many ways the visit of the General had taken a wide range, and what he would say to the Emperor would have great importance, because every word he uttered would be weighed in every Japanese household. General Grant's habit in answering speeches and addresses is to speak at the moment, without previous thought or preparation. On several occasions, when bodies of people made addresses to him, they sent copies in advance, so that he might read them and prepare a response. But he always declined these courtesies, saying that he would wait until he heard the addresses in public, and his best response would be what came to him on the instant. This was so particularly at Penang, when the Chinese came to him with an address which opened up the most delicate issue of American politics, the Chinese question. A copy of this address had been sent to the Government House for him to look over, but he declined, and his first knowledge of the address which propounded the whole Chinese problem was when the blue-buttoned mandarin stood before him reading it. The response was one of the General's longest and most important speeches, and was made at once, in a quiet, conversational tone. The farewell to the Emperor was so important, however, that the General did what he had not done before during our journey. He wrote out in advance the speech he proposed making to his Majesty. I mention this circumstance simply because the incident was an exceptional one, and because it showed General Grant's anxiety to say to the Emperor and the people of Japan what would be most becoming, in return for their kindness, and what would best conduce to good relations between the two nations.

At two in the afternoon the sound of the bugles and the tramp of the horsemen announced the arrival of the escort that was to accompany us to the imperial palace. Mr. Bingham arrived shortly after, looking well, but a little sad over the circumstance that the ceremony in which he was about to officiate was the close of an event which had been to him the source of unusual pleasure—the visit of General Grant to Japan. Prince Dati and Mr. Yoshida were also in readiness, and a few minutes after two the state carriages came. General and Mrs. Grant rode in the first carriage, Mr. Bingham, accompanied by Prince Dati and Mr. Yoshida, in the second, Colonel Grant and the writer in the third. Colonel Grant wore his uniform, the others evening dress. The cavalry surrounded our carriages and we rode off at a slow pace. The road was long, the weather hard and dry, the heat pitiless. On reaching the palace infantry received the General with military honors. The Prime Minister, accompanied by the Ministers for the Household and Foreign Affairs, were waiting at the door when our party arrived. The princes of the imperial family were present. The meeting was not so stately and formal as when we came to greet the Emperor and have an audience of welcome. Then all the cabinet were present, blazing in uniforms and decorations. Then we were strangers, now we are friends. On entering the audience-chamber—the same plain and severely furnished room in which we had been received—the Emperor and Empress advanced and shook hands with the General and Mrs. Grant. The Emperor is not what you would call a graceful man, and his manners are those of an anxious person not precisely at his ease—wishing to please and make no mistake. But on this farewell audience he seemed more easy and natural than when we had seen him before. After the salute of the Emperor there was a moment's pause. General Grant

JAPANESE BONZES.

then took out of his pocket the manuscript of his speech, and read it as follows:

"YOUR MAJESTY: I come to take my leave, and to thank you, the officers of your government, and the people of Japan, for the great hospitality and kindness I have received at the hands of all during my most pleasant visit to this country. I have now been two months in Tokio and the surrounding neighborhood, and two previous weeks in the more southerly part of the country. It affords me great satisfaction to say that during all this stay and all my visiting I have not witnessed one discourtesy toward myself, nor a single unpleasant sight. Everywhere there seems to be the greatest contentment among the people; and while no signs of great individual wealth exist, no absolute poverty is visible. This is in striking and pleasing contrast with almost every other country I have visited. I leave Japan greatly impressed with the possibilities and probabilities of her future. She has a fertile soil, one half of it not yet cultivated to man's use, great undeveloped mineral resources, numerous and fine harbors, an extensive sea-coast abounding in fish of an almost endless variety, and, above all, an industrious, ingenious, contented, and frugal population. With all these nothing is wanted to insure great progress except wise direction by the government, peace at home and abroad, and non-interference in the internal and domestic affairs of the country by the outside nations. It is the sincere desire of your guests to see Japan realize all possible strength and greatness, to see her as independent of foreign rule or dictation as any Western nation now is, and to see affairs so directed by her as to command the respect of the civilized world. In saying this I believe I reflect the sentiments of the great majority of my countrymen. I now take my leave without expectation of ever again having the opportunity of visiting Japan, but with the assurance that pleasant recollections of my present visit will not vanish while my life lasts. That your Majesty may long reign over a prosperous and contented people and enjoy every blessing is my sincere prayer."

When General Grant had finished, Mr. Ishibashi, the interpreter, read a Japanese translation. The Emperor bowed, and taking from an attendant a scroll on which was written in Japanese letters his own address, read it as follows:

"Your visit has given us so much satisfaction and pleasure that we can only lament that the time for your departure has come. We regret also that the heat of the season and the presence of the epidemic have prevented several of your proposed visits to different places. In the meantime, however, we have greatly enjoyed the pleasure of frequent interviews with you; and the cordial expressions which you have just addressed to us in taking your leave have given us great additional satisfaction. America and Japan being near neighbors, separated by an ocean only, will become more and more closely connected with each other as time goes on. It is gratifying to feel assured that your visit to our empire, which enabled us to form very pleasant personal acquaintance with each other, will facilitate and strengthen the friendly relations that have heretofore happily existed between the two countries. And now we cordially wish you a safe and pleasant voyage home, and that you will on your return find your nation in peace and prosperity, and that you and your family may enjoy long life and happiness."

His Majesty read his speech in a clear, pleasant voice. Mr. Ishibashi at the close also read a translation. Then the Empress, addressing herself to Mrs. Grant, said she rejoiced to see the General and party in Japan, but she was afraid the unusual heat and the pestilence had prevented them from enjoying her visit. Mrs. Grant said that her visit to Japan had more than realized her anticipations; that she had enjoyed every hour of her stay in this most beautiful country, and that she hoped she might have in her American home, at some early day, an opportunity of acknowledging and returning the hospitality she had received in Japan.

The Emperor then addressed Mr. Bingham, our Minister, hoping he was well, and expressing his pleasure at seeing him again. Mr. Bingham advanced and said:

"I thank your Majesty for your kind inquiry. I desire, on behalf of the President of the United States and of the government and people I represent, to express our profound appreciation of the kindness and the honor shown by your Majesty and your people to our illustrious citizen."

His Majesty expressed his pleasure at the speech of Mr. Bingham, the audience came to an end, and we drove back to our home at Enriokwan.

The audience with the Emperor was the end of all festivities; for, after taking leave of the head of the nation, it would not have been becoming in others to offer entertainments. Sunday passed quietly, friends coming and going all day. Monday was spent in Yokohama making ready for embarking. The steamer, which was to sail on Tuesday, was compelled to wait another day. On Tuesday the General invited Admiral Patterson, Captain Benham, Commander Boyd, and Commander Johnson, commanding respectively the American men-of-war

"Richmond," "Ranger," and "Ashuelot," Mr. Bingham, General Van Buren, and several members of the Japanese cabinet, with the ladies of their families, to dinner, our last dinner in Japan. In the evening was a reception, or rather what grew into a reception, the coming of all our friends—Japanese, American, and European—to say good-by. The trees in the park were hung with lanterns, and fireworks were displayed, furnished by the committee of the citizens of Tokio. There was the band from the War Department. The night was one of rare beauty, and during the whole evening the parlors of the palace were thronged. There were the princes and princesses of the imperial family, the members of the cabinet, the high officers of the army and navy, Japanese citizens, ministers, and consuls. The American naval officers from four ships, the "Monongahela" having come in from Hakodadi, were in full force, and their uniforms gave color to what was in other respects a brilliant and glittering throng. It was a suggestive, almost a historic assembly. There were the princes and rulers of Japan. Sanjo, the Prime Minister, with his fine, frail, almost womanly face, his frame like that of a stripling, was in conversation with Iwakura, the Junior Premier, whose strong, severe, almost classical features are softened by the lines of suffering which tell of ever-present pain. In one room Ito sits in eager talk with Okuma, the Finance Minister, with his Hamlet-face and eyes of speculation. Okuma does not speak English, but Ito gives you a hearty American greeting. Mrs. Grant is sitting on the piazza, where the fireworks can be seen, and around are Japanese and American ladies. Mr. Bingham, whose keen face grows gentler with the frosty tints of age, is in talk with Sir Harry Parkes, the British Minister, a lithe, active, nervous, middle-aged gentleman, with open, clear-cut Saxon features, the merriest, most amusing, most affable gentleman present, knowing everybody, talking to everybody. One would not think as you followed his light banter, and easy rippling ways, that his hand was the hand of iron, and that his policy was the personification of all that was hard and stern in the policy of England. This genial, laughing, plump Chinese mandarin, with his button of high rank, who advances with clasped hands to salute the General, is Ho, the Chinese ambassador, an intelligent gentleman, with whom I have had many instructive talks about China. His Excellency is anxious about the Loochoo question, and, when he has spoken with the General, advances

THE DINNER AT MR. YOSHIDA'S.

and opens the theme, and hopes the good offices of the General will go as far as his good wishes would have them. This man, with the swarthy features, and full, blazing eyes, who greets you with cordial, laughing courtesy, and who reminds you a great deal in his manners and features of General Sheridan, is the Secretary of War, the famous General Saigo, who commanded the Japanese expedition to Formosa. The General is brother of that still more famous Saigo—a great name and a great character—who threw away his life in that mad and miserable Satsuma rebellion. What freaks fate plays with us all! It was foreordained that this Saigo should be Secretary of War, and directing the troops of the government, while the other Saigo, blood of his blood, brother and friend, should be in arms against the government. General Saigo is in conversation with Colonel Grant, with whom he has become most friendly, and the Colonel is telling how a soldier lives on the Plains, and what a good time Saigo and the other friends who form the group would have if they came to America, and allowed him to be their host and escort in Montana. The other friends are notable men. The one with the striking features—a thin face that reminds you of the portraits of Moltke, a serious, resolute face that mocks the restless, dare-devil eye—is Admiral Kawamura, the head of the navy, famous for his courage, about which you hear romantic stories. Inemoto, who is near him, is Secretary of the Navy. It shows the clemency of Japan when you remember that Inemoto was the leader of a rebellion against the government in whose cabinet he now holds a seat. He owes his life, his pardon, and his advancement largely to the devotion and wisdom of one of the generals who defeated him. That officer is now at his side listening to the Colonel's narrative, General Kuroda, Minister of Colonization. Kuroda looks like a trooper. In another group you see Yoshida, with his handsome, enthusiastic face, and Mori, who looks as if he had just left a cloister, and Wyeno, fresh from England, where he has been Minister, whose wife, one of the beauties of Japan, is one of the belles of the evening, and Inouye, Minister for Public Works—all noted men, and all young men. The men here to-night have made the new Japan, and as you pick them out, one after the other, you see that they are young, with the fire, the force, and the sincerity of youth. The only ones in the groups who appear to be over forty are Sanjo and Iwakura. Sanjo has never put any force upon the government; his mission has been to use his high rank and lofty station to smooth and reconcile and conciliate. As for Iwakura, although he did more than any one else at the time, they say that he has ceased to look kindly upon the changes, that his heart yearns for old Japan, and that his eyes are turned with affection and sorrow toward the lamented and irrecoverable past.

Supper coming, groups go in various directions—some with Mrs. Grant and the ladies to one room, where there are ices and delicate refreshments, and some, especially the Americans, with Saigo and Kawamura and Prince Dati, to drink a joyous toast, a friendly farewell bumper to the Colonel before he

A JAPANESE SHOEMAKER.

sails home. And this special fragment of the company becomes a kind of maelstrom, especially fatal to naval men and Americans, who are sooner or later drawn into its eddy. But the maelstrom is away in one of the wings of the palace. In the drawing-rooms friends come and go, and give their wishes to the General and all of us, and wander about to see the decorations of our unique and most interesting dwelling; or more likely go out under the trees to feel the cool night air, as it comes in from the ocean, and note the variegated lanterns as they illuminate the landscape; or watch the masses of fire and flame and colors that flash against the dense and glowing sky, and shadow it with a beauty that may be seen from afar—from all of Tokio, from the villages around, from the ships that sail the seas. Midnight had passed before our fête was ended, before the last carriage had driven away; and walking through the empty saloons the General and one or two friends sat down on the piazza to smoke a cigar, and have a last look at the beauty of Enriokwan, the beauty that never was so attractive as when we saw it for the last time under the midnight stars.

We were up and stirring in time, but our impedimenta was on board the steamer, and there was really nothing to do but breakfast and take our departure. The day of our leaving Japan was clear and beautiful, and, as the hour for our going was early, the morning shadows made the air grateful. While we were at breakfast the cavalry came trooping into the grounds, and we could hear the notes of the bugle and the word of command. Officials, ministers, and other friends came in to accompany the General. Shortly after eight the state carriages came. We drove slowly away, the cavalry forming around us, the infantry presenting arms. We looked back and took our farewell of Enriokwan, where we had passed so many happy hours. It was like leaving an old home. The servants swarmed on the veranda, and we felt sorry to leave behind us people so faithful and obliging. General Grant's departure from his Tokio residence was attended with as much ceremony as his arrival. Troops formed in double line from the door of the palace along the whole line of our route, even to the railway station. Military officers of high rank rode with the cavalry as a guard of honor. The crowd was enormous and increased as we came to the railway. The station had been cleared and additional troops were posted to keep the multitude out of the way. On entering the station the band played "Hail Columbia," and we found our Japanese and American friends present, some to say farewell, but most of them to go with us as far as Yokohama. The committee of citizens who had received us were drawn up in line in evening costume. The General shook hands with the members and thanked them for their hospitality. Mr. Iwakura escorted Mrs. Grant to the imperial car. Here were Mrs. Mori, Mrs. Yoshida, and other ladies. The Chinese Minister came just as we were leaving, and our train, which was a long one, was filled with friends who meant to see us embark. At twenty-five minutes past eight the train pushed out from Tokio, the troops presenting arms, the band playing our national air, the people waving their farewell, while the General stood on the platform and bowed his acknowledgments. Our engine was draped with the American and Japanese flags. Our train was a special one, and stopped at none of the intermediate sta-

AIRING THE LITTLE ONES.

tions. But as we whirled past each station we observed the crowds assembled to have a last glimpse of the General. As we passed Kanagawa and came in sight of Yokohama bay we saw the ships dressed from stem to stern with streamers, flags, and emblems. When we entered the Yokohama station the crowd was apparently as large as what we had left in the capital. There were troops presenting arms, a band to play "Hail Columbia," and the Governor to welcome us. The merchants and principal citizens, in European evening dress, stood in line. The Governor escorted Mrs. Grant to her carriage, and we drove to the Admiralty wharf. The road was decorated with Japanese and American flags, and when we came to the Admiralty there was a display of day fireworks, an exquisite combination of gray and blue, of colors that do not war with the sun, spreading over the sky gossamer shapes, delicate tints, showers of pearl-like spray. There in waiting we found the Consul-General, Admiral Patterson, Captain Benham, Captain Fitzhugh, Commander Boyd, and Commander Johnson, who had come to escort the General on board his steamer. We remained at the Admiralty several minutes while light refreshments were served. The General then went on the Admiralty barge, Mrs. Grant being escorted by Admiral Kawamura, and amid the noise of the exploding fireworks and strains of the naval band we pushed off.

We came alongside of the steamer and were received by Commodore Maury, who began at once to prepare for sea. During the few minutes that were left for farewells the deck of the "City of Tokio" formed a brilliant sight. Boats from the four men-of-war came laden with our naval officers, in their full uniforms, to say good-by. All of them were friends, many of them had been shipmates and companions, and the hour of separation brought so many memories of the country, the kindness, the consideration, the good-fellowship they had shown us, that we felt as if we were leaving friends. Steam-tugs brought from Yokohama other friends.

In saying farewell to our Japanese friends, to those who had been our special hosts, General Grant expressed his gratitude and his friendship. But mere words, however warmly spoken, could only give faint expression to the feelings with which we took leave of many of those who had come to the steamer to pay us parting courtesy. These gentlemen were not alone princes—rulers of an empire, noblemen of rank and lineage, ministers of a sovereign whose guests we had been—but friends. And in saying farewell to them we said farewell to so many and so much, to a country where every hour of our stay had a special value, to a civilization which had profoundly impressed us, and which awakened new ideas of what Japan had been, of her real place in the world, and of what her place might be if stronger nations shared her generosity or justice. We had been strangely won by Japan, and our last view of it was a scene of beauty. Yokohama nestled on her shore, against which the waters of the sea were idly rolling. Her hills were dowered with foliage, and here and there were houses and groves and flagstaffs, sentinels

FAREWELL TO JAPAN.

of the outside world which had made this city their encampment. In the far distance, breaking through the clouds, so faint at first that you had to look closely to make sure that you were not deceived by the mists, Fusiyama towered into the blue and bending skies. Around us were men-of-war shimmering in the sunshine, so it seemed, with their multitudinous flags. There was the hurry, the nervous bustle and excitement, the glow of energy and feeling which always mark the last moments of a steamer about to sail. Our naval friends went back to their ships. Our Yokohama friends went off in their tugs, and the last we saw of General Van Buren was a distant and vanishing figure in a state of pantomime, as though he were delivering a Fourth of July oration. I presume he was cheering. Then our Japanese friends took leave, and went on board their steam-launch to accompany us a part of our journey. The Japanese man-of-war has her anchor up, slowly steaming, ready to convoy us out to sea. The last line that binds us to our anchorage is thrown off, and the huge steamer moves slowly through the shipping. We pass the "Richmond" near enough to recognize our friends on the quarter-deck—the Admiral and his officers. You hear a shrill word of command, and seamen go scampering up the rigging to man the yards. The guns roll out a salute. We pass the "Ashuelot," and her guns take up the iron chorus. We pass the "Monongahela," so close almost that we could converse with Captain Fitzhugh and the gentlemen who are waving us farewell. Her guns thunder good-by, and over the bay the smoke floats in waves— floats on toward Fusiyama. We hear the cheers from the "Ranger." Very soon all that we see of our vessels are faint and distant phantoms, and all that we see of Yokohama are lines of gray and green. We are fast speeding on toward California. For an hour or so the Japanese man-of-war, the same which met us at Nagasaki and came with us through the Inland Sea, keeps us company. The Japanese cabinet are on board. We see the smoke break from her ports and we hurry to the side of our vessel to wave farewell—farewell to so many friends, so many friends kind and true. This is farewell at last, our final token of good will from Japan. The man-of-war fires twenty-one guns. The Japanese sailors swarm on the rigging and give hearty cheers. Our steamer answers by blowing her steam-whistle. The man-of-war turns slowly around and steams back to Yokohama. Very soon she also becomes a phantom, vanishing over the horizon. Then, gathering herself like one who knows of a long and stern task to do, our steamer breasts the sea with an earnest will—for California and for home.

ULYSSES S. GRANT

Notes for Chapter XLIV
Page numbers refer to pagination of facsimile document.

(1) p. 590 Edward H. House came to Japan as a journalist in 1870. He wrote for the *Tribune* and also contributed to *Harpers* and the *New York Times*. Several years before Grant's visit he had established his own English language newspaper, *Tokio Times*. For a full treatment of House's career see: Huffman, *A Yankee in Meiji Japan – the Crusading Journalist, Edward H. House*.

House's house was in Tsukiji an area in Tokyo where many foreigners lived. American minister Bingham had moved the legation from its dilapidated temple location in Azabu in what was then the southern outskirts of Tokyo into the center of the city and had a legation office and official residence constructed on the site in Tsukiji.

(2) p. 595 19th century karaoke. Colonel Grant is the president's older son, Frederick "Fred" Grant. Fred had been a West Point classmate of James Wasson, who had met and married Minister John Bingham's daughter, Marie. Wasson had vacationed with the Grant family and after West Point took a job in Japan where he married Marie. By the time of Grant's visit, Wasson had ended his term in Japan and had been assigned to an outpost in West Texas. At first Marie had joined her husband in Texas but by the time of Grant's visit had returned to Tokyo with their young son. The marriage ended not long after that and Wasson was arrested, charged, tried, convicted and imprisoned for stealing the army payroll. See Kidder, *Of One Blood All Nations*, p. 185.

ANDREW CARNEGIE

Picture of Carnegie taken several years after his trip around the world. Public Domain

KEYSTONE BRIDGE CO. WORKS,
PITTSBURGH, PA.

1875

Courtesy of Angela Schad Head of Reference Services
Hagley Museum and Library Wilmington, Delaware, USA

ANDREW CARNEGIE

Introduction by John Sagers

John Sagers is Professor of History at Linfield University in McMinnville, Oregon, where he teaches courses on the history of Japan, China, and East Asia. Recently, he developed a new course on epidemics in world history. His research specializes on the intellectual and economic history of modern Japan. Professor Sagers earned his BA in history from the University of California at Berkeley, his MA in international affairs from the University of California at San Diego, and Ph.D. in East Asian history from the University of Washington in Seattle. He has been a Fulbright Fellow at Rikkyo University in Tokyo and a recipient of a Japan Foundation Fellowship. His publications include the books Origins of Japanese Wealth and Power: Reconciling Confucianism and Capitalism, 1830 – 1885 *and* Confucian Capitalism: Shibusawa Eiichi, Business Ethics, and Economic Development in Meiji Japan.

In the 1870s, Andrew Carnegie became wealthy running the Keystone Bridge Company and the Union Iron Mills and was beginning to supply steel to railroads. In October 1878, he embarked on a trip around the world both for leisure and to gather material for a book which he hoped would launch him as a literary figure. Upon his return, he had his notes transcribed and published them as a book that he distributed to his friends and colleagues. This chapter comes from a later edition, for a broader commercial readership, entitled *Round the World* published by Charles Scribner in 1884 and includes updated information on Japan that Carnegie added after his 1878 visit. With this in mind, we can see that Carnegie was not so much interested in creating a comprehensive record of his visit to Japan as in displaying his literary abilities describing scenes that would most resonate with his intended readers. (Nasaw, 188-195) For example, he described the grandeur of Mt. Fuji, his visits to temples and shrines, and his impressions of evening entertainment, but says little about his personal interactions with individual Japanese people.

ANDREW CARNEGIE

When Carnegie arrived in November, 1878, Japan was about a decade into the government-sponsored program of rapid modernization that followed the Meiji Restoration. Carnegie reviewed recent history and noted that shogun (which he calls "tycoon" from the Japanese *taikun* meaning "great lord"), daimyo, and samurai have been replaced by a new government headed by the emperor and new bureaucratic officials. The emperor's capital had been moved from Kyoto to the shogun's city of Edo and renamed Tokyo. Tokyo was the center of Japan's modernization efforts, and Carnegie noted that most government officials wore European-style clothing. The hotel where Carnegie stayed had a French cook and, except for an evening of traditional-style entertainment, he did not say much about Japanese food. When he visited Kyoto, he was not very impressed with the city which had no buildings over one story.

Like many travelers, Carnegie paid much attention to social customs that struck him as unusual. He compared workers wearing loincloths to the scantily clad "demons" of a popular American play. He thought people wearing geta (elevated sandals) looked like they were walking on stilts. He was repulsed by both the Japanese fashion of women blackening their teeth and Japanese music which he found grating and difficult to listen to. He also thought Japanese art to be purely decorative and not as elevated as European works. Consequently, he consistently praised Japanese who were adopting European fashions. In religion, he noted especially the popularity of inari fox shrines and images of the goddess Enma. He also described Shinto shrines and the rituals he observed there as well as marriage ceremonies.

Perhaps most important in understanding Carnegie's view of Japan was his devotion to Herbert Spencer's ideas of evolutionary change that led to material and moral progress (Nasaw, 228-229). Like many in the late nineteenth century, Carnegie had a strong belief in natural and moral laws that, if followed properly, necessarily led to prosperity and intellectual achievements. Societies that remained mired in superstition and ignorance, however, were doomed to remain in a subordinate position to more advanced civilizations. This view both reinforced existing racial hierarchies in Carnegie's mind and gave him great optimism for countries that adopted Western practices. In his account of Japan, he praises Japan's relatively weak traditional religion which allows the Japanese to adopt more progressive creeds. He is also impressed how Japanese society was moving away from hereditary ranks and toward a more objective system of recruitment based on merit. As an example of Japanese promise, he cites the growth of newspapers, telegraphs, and the postal system as examples of "the rapid progress of this strange country in the ways of the West."

Carnegie noted with approval several of Japan's economic reforms including land tax reform, a modern banking system, and moves toward industrialization. He was also aware of the problem of currency inflation that the Meiji government faced after buying out the samurai classes' stipends and paying the costs of suppressing the 1877 Satsuma Rebellion. He compared Japan's problems with inflation to similar issues that occurred in the United States during the Civil War. Japan's industrial revolution would not take off until the mid-1880s, but Carnegie saw signs of progress and expressed confidence in Japan's government and people to industrialize. When invited to visit an arsenal, he noted the wages and wage structure and working conditions, but was most intrigued with workers bowing deeply to their superiors and concluded that obsequious behavior was necessary for advancement. In scenes like this, he implied that there was still much work to do to overcome the psychological remnants of the recently abandoned feudal system.

Carnegie was especially impressed with changes in Japan's political system that seemed to be moving toward democratic government. By the time of the 1884 printing of his book, Japan's government had promised a constitution and representative government which was to come into effect in 1889. Carnegie noted this development and was optimistic that Japan would become increasingly democratic. Of plans to create a constitution, he remarked, "Presto, change! And here before our eyes is presented the strange spectacle of the most curious, backward, feudalist, Eastern nation turning into a Western one of the most advanced type."

In his account, Carnegie was most interested in describing scenes that would impress his audience and showcase his skills as an aspiring writer. He was also interested in locating Japanese civilization in his imagined hierarchy of nations, often using racial terminology that is shocking to readers today. Japan's series of modernizing reforms seem to have captured Carnegie's imagination and reinforced his faith in Western science, industry, and political institutions to liberate any nation that diligently adopted them. In Carnegie's mind, the willingness

ANDREW CARNEGIE

of the Japanese to become pupils of the West set them apart from the people of China and other nations who held on more tightly to their own traditions.

Editor's Note: *Professor Sagers' referral to the Nasaw book is significant. Other Carnegie biographers did not appreciate the positive impact the Japan visit had on the steel baron. In* Carnegie, *Peter Krass ends a single paragraph on Carnegie's time in Japan quoting* Round the World *writing "...the odor of the toyshop pervades everything, even their temples." Generations earlier, Burton Hendrick in his two volume* The Life of Andrew Carnegie, *uses the odor of the toyshop quote in one of only two sentences on the Japan visit. It would appear that Hendrick in 1932 did not read or was uninterested in the many positive descriptions of Japan and its prospects for advancement contained in Carnegie's account of his time in Japan.*

I have left the spelling and other items as printed in the original published text of Round the World. Instances where I have added comments and notes are indicated with an endnote. Round the World *had no illustrations or photographs. I have added several that I hope may be of interest. The origin of the illustrations contained in this volume, if known, is indicated below the pictures. Words or passages in parentheses are explanatory notes added by Carnegie. Items or phrases in brackets were inserted by me. Places where the full text in a given entry date was not provided, are indicated as follows ...*

Although offensive to readers today, Carnegie's terms for Chinese and Japanese people were in common usage in the nineteenth century. The original text has been maintained to understand Carnegie's experience of Japan in his own words.

Sources

Hendrick, Burton J. *The Life of Andrew Carnegie*. Garden City, New York: Doubleday, Doran & Company, Inc., 1932

Krass, Peter. *Carnegie*. Hoboken, New Jersey: John Wiley & Sons, 2002.

Nasaw, David. *Andrew Carnegie*. New York: Penguin Press, 2006.

ANDREW CARNEGIE

PITTSBURGH, Thursday, October 17.

What is this? A telegram! "Belgic sails from San Francisco 24th instead of 28th." Can we make it? Yes, travelling direct and via Omaha, and not seeing Denver as intended. All right! through we go, and here we are at St. Louis Friday morning, and off for Omaha to catch the Saturday morning train for San Francisco. If we miss but one connection we shall reach San Francisco too late. But we sha'n't. Having courted the fickle goddess assiduously, and secured her smiles, we are not going to lose faith in her now, come what may. See if our good fortune doesn't carry us through!

HARBOR OF SAN FRANCISCO, Thursday, October 24.

At last! noon, 24th, and there she lies – the *Belgic* at her dock! What a crowd but not of us; eight hundred Chinamen are to return to the Flowery Land. One looks like another, but how quiet they are! Are they happy? overjoyed at being homeward bound? We cannot judge. Those sphinx-like, copper-colored faces tell us no tales. We had asked a question last night by telegraph, and here is the reply brought to us on the deck. It ends with a tender good-bye. How near and yet how far! but even if the message had sought us out at the Antipodes, its power to warm the heart with the sense of the near presence and companionship of those we love would only have been enhanced. In this we seem almost to have reached the dream of the Swedish seer **(1)**, who tells us that thought brings presence, annihilating space in heaven.

We start promptly at noon. Our ship is deeply laden with flour, which China needs in consequence of the famine prevailing in its northern provinces, not owing to a failure of the rice, as I had understood, but of the millet, which is used by the poor instead of rice. Some writers estimate that five millions of people must die from starvation before the next crop can be gathered; but this seems incredible. And now America comes to the rescue, so that at this moment, while from its Eastern shores it pours forth its inexhaustible stores to feed Europe, it sends from the West of its surplus to the older races of the far East. Thus from all sides, fabled Ceres **(2)** as she is, she scatters to all peoples from the horn of plenty. Favored land, may you prove worthy of all your blessings and show to the world that after ages of wars and conquests there comes at last to the troubled earth the glorious reign of peace. But no new steel cruisers, no standing army. These are the devil's tools in monarchies; the Republic's weapons are the ploughshare and the pruning hook.

For three hundred miles the Pacific is never pacific. Coast winds create a swell, and our first two nights at sea were trying to bad sailors, but the motion was to me so soft after our long railway ride that I seemed to be resting on air cushions. It was more delightful to be awake and enjoy the sense of perfect rest than to sleep, tired as we were; so we lay literally "Rocked in the cradle of the rude imperious surge." (Shakespeare, King Henry IV Part II, Act 3, Scene 1) and enjoyed it. **(3)**

To some of my talented New York friends who are touched with Buddhism just now and much puzzled to describe, and I judge even to imagine, their heaven, I confidently recommend a week's continuous jar upon a rough railway as the surest preparation for attaining a just conception of Nirvana, where perfect rest is held the greatest possible bliss. Lying, as I did apparently, upon air cushions, and rocked so softly on the waves, I had not a wish; desire was gone, I was content; every particle of my weary body seemed bathed in delight. Here was the delicious sense of rest we are promised in Nirvana.

The third day out we are beyond the influence of the coast, and begin our first experience of the Pacific Ocean. So far it is simply perfect; we are on the ideal summer sea. What hours for lovers, these superb nights! They would develop rapidly, I'm sure, under such skyey influences. The temperature is genial, balmy breezes blow, there is no feeling of chilliness, the sea, bathed in silver, glistens in the moonlight; we sit under awnings and glide through the water. The loneliness of this great ocean I find very impressive – so different from the Atlantic pathway – we are so terribly alone, a speck in the universe; the sky seems to enclose us in a huge inverted bowl, and we are only groping about, as it were, to find a way out; it is equidistant all around us; nothing but clouds and water. But as we sail westward we have every night a magnificent picture...

ANDREW CARNEGIE

THURSDAY, October 31.

While on the subject of the Chinaman I may note that of course we did not get through California without hearing the Chinese problem warmly discussed. It is the burning question just now upon the Pacific coast, but it seems to me our Californians' fears are, as Colonel Diehl would put it, "slightly previous." There are only about 130,000 Chinese in America, and great numbers are returning as the result of hard times, and I fear harder treatment. There is no indication that we are to be overrun by them, and until they change their religious ideas and come to California to marry, settle, die and be buried there, it is preposterous to believe there is any thing in the agitation against them beyond the usual prejudice of the ignorant races next to them in the social scale.(4)

I met the owner of a quicksilver [mercury] mine, whose remarks shed a flood of light on the matter. The mine yields a lean ore, and did not pay when worked by white labor costing $2 to $2.50 per day. He contracted with a Chinaman to furnish 170 men at one-half these rates. They work well, doing as much per man as the white man can do in this climate. He has no trouble with them – no fights, no sprees, no strikes. The difference in the cost enables him to work at a profit a mine which otherwise would be idle; and to such as talk against Chinese labor in the neighborhood, he replies, "Very well, drive it off if you please, but the mine stops if you do." The benefit to the district of having a mine actively at work has so far insured protection. This is the whole story. Our free American citizen from Tipperary and the restless rowdy of home growth find a rival beating them in the race, and instead of taking the lesson to heart and practicing the virtues which cause the Chinaman to excel, they mount the rostrum and proclaim that this is a "white man's country," and "down with the n....r and the Heathen Chinee," and "three cheers for whiskey and a free fight!" The Chinese question has not reached a stage requiring legislation, nor, if let alone, will it do so for centuries to come – and not then unless the Chinese change their religious ideas, which they have not done for thousands of years, and are not likely to do in our time.

ANDREW CARNEGIE

FRIDAY, November 15.

Land ahoy! The islands of Japan are in sight, and the entrance to the bay is reached at 4 P.M. The sail up this bay is never to be forgotten. The sun set as we entered, and then came such a sky as Italy cannot rival. I have seen it pictured as deluging Egypt with its glory, this we have yet to see. Fujiyama itself shone forth under its rays, its very summit clear, more than 14,000 feet above us. The clouds in large masses lay east and west of the peak, but cowering far below, as if not one speck dared to rise to its crown. It stood alone in solitary grandeur, by far the most impressive mountain I have yet seen; for mountains, as a rule, are disappointing, the height being generally attained by gradations. It is only to Fujiyama and such as it, that rise alone in one unbroken pyramid, that one can apply Schiller's grand line, "Ye are the things which tower,"

Fujiyama towers beyond any crag or peak I know of; and I do not wonder that in early days the Japanese made the home of their gods upon its crest.

It was nine o'clock when the anchor dropped, and in a few minutes after small boats crowded alongside to take us ashore. Until you are rowed in a sampan in style, never flatter yourself you have known the grotesque in the way of transportation. Fancy a large, wide canoe, with a small cabin in the stern, the deck in front lower than the sides and on this four creatures, resembling nothing on earth so much as the demons in the *Black Crook* **(5)** minus most of the covering. They stand two on one side, but not in a line, and each works with a long oar scull-fashion accompanying each stroke with shouts such as we never heard before, the last one steers as well as sculls with his oar, and thus we go propelled by these yelling devils, who apparently work themselves into a state of fearful excitement. We land finally, pass the Custom House without examination and with sea-legs which are far from steady reach our hotel. A bite of supper – but what fearful creatures again to bow and wait on us! More demons. We laugh every minute at some funny performance, and wonder where we can be; but how surprisingly good every thing is which we eat or drink on land after twenty-two days at sea!

ANDREW CARNEGIE

TUSEDAY, November 19.

We have been three days in Japan, and all we can tell you is that we are powerless to convey more than the faintest idea of that which meets us at every turn. Had we to return tomorrow, we should still feel that we had been fully compensated for our journey. Though we have seen most of the strange and novel which Europe has to show, a few hours' stroll in Yokohama or Tokio has revealed to us more of the unexpected than all we ever saw elsewhere. No country I have visited till now has proved as strange as I had imagined it; the contrary obtains here. All is so far beyond what I had pictured it that I am constantly regretting so few of my friends will probably ever visit Japan to see and enjoy for themselves. Let me try to describe a walk. We are at the hotel door, having received the repeated bows, almost to the ground of numerous demons. A dozen big fellows rush up, each between the shafts of this "jinrikshaw" like a cab-horse, and invite us to enter, just as cabmen do elsewhere. But look at their costume, or shall I rather say want of costume? No shoes, unless a mat of straw secured with straw strings twisted around and between the big toe and the next one may be called a shoe; legs and body bare, except a narrow strip of rag around the loins, and such a hat! It is either of some dark material, as big as the head of a barrel (I do not exaggerate), to shelter them from sun and rain, or a light straw flat of equal size. These are the Bettoes, who will run and draw you eighteen miles in three hours and a quarter, this being the distance and time by "jinrikshaw" to Tokio. We decline their proffers and walk on. What is this? A man on stilts! His shoes are composed of a flat wooden sole about a quarter of an inch thick, on which the foot rests, elevated upon two similar pieces of board, about four inches high, placed crosswise about three inches apart. On the edges of these cross-pieces he struts along. A second has solid wood pieces of equal height, a third has flat straw shoes, a fourth has none. Look out behind! What is this noise? "Hulda, hulda, hulda!" shouted in our ears. We look around, and four coolies, as naked as Adam, one at each corner of a four-wheel truck, pushing a load of iron and relieving themselves at every step by those unearthly groans. Never have we seen that indispensable commodity transported in that fashion before. But look there! A fishmonger comes with a basket swinging on each end of a bamboo pole carried over the shoulder – all single loads are so carried – and yonder goes a water-carrier, carrying his stoups in the same manner, while over his shoulders he has flung a coat that would make the reputation of a clown in the circus. The dress of the women is not so varied, but their painted lips and whitened necks, and , in the case of the married women, their blackened teeth, afford us much cause for staring, although I cannot bear to look upon these hideous-locking wretches when they smile; I have to turn my eyes away. How women can be induced to make such disgusting frights of themselves I cannot conceive, but Fashion – Fashion does anything. The appearance of the children is comical in the extreme. They are so thickly padded with dress upon dress as to give them the look of little fat Esquimaux. The women invariably carry them on their backs, Indian fashion. Here are two Japs meeting in the middle of the street. They bow three times, each inclination lower and more profound than the preceding one, infinite care being taken to drop the proper number of inches befitting their respective ranks, and then shake their own hands in token of their joy. We soon reach the region of the shops. These are small booths, and squat on the floor sit four or five men and women around a brazier, warming their hands while they smoke. All the shops are of wood, but a small part is constructed of mud, and is said to be fire-proof. In this the valuables are instantly thrown when one of the very frequent fires occurs. The floors are matted, and kept scrupulously clean. No one thinks of entering without first taking his shoes off. The shop floors are raised about eighteen inches above the street, and on the edges purchasers sit sidewise and make their bargains. The entire street is a pavement, as no horses are to be provided for.

We visited the tea factories at Yokohama. Japan has become of late years an exporter of tea to America, no less than five thousand tons being shipped last year. Tea when first gathered is tasteless, but after being exposed to the sun it ferments like hay. It is then curled, twisted, baked, and brought to the dealers, who again pick it over carefully and roll it into the form in which it reaches us. We saw many hundreds of women and girls in the establishment of Messrs. Walsh, Hall & Co.(6) rolling rapidly about with their hands a quantity of the leaves in large round pots under which a small charcoal fire was burning. And now, for the benefit of my lady friends, let me explain that the difference between black and green tea is simply this: the former is allowed to cure or ferment in the sun about fifty minutes longer than the latter, and during this extra fifty minutes certain elements pass off which are thought to affect the nervous system, hence green tea has a greater effect upon weak nerves than the black, but you see the same leaf makes either kind, as the owner elects. But here comes in a strange prejudice. Green tea of the natural color could not be sold in the American market. No we insist upon having a "prettier green," and we are accommodated, of course. What can a dealer do but meet the imperious demands of his patrons? The required color is obtained by adulterating the pure tea with a mixture of indigo and gypsum, which the most conscientious dealers are compelled to do. But we saw used in one case Prussian blue, which is poisonous – this, however, was not in Messrs. Walsh, Hall & Co.'s – and I was told that ultramarine is sometimes resorted to. These more pernicious substances produce even a "prettier green" than the indigo and gypsum, and secure the preference of ignorant people. Moral – Stick to black tea and escape poison. For all of which information, and many kind attentions, I have to thank Mr. Walsh, our banker.

One hears very often in Japan during the night a long, plaintive kind of whistle, which, upon inquiry, I found proceeded from blind men or women, called shampooers, who are employed to rub or pinch those suffering from pain, and who cure restlessness by the same means. It is a favorite cure of the Japanese and some foreigners tell us they have employed it with success. I suppose, this climate being productive of rheumatism and kindred pains, the people are prone to fly to anything that secures temporary relief; but it is a new idea, this, of being pinched to sleep.

We live well at the hotels here. Japan abounds in fish and game in great variety. Woodcock, snipe, hares, and venison are cheap, and all of excellent quality. The beef and mutton are also good, as are the vegetables. Turnips, radishes and carrots are enormous, owing, I suppose to the depth and fineness of the soil. Vandy [7] measured some of each, and reports: "Radishes, eighteen inches, and beautifully white; carrots, twenty inches, and splendid."

ANDREW CARNEGIE

WEDNESDAY, November 20.

We started this morning from Yokohama for Tokio, the great city of the Empire, which contains 1,030,000 inhabitants, according to a census taken last year. Until within a few years past Japan had two rulers – the Mikado, or spiritual, and the Tycoon, or secular ruler, although strictly speaking, the former was theoretically the supreme ruler, the latter obtaining his power through marriage with the family of the former. The seat of the Mikado was at Kioto, a fine city near the centre of the island, while the Tycoon resided at Tokio, or Yeddo, as it was then called. The Mikado was invisible, being the veritable veiled prophet, none but a privileged few being ever permitted to gaze upon his divine person. A few years ago it was decided to combine the two powers, and make Yeddo the only capital. The Mikado was carried to Yeddo closely veiled, in triumphal procession, and the vast crowds, assembled at every point to see the cavalcade, prostrated themselves, and remained with eyes bent upon the ground as the sacred car approached. An eye-witness describing the entry into Tokio says that few dared to look up as the Presence passed. Lately, the same Mikado has made a royal progress through the country, meeting the principal men in each district, and travelling in view of the entire population, so rapidly have manners changed in Japan. When the Mikado was elevated to supreme power, the feudal system, which had existed up to that time, was abolished, and we now see no more of the Samurai, or two-sworded men, or of the Daimios, the petty princes who formerly promenaded the streets in gorgeous dresses, accompanied by their military retainers. The soldiers, sailors, policemen, and all the official classes are dressed in European style. It is the reigning fashion to be European, and even furniture after our patterns is coming into use. It is the same with food. The hotel where we are rejoices in a French cook, expressly imported, and every night we have parties of wealthy Japanese dining at this Tokio Delmonico's. Last night we had a party of the most celebrated actors enjoying a dinner to commemorate the successful completion of a new piece which had enjoyed a great run. I amused myself trying to select the Montagu, Gilbert, Becket, and Booth(8) of the party, and succeeded well, as I afterward heard. Actors are held in estimation in Tokio, and these attracted great attention as they dined. Matters are much as with us, I fancy. Our

ANDREW CARNEGIE

interpreter, in his broken English, told us in regard to the two young lovers, "Very high thought by much high ladies – oh, very high!" I do not think European dress improves the appearance of the Japanese gentlemen; they are very short **(9)**, and – I regret to report it – generally quite crooked in the legs, and their own flowing costumes render them dignified and graceful. Indeed, after a residence in the East for a while one agrees with the opinion he hears often expressed there that our costume is the most unpicturesque dress in the world.

We were fortunate in having as shipmates Captain Totaki, of the navy and a young lady, Mlle. Rio **(10)**, who had been in America several years, and had acquired an English education. They were excessively kind to us during our entire stay, and much of the pleasure derived is due to them. The captain gave us one evening an entertainment at a fashionable tea-house, and introduced us to the celebrated singing and dancing girls of Japan, of whom all have heard. We were shown into a large room, the floor of which was covered with bamboo matting laid upon some soft substance. [tatami mat] Of course our shoes were laid aside at the door of the house. There were neither chairs nor furniture of any kind, but subsequently chairs were found for us. The salutations on the part of the numerous women servants were most profound, each prostrating herself to the floor, and touching the mat with her forehead every time she entered or left the apartment. Velvet mats were carried into the room by a servant and placed around a brazier of charcoal. In a few minutes servant after servant entered, prostrating herself to the ground, and placing before us some Japanese delicacy. One served soup in small lacquer bowls, another fish, a third cakes, a fourth tea in very tiny cups, and other various things, and finally saki, [sake] the wine of the country, was produced, served in small cups like the tea. Then came the girls. Seven approached, each carrying a musical instrument of queer construction. They bowed profoundly, but I noticed did not touch the mat with their foreheads, their rank being much superior to that of the servants, and began to play and sing.

No entertainment is complete without a troop of these Gahazi [geisha] girls, and such entertainments form about the only social amusement of the Japanese. And now for the music. Please understand that the Japanese scale is not like ours, and nothing like melody to our ears can be produced by it. They have a full tone between each first and second note, and a semitone between each third and fourth, and yet the same feelings are awakened in them by their music as in us by ours, so that harmony itself is simply a matter of education after all, and the glorious Fifth Symphony itself, "Lohengrin," or "Scots what hae," played or sung as I have heard them, would convey no more meaning to these people than so much rattling of cross-bones; but imagine the Fifth Symphony on any scale but ours! I cannot reconcile myself to the idea that we have not the only scale for such a theme; but one has to learn that there are different ways for every thing, and no one who knows much will assume that he has the best. Owing to the change of the scale, I suppose I missed the sentiment of every piece performed. When I thought they were giving us a wail for the dead it turned out to be a warm welcome, and an assurance on the part of these pretty maidens of their happiness in being permitted the great honor of performing before such illustrious visitors. Our companion, Mlle. Rio, took one of the instruments and played and sang a piece for us, but I was not more fortunate in my guess with her. It was a wedding chorus, which I was willing to wager was the Japanese "Miserere"; but this error may have its significance after all. To us, in short, the music was execrable. A falsetto, and a grinding, singsong falsetto at that – the most disagreeable sound I ever heard in music – is very common, and highly esteemed. The instruments resemble banjos, and there is a harsh kind of drum accompaniment; but there is one larger string instrument, the Japanese piano, upon which much older women play, the younger girls not being sufficiently skilled to perform upon it.

After a few songs had been sung, several of the girls laid down their banjos, and after obeisance prepared to dance. Instead of being a sprightly performance to lively music, "first ae caper syne anither," Japanese dancing is a very stately and measured performance, the body instead of the feet being most brought into requisition. With the aid of the indispensable fan the girls succeed in depicting many different emotions, and all with exquisite grace. It is the very poetry of motion. Each dance illustrates a story, and is as well known by name as is the "Highland Fling" or the "Sailor's Hornpipe." Here there was no difficulty in following the story. Unlike music, acting is a universal language, and in its domain "one touch of nature makes the whole world kin." [Shakespeare. Troilus and Cressida, Act III, Scene 3] there are no

ANDREW CARNEGIE

different scales for the expression of feeling. Love, in some of its manifold forms, as was to have been expected, is the theme of most of these dances. I redeemed my reputation here as a guesser, I think. I could give a very fair report to Mlle. Rio of most that took place in the dances, and we enjoyed this portion of the entertainment highly. To a Japanese, how stupid our people must appear whirling round a room until fatigued or dizzy, all for the fun of the thing!

The dresses of the girls were of the richest and most fashionable description, the quietness of the colors surprising us, and their manners those of high-born women. Indeed, they set the fashions, and are the best educated and most accomplished of their sex. These girls are sent for to furnish entertainment for an evening such as we would engage a band for a party. They are said to be highly respectable as a class, invariably reside with their parents, who educate them at great expense, and often make, we were told, very favorable marriages. The contrast between them and their less accomplished sisters is so great as to strike even us, who have been here only a few days, and must be held ignorant of style.

The most wonderful sights of Tokio are the temples and the famous tombs of the Tycoons. There is much similarity in the latter, but that of the sixth Tycoon, at Shibba [Shiba], is by far the most magnificent. It has been rendered familiar by photographs and engravings and at any rate no description would convey a just idea of it. It is gorgeous in color, and the extreme delicacy of the gold is surprising; upon it, too, are found the finest known specimens of the old lacquer. But these tombs totally failed to impress me with any feeling akin to reverence; indeed, nothing in Japan seems calculated to do so – the odor of the toy shop pervades everything, even their temples. As for their religious belief, it is hard to tell what it is, or whether they have any. One thing is sure, the educated classes have discarded the faith of the multitude, if they ever really entertained it, and no longer worship the gods of old. The ignorant classes, however, are seen pouring into the temples with their modest offerings, and asking for prayers in their behalf. It is in Japan as it was in Greece – one religion for the masses, and another, or rather none in the ordinary sense, for the educated few.

As in Catholic countries, some shrines are esteemed more than others. The Temple of the Foxes is the most popular in the Empire. [Inari

Shrines] It is adorned with statues of Master Reynard in various postures. His votaries are numerous, for the sagacity of the fox has passed into a proverb, and these people hope by prayers and gifts to move the fox-god to bestow upon them the shrewdness of the symbol. The fox may be justly related as the most successful preacher in Japan: he draws better than any other, and his congregation is the largest; but he has a rival not without pretensions in the favorite goddess "Emma." We found her to be a large, very fat woman, sitting in Japanese style, and surrounded by images of children. Babies cluster like cherubs around the principal figure, while an attendant sells for a cent apiece ugly painted ones made out of clay, many of which have been placed by worshippers before the goddess. As we approached, a young woman – married, for her teeth were black, and respectably but not richly dressed – was on her knees before the goddess so earnestly engaged in prayer that she appeared to be wholly unconscious of our presence. There was no mistaking that this was sincere devotion – a lifting up of the soul to some power considered higher than itself. I became most anxious to know what sorrow could so move her, and our interpreter afterward told us that she asked but one gift from the goddess. It was the prayer of old that a man-child should be born to her; and, poor woman! when one knows what the life must be in this country should this prayer remain unanswered, it saddens one to think of it. A living death; another installed in her place; all that woman holds dear trembling in the balance. How I pitied her! I also saw men praying before other idols and working themselves into a state of frenzy. Indeed I saw so much in the temples to make me unhappy that I wished I had never visited any of them. It gives one such desponding hopes of our race, of its present and of its future, when so many are so bound down to the lowest form of superstition.

At one of the principal Shinto temples I saw the sacred dance with which that great god is propitiated. In a booth two stories high, in front of the temple, was a small stage upon which sat three old priests. One beat a drum, the second played a flute, while the third fingered a guitar. To this music a very pretty young daughter of a priest, gorgeously arrayed in sacred robes, postured with a fan, keeping time to the music. This was all. But, like the tom-tom beating of the Buddhist which we heard at the same moment from an opposite temple, the dance is thought to dispose the gods to receive favorably the gifts and prayers of the devotees. We saw at the same temple a large wooden figure which is reputed able to cure all manner of diseases. So much and so hard had this figure been rubbed by the poor sufferers that the nose is no longer there; the face is literally rubbed smooth. The ears are gone, and it is only a question of time when all traces of human form will have vanished. It reminded us of the toe of St. Peter, in the cathedral of Rome, which has been worn smooth by the osculations of devout Christians.

Japan is rapidly adopting the manners and customs of European civilization. There is at present a cry for representative government, and one need not be surprised to hear by and by of the Parliament of Japan. War-ships are building at the arsenal, which are not only constructed but designed by native genius. A standing army of about 50,000 men is maintained. Gas has been introduced in some places, and railroads and telegraphs are in operation; and, not to be behind their neighbors, a public debt and irredeemable currency (based upon the property of the nation, of course,) have been created. The currency is now at 22 per cent. discount as compared with gold, and further depreciation is apprehended. (It has since reached 50 per cent. discount.) It is modelled on our American paper money, and is actually printed in New York. Let us hope that Japan may soon be able to follow the Republic farther by making it convertible – as good as gold. Notwithstanding its wise "base" – in short, our greenbackers' "base" – it doesn't seem to work here any better than at home.

Art in Japan is utilitarian; in no other country are the articles of common use so artistic. The furniture of the Japanese house is scanty. We see no walls hung with pictures with showy gilt frames, no portieres or curtains, none of the sofas, chairs, tables, brackets, chandeliers, etc., which give our rooms so crowded an appearance. The bareness of the rooms strikes one at once upon entering, but when one examines the utensils in daily use even by the poorer classes he sees that they are of uncommon beauty. Sure this is of more moment than to have art confined to the few, both as to articles and to persons. In Japan, art may be said to be democratic; all classes are brought under its sway.

One thing must be said, however, about art throughout the East, in China and in India as well as in Japan: up to this time it has been content to remain solely decorative. The higher creative and imaginative power has yet to be reached. Why this should be so is an interesting question, and I resolve to read up the authorities when opportunity offers and see how they account for it. May not the poverty of the East have much to do with it? So very few are rich; indeed, scarcely any are opulent in our sense, and very few, even of the higher classes, possesses as much. In China and India it is much the same, a few rajahs in the latter country excepted.

The start which religion gave to art in Europe is wanting in the East, for the temples are mean and destitute of costly works. Rich commercial and manufacturing classes do not exist in the East – as wealth does not run into "pockets" as it does in Europe – especially in England – and in America. I fear, therefore, that art in the East will not advance much beyond the decorative stage for centuries to come.

SATURDAY, November 23.

Vandy and I walked to-day through the principal street of Tokio from end to end, a distance of three miles. It is a fine, broad avenue, crowded with people and vehicles drawn or pushed by men. There is also a line of small one-horse wagons running as omnibuses on the street – novel feature, unknown anywhere else in the Empire. Our appearance attracted such crowds whenever we stopped at a shop, that the police had to drive the gazers away. The city is built upon a plain, and supplied with water by wells only. Fires are of frequent occurrence. Japanese cities are such piles of combustible material that I wonder they exist at all. But fires are little used – only a brazier of charcoal now and then for cooking purposes; and as most of the people eat at cook-shops, there is never any fire at all in many of the houses. Long ladders are erected as fire-towers and upon these watchmen sit through the night to give the alarm. It is only by tearing down or blowing up surrounding houses that the progress of a fire can generally be stayed. There is no such thing as insurance in Japan, the risks being much too great.

The Japanese go to the theatre early in the morning and remain until five o'clock in the evening. Doors open at five A.M., but the rich classes do not appear before six or seven o'clock, at which hour the performance begins. Breakfast is served in the theatre about noon. The audience smoke, eat, sip tea, and enjoy themselves as they choose. No seats are provided, but a small mat is put down for each person as he enters, and beside it a box filled with sand, in the middle of which are two pieces of glowing charcoal, at which pipes are lighted. Ladies, as well as gentlemen, be it remembered, invariably smoke in Japan. Every one carries a small pipe with a long stem, and a tobacco-pouch attached to it. At short intervals a little tobacco is put into the pipe – just enough to give two whirls of smoke – after which the tobacco is knocked out and the pipe again replenished. In no case have I ever seen more than two very small whiffs taken at one time. Even young ladies smoke in this manner, and to one who detests tobacco, as I instinctively do, it may be imagined this habit did not add to their attractiveness. A sweetheart who defiled her lips with tobacco! "Phew!" Neither is it considered disrespectful in any degree to begin smoking in the presence of others. Deferential as the singing girls were, when at leisure they lighted their pipes as a matter of course, wholly unconscious that they were taking a liberty.

The marriage ceremony differs greatly from ours. The priests have nothing to do with it, nor is there any religious ceremony. The parents of a young man select a proper wife for him when he is about twenty years of age, and manage the whole affair. They consult the young lady's parents, and if the match is a satisfactory one to them, writings are exchanged between the parents of the young couple, the day is appointed, and the bride and groom drink saki from the same cup; feasting and rejoicings follow, sometimes continued for several days if the parents are wealthy, and the marriage is consummated. In all cases the bride goes to reside with the husband's parents, to whom, much more than to the husband, it is necessary she should continue to be satisfactory. Very often three generations live together, and an amount of deference is paid to the oldest such as we have no conception of.

The custom of blackening the teeth by married women is the most revolting practice I have yet seen. I have been in the houses of fine people in Japan, and seen women, otherwise good-looking, who had only to open their lips to convert themselves into objects of disgust. I rejoice, therefore, to hear that fashion is setting in against this abomination, and that some of the more recent brides have refused to conform to the custom.

One readily gets used to anything, earth quakes included, and Japan has many of these unruly visitors. One night we had three shocks at Tokio, one sufficiently strong to wake me from sleep. My bed shook violently, and the house threatened to fall upon us. The same night we had a large fire in the city, and a hundred shrill, tinkling bells, like so many cows in the woods, were run to give the alarm. The clapping of the night watchmen about our street assured me, however, that it was all right with us, and I lay still. The night watchmen here use two small square pieces of hard wood which they strike frequently against each other as they go the rounds as the "All's well" signal; but I think strangers, as a rule, fail to appreciate the point in being awakened every now and then simply to be assured that there is not the slightest occasion for their being awake at all.

MONDAY, November 25.

To-day we took a small steamer and visited the arsenal upon the invitation of our friend Captain Totaki, Mlle. Rio being of the party. It is finely situated on the bay about fifteen miles below Yokohama, and is quite extensive, having good shops filled with modern tools. **(11)** Several ships have already been built here, and two men-of-war are now upon the stocks – another evidence of so-called civilization. Japan, you see, is ambitious. All the officials, foremen, and mechanics, are natives, and these have proved their ability in every department. The wages paid surprise us. All branches are about upon an equality. Painters, moulders, blacksmiths, carpenters, machinists, all get the same compensation – from 25 to 40 cents per day, according to their respective value as workmen; common labor, outside, 18 cents; shop labor inside, 25 cents, foreman of department, $80 per month. Work nine hours per day, every tenth day being a day of rest corresponding to our Sunday. In addition to the two men-of-war under construction, the machinery for which is all designed and manufactured here, the Emperor is having built for his private use a large side-wheel yacht, which promises to be magnificent. However poor a nation may be, or however depreciated its currency, if it set up an emperor, king, or queen, improper personal expenditure inevitably follows. Even as good a woman as Queen Victoria, probably the most respectable woman who ever occupied a throne – such a character as one would not hesitate to introduce to his family circle, which is saying much for a monarch – will squander thirty thousand pounds per annum of the people's money on a private yacht which she has used but a few times, and which is one of three she insists upon keeping at the State's expense. It is the old story: make any human being believe his is born to position and he becomes arbitrary and inconsiderate of those who have exalted him. Serves the foolish ones right, I suppose is the proper verdict. But one is not indignant at the worship of their emperor by the Japanese: he is a real ruler, has power, and stands firmly upon divine right. The Japanese are yet children politically; but the English should be out of their swaddling-clothes, surely.

Illustrated London News 1878 Public Domain.

The captain being high in command, and this being his first visit to the arsenal since his return from a tour round the world, he was received by the officials with manifestations of delight. We had another opportunity of seeing the bowing practice in its fullest development. The various foremen as they approached bowed three times almost to the ground, and in some cases they went first upon their knees and struck the floor three times with their foreheads. We were afterward informed that only a few years ago these would have added to the obeisance by extending the arms to their full length and placing the palms of the hands flat upon the ground, now this is omitted, and I have no doubt, as intelligence spreads, less and less of this deference will be exacted. But up to this date it may safely be said Japan is in the condition of Sir Pertinax MacSycophant, who, it will be remembered, admitted that his success came from "booing"[bowing] He "never could stand strecht in the presence of a great man;" no more can a Japanese.

My writing has just been interrupted by another earthquake shock. My chair began to tremble, then the house; I could not write, and looking up I saw Vandy standing in amazement. For a few moments it seemed as if we were rocking to pieces, and that the end of all things had come. I shall never forget the sensation. The motion of a ship rolling at sea transferred to land, where you have the solid earth and heavy stone wall surrounding and threatening to fall upon you, is far from agreeable; but it passed away, and old Mother Earth became steady once more.

The way to buy in Japan is not by visiting the shops, for there is nothing displayed, and a stranger has infinite difficulty in learning where certain articles are to be found, but just intimate to your "boy" what you wish, and at your door in a few minutes stand not one or two merchants, but five or six, all bowing as you pass in or out, and awaiting master's pleasure to examine their wares. They leave any articles you may wish to decide upon, and the result is that one's rooms become perfect bazaars. The most unpleasant feature connected with purchasing is that everything is a matter of bargain. A price is named and you are expected to make an offer. Vandy is a great success at this game, and seems to enjoy it. I am strictly prohibited from interfering, and so escape all trouble. It is always comforting to know that one's interests are in much abler hands than his own, and I always have this pleasure when Vandy is about.

Wherever we go, Fujijama looks down upon us. What a beautiful cone it is, and how grandly it pierces the heavens, its summit clad with perpetual snow! No wonder that the Japanese represent it on so many of their articles. Thousands of pilgrims flock to it annually from all parts of the Empire, for it is their sacred mount and the gods reward such

ANDREW CARNEGIE

as worship at this shrine. It was once an active volcano, but there has been no eruption since about 1700, when ashes were thrown from it into Yeddo, sixty miles away The crater is nearly five hundred feet deep. Fujiyama stands alone among mountains, a vast pyramid rising as Cheops does from the plain, no "rascally comparative" near to dispute its sway.

WEDNESDAY, November 27.

We sail to-day for Shanghai, leaving Yokohama with sincere regret; nor shall we soon forget the good, kind faces of those who have done so much to make our visit to Japan an agreeable one. Had it been possible to remain until Saturday I should have been greatly tempted to do so to accept an invitation received to respond to a toast at St. Andrew's banquet. It would surely have stirred me to hold forth on Scotland's glory to my fellow-countrymen in Japan; but this had to be foregone. At Kiobe the steamer lay for twenty-four hours, and this enabled us to run up by rail to Kioto, the former residence of the Mikado, reputed to be the Paris of Japan. The city itself deserves the reputation about as well as Cincinnati does that of our American Paris, which I see some one has called it. Kioto is only a mass of poor one-story buildings, but its situation is beautiful, and cannot probably be equalled elsewhere in the Empire, and this one can justly say of Cincinnati as well, while the beauty of Paris is of the city and not at all rural. There are more pretty toy villas embowered in trees upon the little hills about Kioto than we saw in all other parts of Japan. The temples at Kioto are much inferior to those at Shibba. Our journey enabled us to see about seventy miles of the interior, and we were again impressed by the evidences on every hand of a teeming population. Gangs of men and women were everywhere at work upon small patches of ground, six or seven persons being busily engaged sometimes on less than one acre. It is not farming; there is in Japan scarcely such as thing as farming in our sense, it is a system of gardening such as we see in the neighborhood of large cities. Compared with that prevalent throughout the whole country, I have seen nothing equal to it in thoroughness, not even in Belgium.

We are upon the old steamer *Costa Rica*, now belonging to the Japanese Company, which recently purchased this and other boats from the Pacific Mail Company.(12) Among our cargo is a large lot of live turkeys which some pushing Jap is taking over to Shanghai for Christmas; and listen, you favored souls who revel in the famous bird at a dollar a head, your fellow countrymen in China have to pay ten dollars for their Christmas turkey. It is said the Chinese climate is too damp for the noble bird; but in flourishes in Japan. I wish the exporter who thus develops the resources of his country much profit on his venture. But it strikes me that, instead of the eagle, the more useful gobbler has superior claims to be voted the national bird of America. "A turkey for a dollar – what a country!" The climate of Northern China is not favorable for Europeans, and many take a run over to Japan to recuperate, a fact which argues much for the future of Japan. Although our ship belongs to the Japanese, the servants are generally Chinamen, and the agent explains this by informing us that while the former do very well until they arrive at the age of manhood, they then begin to develop more ambitious ideas and cannot be managed, while with the Chinese a "boy" (a servant throughout the East is called "boy") is always a boy, and is constantly on the watch to serve his master. Again, the Japs are pugnacious, a race of little game-cocks, always in for a fight, especially with a Chinaman. The captain told us the other day a great big Chinaman had complained to him that one of the Japs had abused him. Upon calling up the belligerent, he proved to be such a small specimen that the captain asked the sufferer why he hadn't picked him up and thrown him overboard. The complaint was dismissed: served the big fellow right. But some missionary should expound the civilized doctrine to him, per revised edition, which reads: "When smitten on the one cheek, turn to the smiter the other also, but if he smites you on that, go for him." Tomorrow is one of the great days of our trip, for we shall enter the famous inland sea of Japan at daybreak. Will it be fine tomorrow? The sun sets favorably, and I quote Shakespeare to them, which settles the question:

> "The weary sun hath made a golden set,
> And by the bright track of his fiery car
> Gives token of a goodly day to-morrow"
> [Shakespeare, *Richard III*, Act V, Scene 3.]

ANDREW CARNEGIE

Let to-morrow be fair, whatever we may miss hereafter. This is the universal sentiment.

SATURDAY, November 30.

What a day this has been! Many a rich experience which seemed grand enough never to fade from the memory may pass into oblivion, but no mortal can ever sail through the inland sea of Japan on a fine day and cease to remember it till the day he dies. It deserves its reputation as the most beautiful voyage in the world; at least I cannot conceive how, taking the elements of earth, water and sky, anything more exquisitely beautiful could be produced from them. Entering the narrow sea at sunrise, we sail for three hundred and fifty miles through three thousand pretty islands.

> "Which seem to stand
> To sentinel enchanted land."
> [from the *Lady of the Lake* by Sir Walter Scott]

These divide the water, making, not one but a dozen pretty lakes in view at once. It is the Lakes of Killarney, or the English or Scotch lakes, multiplied a hundred-fold; but instead of the islands and mountains being in pasture, they are cultivated to their very tops, terraced in every form, in order to utilize every rod of ground. On the shores cluster villages, nestling in sheltered nooks, while the water swarms with the sails of tiny fishing boats, giving a sense of warm, happy life throughout. These sail-boats add greatly to the beauty of the scene. I counted at one time from the bow of our steamer, without looking back, ninety-seven sails glistening in the sun, while on the hills were seen everywhere gangs of people at work upon their little farm-gardens. It is a panorama of busy, crowded life, but life under the most beautiful surroundings, from beginning to end, and we all vote that never before have we, in a like space of time, seen so much of fairy-land as upon this ever-memorable day. We begin to understand how the thirty odd millions of the Japanese exist upon so small an area. The rivers and seas abound in fish; the hills and valleys under irrigation and constant labor grow their rice, millet, and vegetables. A few dollars per year supply all the clothing needed, and a few dollars build their light wooden houses. Thus they have everything they need, or consider necessary, and are happy as the day is long, certain of one established fact in nature, to wit, that there is no place like Japan; and no doubt they daily and hourly thank their stars that their lines have fallen in pleasant places, and pity us – slaves to imaginary wants – who deny ourselves the present happiness they consider it their wisdom to enjoy, in vain hopes of banqueting to surfeit at some future time, which always comes too late.

On emerging from this fairy scene, we encountered a gale upon the China Sea, which lasted for the few hours we were upon it before reaching Nagasaki, the last port of Japan. Here, two hundred years ago, the Dutch secured a small island, from which they traded with Japan long before any other nations was permitted to do so. The Catholics also had their headquarters here. They were so successful in converting the natives that the government became alarmed, and several thousand Christians were driven to the island and all massacred. This was in the sixteenth century; but it is only a few years ago that seven thousand native Catholic were banished from this region. To-day all is changed. These fugitives have been permitted to return, and there is entire freedom of religious worship. Last month a return was made of professing Christians (Catholics) in this district, and thirty-five thousand were reported. Protestants are very few indeed.

As far as I saw in the East, here is the only real and considerable advance made toward Christianising a people. At other stations throughout my journey I saw only a few ignorant natives who professed Christianity – sometimes a dozen or two, rarely more. European residents invariably told me that these were the dependents or servants of foreigners who held their places mainly because of their conversion to the new faith. If dismissed, they relapsed. One can readily see that the lowest and most unscrupulous would be the first to fall before the almost irresistible temptation, for a means of comfortable livelihood seems the one serious concern of life in all the East to a degree difficult for us in America at least, to imagine.

I remember the dear, kind Catholic Bishop of Canton telling me with such delicious simplicity that every workman engaged in building the Cathedral – a work of many years and yet unfinished – had by the grace

ANDREW CARNEGIE

of God been converted to Holy Mother Church. The hotel-keep told me afterward this so-called conversion was a source of much amusement among the natives. Well, be it so. I believe, myself, that the holy father is the victim of misplaced confidence. But here in Nagasaki nothing like this can be said. Thirty-five thousand professing Christians in a district where there are not a hundred foreign Christian families, if half so many, and where to be a Christian is to declare one's self of the minority and so out of fashion, surely this does prove that the Church has succeeded, and justifies it in hoping that ere long this part of Japan at least will one day enter the fold.

One great reason for this undoubted success is probably that neither the Government nor the people have the slightest objection to missionaries, for their own religion sets but lightly on the Japanese. With the Chinaman it is totally different. His own religion is to him a vital force, and his gods must not be defamed. He stands by his faith like a Covenanter. It touches the most sacred feelings of his nature, and is everything to him. Mrs. D.O. Hill's celebrated statue of Livingstone in Prince's Garden, Edinburgh, therefore, represents too truly the attitude of our missionaries in the flowery land as well as in other so-called heathen lands: the Bible in one hand and the pistol in the other The man of Japan regards the missionaries as harmless curiosities, and if not disposed to trouble himself about their new ideas, he has not the least objection to their being expounded.

There is now no established religion in Japan, Buddhism having been abolished in 1874.**(13)** The temples and priesthood are maintained by voluntary contributions. The poor laws are simple: government gives nine bushels of rice to every person over seventy or under fifteen years of age, who cannot work, and the same to foundlings under thirteen. Out of the total population of thirty-six millions, there are only ten thousand and fifty paupers, and of these more than a thousand are at Tokio in the workhouse.

HARBOR OF NAGASAKI, MONDAY, December 2.

Vandy and I were off early this morning for the shore, and did not return to the ship until late in the afternoon, having walked over the high hills and down into the valleys beyond. We had a real tramp in the country. It is here just as elsewhere, terrace upon terrace, every foot of ground under cultivation; water carried by men in pails, or on the backs of oxen, to the highest peaks, which it is impossible to irrigate, and every single plant, be it rice, millet, turnip, cabbage, or carrot, watered daily. What good Mother Earth can be induced to yield under such attention is a marvel. The bountiful earth has another meaning when you see what she can be made to bring forth. Although we are in December, the sun shines bright and it is quite warm. I sat down several times under the hedge-rows, and heard the constant hum of insect life around me. Butterflies flitted about, the bees gathered honey, and all looked and felt like a day in June. The houses of the people which we saw were poor, and the total absence of glass causes them to look like deserted hovels; but closer inspection showed fine mats on the floors, and everything scrupulously clean. I counted upon one hillside forty-seven terraces from the bottom to the top. There are divided vertically, so that I think twenty-five feet square would be about the average size of each patch; and as the division of terraces is made to suit the ground, and hence very irregularly, the appearance of a hillside in Japan is something like that of a bed-quilt of irregular pieces. The terrace-walls are overgrown with vines, ferns, etc., so that they appear like low green hedges: and this adds much to the beauty of the landscape. No wonder the cultivators of these lovely spots never dream of leaving them. Animal food is not half as important to the Japanese as the supply of fish – indeed the former is said to be comparatively little used, while fish of some kind or in some form is ever present at meals. The favorite fish is the tai [sea bream] which is red when taken from the streams with sandy bottoms, but black when caught at the mouths of the same streams, where the dark soil of the sea begins. A curious parallel case is seen in the black and red pines of this country; in sandy soils they grow red, while in the softer black soil they are dark. Transplant the two varieties and they change color. The same law, you see, with fish and plant. We are all creatures of our environment. Therefore let us choose our companions and surroundings well. To know the best that has been said and done in the world is no doubt much; to be planted and to grow among those who have done the greatest work and who live up to the best standard in our day and generation is surely equally important.

ANDREW CARNEGIE

We had an alarm of fire off the *Belgic* in mid-ocean, but this morning we had the real article. I had just parted from the captain at the stern of the ship, intending to go ashore, when, walking forward, I saw dense volumes of smoke issuing from the walking-beam pit, and in a few moments I heard the cry of fire from below. All was in a bustle at once, but the crew got finely to work. Fortunately, although there was no steam in the main boilers, the small donkey boiler was full, and the pumps were put to work. Meanwhile boats from the various men-of-war in the harbor with hand fire-engines came to our assistance. The steamer is an old wooden craft, and I knew her cargo was combustible. Were the smoke ever to give place to flame, panic was sure to ensue, and not one of the small native boats that had until now been clustering around us could then be induced to approach; indeed, they had already all rowed off. There was only one lady on board, Mrs. McK., a veritable *Princess of Thule* (14) from the Island of Lewes, and I decided that she had better be taken off with her sick child at once; so, bribing a greedy native by the immense reward of a whole dollar (a large fee here small as it seems at home) to come alongside, I grasped the baby and followed the mother down the gangway, and remained at a safe distance until the danger was over. A few minutes more and the *Costa Rica* would have followed her sister ship the *America*, which some years ago took fire under similar circumstances in the harbor of Yokohama, and was completely destroyed. Fortunately we are about done with wood steamships; otherwise they should not be permitted to run as passenger vessels.

The post-office department of Japan is of recent origin, having been established in 1871; yet in 1881, after only ten years' growth, it carried ninety-five millions of letters, newspapers, books, etc. Thirty millions of these were post-cards. Three million of telegrams were also transmitted that year. Perhaps no statement will give one a clearer idea than this of the rapid progress of this strange country in the ways of the West.

Japan has only two short lines of railway for thirty-six millions of people – a population nearly equal to that of Great Britain: one eighteen miles from Yokohama to Tokio, the other seventy miles from Hiogo to Kioto. This seems a scanty allowance; nevertheless it is not probable that more than a few hundred miles of rail will be built for centuries. The habits and poverty of the people, and in many districts the topography of the country, are such as to render railways unsuitable. The main highways are, however, kept in admirable order. I was amused with the classification of these. Those of the first class are such as lead from the capital to the treaty ports; of the second class those lines leading to the national shrines. Commerce has thus usurped the first place. Both the first and second class roads are maintained by the General Government as being national affairs. Various grades of roads follow, some being maintained by large districts; others, of local importance, by taxes upon a smaller area; but all under the strict supervision of central officials at Tokio.

Not the least surprising feature in the revolution growing forward so peacefully in Japan is the prompt adoption of the newspaper as one of the essentials of life. A few years ago the official *Gazette*, read only by officials and containing nothing of general interest, was the only publication in the Empire; today several hundred newspapers are published, many of them daily. A censorship of the press still exists, however, and leads to the usual mode of evasion. Pungent political articles are conveyed under cover of criticisms ostensibly upon the blunders of lands not so enlightened as Japan. Here is a specimen: "In America during the Civil War paper currency was issued and made legal tender. At every successive issue the premium rose higher and higher till the currency was not worth more than a third of it face. The Southern States followed in the same path, but they kept on till their issues were found to be good for about one purpose only – to line trunks withal – such fools these Americans be. Happy Japan! blessed with rulers of preeminent ability, who keep the finances of our land in such creditable form."

The fact was that Japanese currency was then at 22 per cent, discount and rapidly declining in value under successive issues, just as it had done in America. Such articles are no doubt far more effective than open, undisguised assaults could possibly be, for the cleverness of the evasion gives additional zest to the attack. The Press is a hard dog to muzzle, and, like dogs in general, only vicious when muzzled. The Japanese will soon find it safe to "let Truth and Error grapple" in the full face of day, for they are not slow to learn.

TUESDAY, December 3.

The turbulent China Sea has passed into a proverb. The Channel passage in a gale, I suppose, comes nearest to it. We started to cross this sea at daylight, and surely we have reason to be grateful. It is as smooth as a mirror, the winds are hushed, and as I write the shores of Japan fade peacefully from view. I cannot help thinking how improbable that I shall ever see them again; but, however that may be, farewell for the present to Japan. Take a stranger's best wishes for your future.

Our cargo shows something of the resources of the country. It amounts to eight hundred tons, comprising seaweed – a special kind of which the Chinese are fond – ginseng, camphor, timber, isinglass, Japan piece-goods, ingot copper, etc. Every week this line takes to China a similar cargo, and the trade is rapidly extending. This steamship company is worth noting as an evidence of what Japanese enterprise is doing. The principal owner, the Commodore Garrison of Japan, had a small beginning, but now runs some thirty-seven steamers between the various Japanese ports. Under the management of Mr. Krebs, a remarkable Dane, this company beat off the Pacific Mail company from the China trade, and actually purchased their ships. There are many things found on these vessels which our Atlantic companies might imitate with advantage.

I believe I mentioned that Japan, not to be behind her Western neighbors, had created a public debt, which now amounts to about $300,000,000, but $250,000,000 of this was used in payment of the two hundred and sixty-six daimios and their numerous retainers, when government took over the land to itself. Each of these potentates had vested rights in a certain proportion of the yield of the soil of his district, and this was commuted by the government into so much in its bonds, a fixed land tax being substituted for the irregular exactions of former landlords. On every side I hear that this has greatly improved the condition of the population – made the people more contented, and at the same time vastly augmented the products of the soil. Not less than three millions of the population shared in this operation.

The nationalization of the land is under discussion in England, and it is conceded that some change has to be made. Here is Japan proving the results of nationalization, while Denmark shows what private ownership of small pieces of land can do under a system of cumulative taxation in proportion to the size of the estate held. One of these two systems is likely to prevail in England some day. Meanwhile, here is food for thought for the British tax-payer: out of 74 million yens (Pounds 15,000,000) of revenue raised by Japan, forty-three million comes from the land tax. The tax on alcoholic liquors yields about seventeen millions more.

Since my visit to Japan an imperial decree has been published, promising that a national assembly shall meet in 1890; so we have the foundations of representative government almost at hand. Sure no other nation ever abandoned its traditions and embraced so rapidly those of a civilization of an opposite character. This is not development under the law of slow evolution; it seems more like a case of spontaneous generation. Presto, change! and here before our eyes is presented the strange spectacle of the most curious, backward, feudalist Eastern nation turning into a Western one of the most advanced type.

That Japan will succeed in her effort to establish a central government, under something like our ideas of freedom and law, and that she has such resources as will enable her to maintain it and educate her people, I am glad to be able to say I believe; but much remains to be done requiring in the race the exercise of solid qualities, the possession of which I find some Europeans disposed to deny them. They have travelled, perhaps, quite fast enough, and I look for a temporary triumph of the more conservative party. But the seed is sown, and Japan will move, upon the whole, in the direction of progress. And so, once more, farewell, Japan; and China, now almost within sight, all hail!

ANDREW CARNEGIE

Notes

(1) Carnegie's contemporary readers would have recognized this reference to the Christian theologian and mystic Emanuel Swedenborg (1688-1772) and his family's involvement with the movement.

(2) Ceres is the Greek goddess of agriculture.

(3) David Nasaw, author of *Andrew Carnegie*, discusses Carnegie's frequent use of poetry, particularly Robert Burns and William Shakespeare, in conversation and in his writings. Nasaw says that Carnegie's prodigious memory of such bon mots not only spiced up his energetic conversation but help compensate for his lack of formal education, an important compensation in some but not all of the social circles in which he travelled and revelled.

(4) In 1879 Congress passed and President Rutherford Hayes vetoed legislation to restrict Chinese immigration. In 1882 the Chinese Exclusion Act was passed and signed by President Chester Arthur. For Carnegie and his generation, the use of the term race is somewhat different than common usage today. Race would include cultural identity and is closer to what today is more often termed ethnic or national identity.

(5) *Black Crook* was a musical extravaganza and first opened in New York in 1866. It is often called the first American musical.

(6) Walsh, Hall & Co. was the most prominent American company in Japan in the late 19th and early 20th century. Thomas Walsh managed the company's interests in Yokohama and his brother John ran the operation in Nagasaki. Thomas Walsh is also mentioned in Olive Ridley's book on William Seward.

(7) John W. Vandewort had known Carnegie since early in their careers in Pittsburgh. "Vandy" accompanied Carnegie on several long trips.

(8) Edwin Booth, noted actor, particularly famous for his role in Shakespeare's *Hamlet*. Brother of Lincoln's assassin John Wilkes Booth

(9) Carnegie himself was a short man, reported to be 5'2" or 157.5 cm. David Nasaw in his biography, *Andrew Carnegie*, believes Carnegie may not have reached 5' or 152.4cm.

ANDREW CARNEGIE

(10) Ryo Yoshimasu, 14 years old at the time, was one of 5 young women brought from Japan with the Iwakura Mission, and stayed as students, lodging in American homes. Janice Nimura's *Daughters of the Samurai*, tells the story of these remarkable women. Ryo returned to Japan after less than a year in the United States due to eye problems.

(11) The place described is Yokosuka, site then and since of a major naval base.

(12) Iwasaki Yotaro, whom Charles Longfellow mentions as a dinner companion in his first year in Tokyo, renamed the shipping company he had established, Mitsubishi, and by Carnegie's visit, Mitsubishi had replaced the Pacific Mail company on the Tokyo-Shanghai run.

(13) Carnegie's statement that Buddhism was abolished in 1874 is a misstatement or at best an exaggeration. During early Meiji, the government did move to blunt the institutional power of Buddhism and to promote Shinto and the status of the Imperial institution.

(14) Popular romantic novel of 1873 by William Black.

PRIMARY SOURCES

Carnegie, Andrew. *Round the World.* New York: Charles Scribner's Sons, 1884.

Seward, Olive Risley, editor. *William H. Seward's Travels Around the World.* New York: D. Appleton and Co., 1873.

Young, James Russell. *Around the world with General Grant : a narrative of the visit of General U. S. Grant, ex-President of the United States, to various countries in Europe, Asia, and Africa, in 1877, 1878, 1879 : to which are added certain conversations with General Grant on questions connected with American politics and history.* In two volumes. New York: Subscription Book Department, the American News Company, 1879.

Additional Primary Sources of Interest

Bird, Isabella. *Unbeaten Tracks in Japan.* London: John Murray, 1880.

Coffin, Charles Carleton. *Our New Way Round the World.* Boston: Fields, Osgood, & Co., 1869.
https://archive.org/details/newwayroundworld00coffiala/mode/2up

Dana, Richard Henry. *Two Years Before the Mast. A Personal Narrative of Life at Sea.* New York, New York: Harper & Brothers, 1840.

Dickins, F.V. and Lane-Poole, Stanley. *The Life of Harry Parkes: Minister Plenipotentiary to Japan and China.* London: Macmillan & Co., 1894. (Reprint edition, Tokyo: Edition Synapse, 1999.)

Fogg, William Perry. *Round the World: Letters from Japan, China, India, and Egypt.* Cleveland, Ohio: 1872. (Originally published in a series in *The Cleveland Leader* newspaper.)

Perry, Matthew Calbraith. *Narrative of the Expedition of an American Squadron to the China Seas and Japan, performed in the years 1852, 1853, and 1854, under the Command of Commodore M. C. Perry, United States Navy, by Order of the Government of the United States. Compiled from the Original*

Notes and Journals of Commodore Perry and his Officers, at his request, and under his supervision, by Francis L. Hawks, D.D., L.L.D. (Washington, D.C.: Published by Order of the Congress of the United States, 1856–1858). Three quarto volumes.
https://archive.org/details/narrativeofexpe01perr/page/n5/mode/2up

Pumpelly, Raphael. *Across America and Asia: notes on a five years' journey around the world and of residence in Arizona, Japan and China.* New York: Leypoldt & Holt, 1871.
https://archive.org/details/acrossamericaan00pumpgoog

Seward, William H. "Commerce in the Pacific Ocean." Speech of William H. Seward, in the Senate of the United States, July 29, 1852 Washington, D.C: Buell & Blanchard ,1852.

Verne, Jules, *Around the World in Eighty Days*, (English translation by George Makepeace Towle), 1873.

Editor's Note: *Both the primary sources used for this book and the additional primary sources listed above are available in various ways. Most are available online at Project Gutenberg or Internet Archive. Several are available in a number of print editions produced in the 19th century or more recently, often with introductions by scholars. Dana's* Two Years Before the Mast, *popular for generations of American readers, is a good example. For many of the others, there are recent scanned editions by a variety of publishers. While the online or scanned editions are useful and do provide the full content, I highly recommend seeing if original editions may be available in university or public library collections near you. Librarians will be pleased to see your interest. And holding and examining books that are a century and a half old truly brings the past alive.*

Suggested Secondary Reading

Beasley, W. G. *The Meiji Restoration.* Stanford: Stanford University Press, 1972.

Benfey, Christopher. *The Great Wave: Gilded Age Misfits, Japan's Eccentrics.* New York: Random House, 2003.

Campbell, Edwina. *Citizen of a Wider Commonwealth: Ulysses S. Grant's Postpresidential Diplomacy.* Carbondale, Illinois: Southern Illinois University Press, 2016.

Chang, Richard. "General Grant's 1879 Visit to Japan." *Monumenta Nipponica 24. No. 4.* (1969).

Chernow, Ron. *Grant.* New York: Penguin Press, 2017.

Farrow, Lee A. *Seward's Folly: a new look at the Alaska Purchase.* Fairbanks, AK: 2016.

Free, Dan. *Early Japanese Railways, 1853-1914.* Tokyo, Rutland, Vermont: Tuttle Publishing, 2008.

Fuess, Harald. "Informal Imperialism and the 1879 Hespira Incident: Containing Cholera and Challenging Extraterritoriality." *Japan Review 27* (2014): 103-40.

Fujita, Fumiko. *American Pioneers and the Japanese Frontier.* Westport, CT, London: Greenwood Press, 1994.

Gordon, Andrew. *A Modern History of Japan: From Tokugawa Times to the Present.* Berkeley, CA: University of California Press, 1998.

Green, Michael J. *By More Than Providence Grand Strategy and American Power in the Asia Pacific Since 1783.* New York: Columbia University Press, 2017.

Hammersmith, Jack L. *Spoilsmen in a "Flowery Fairyland."* Kent, Ohio: Kent University Press, 1998.

Hendrick, Burton J. *The Life of Andrew Carnegie.* Garden City, New York: Doubleday, Doran & Company, Inc., 1932.

Huffman, James A. *A Yankee in Meiji Japan.* Lanham, MD: Rowman and Littlefield Publishers, Inc., 2003.

Ion, Hamish. *American Missionaries, Christian Oyatoi, and Japan 1859-73.* Vancouver, British Columbia: University of British Columbia Press, 2009.

Iryie, Kira. *Japan and the Wider World from the Nineteenth Century to the Present.* London and New York: Longman, 1997.

Jansen, Marius. *The Making of Modern Japan.* Cambridge, MA: The Belknap Press of Harvard University, 2000.

Japan Weely Mail Periodical available at the Yokohama Archives of History.

Jones, H.J. *Live Machines: Hired Foreigners in Meiji Japan.* Vancouver, British Columbia: University of British Columbia Press, 1980.

Keene, Donald. *Emperor of Japan: Meiji and His World, 1852-1912.* New York: Columbia University Press, 2002.

Krass, Peter. *Carnegie.* Hoboken, New Jersey: John Wiley & Sons, 2002.

Laidlaw, Christine Wallace. *Charles Appleton Longfellow: Twenty Months in Japan, 1871-1873.* Cambridge: Friends of the Longfellow House, 1998.

Mackowski, Chris and Scaturro, Frank J. with forward by Williams, Frank J. *Grant at 200.* El Dorado Hills, CA: Savas Beatie, 2023. (Published in cooperation with the Ulysses S. Grant Association)

McHale, Jonathan. *A History of the American Ambassador's Residence in Tokyo.* Tokyo Japan: American Embassy, 1995.

Miyoshi, Masao. *As We Saw Them, the First Japanese Embassy to the United States.* Paul Dry Books: Philadelphia, 2005.

Murphy, Kevin. *The American Merchant Experience in Nineteenth Century Japan.* London and New York: Routledge, Curzon, Taylor and Francis Group, 2003.

Nakajima, Koji. "Diplomacy and Missionaries in Modern Japan." Yoshikawa Kobunkan. (2012) (Japanese)

Nasaw, David. *Andrew Carnegie.* New York: The Penguin Press, 2006.

Neuman, William L. *America Encounters Japan from Perry to MacArthur.* Baltimore: Johns Hopkins University Press, 1963.

Nimura, Janice. D*aughters of the Samurai: A Journey to East and West and Back.* W&W Norton and Company: New York. 2015.

Nish, Ian. *The Iwakura Mission to America and Europe: A New Assessment.* Abington, UK: Routledge, 2008.

Nootbaar, Julie Joy. "Charles Longfellow's Twenty Months in Japan". *Oita College of Art and Cultural Journal* 52 (2015): 107-121.

Noteheller, F.G. *American Samurai Captain: L.L. Janes and Japan.* Princeton, NJ: Princeton University Press, 1985.

Notefeller, F.G. *Japan Through American Eyes: The Journal of Francis Hall 1859-1866.* Boulder, CO: Westview Press, 2001. (original journal in possession of Cleveland Public Library)

Perry, John Curtis. *Facing West: Americans and the Opening of the Pacific.* Westport, CT., London: Praeger, 1994.

Ravina, Mark. *To Stand with the Nations of the World.* New York: Oxford University Press, 2017.

Sagers, John. *Confucian Capitalism: Shibusawa Eiichi, Business Ethics, and Economic Development in Meiji Japan.* London, New York: Palgrave, Macmillan, 2018.

Seidensticker, Edward. *Tokyo: from Edo to Showa 1867-1989.* Tokyo, Rutledge, VT: Tuttle Publishing, 2010.

Sexton, Jay. "William H. Seward and the World." *Journal of the Civil War Era* 4.3 (September 2014): 398-430.

Shavit, David. *The United States in Asia: A Historical Dictionary.* New York: Greenwood Press, 1990.

Shibusawa Eiichi. Craig Teruko, translator. *The Autobiography of Shibusawa Eiichi: from Peasant to Entrepreneur.* Tokyo: Tokyo University Press, 1994.

Taylor, John. *William Henry Seward: Lincoln's Right Hand.* New York: HarperCollins, 1991.

Tokio Times. Periodical available at the Yokohama Archives of History.

Treat, Payson Jackson. T*he Early Diplomatic Relations Between the United States and Japan, 1853-1865.* Baltimore: Johns Hopkins Press, 1917.

Umetani Noboru. "The Role of Foreign Employees in the Meiji Era in Japan." *Institute of Developing Economies Occasional Papers*, Series 9 (1971).

Van Deusen, Glyndon G. *William Henry Seward.* Oxford University Press, New York, 1967.

Weir, David. *American Orient: Imagining the East from the Colonial Era through the Twentieth Century.* Amherst and Boston: University of Massachusetts Press, 2011.

White, Ronald C. *American Ulysses: A Life of Ulysses S. Grant.* New York: Random House, 2017.

Whitney, Clara. William Steele and Tamiko Ichimata, editors. *Clara's Diary: An American Girl in Japan.* Kodansha International Ltd., 1979.

Yanoff, Stephen G. T*urbulent Times: The Remarkable Life of William H. Seward* Author House, Bloomington, Indiana. 2017.

Editor's Note: *The sources listed are representative, not exhaustive. Longfellow House, the Seward House and Museum and the Grant Library and the deep bench of Grant scholars accessible through the Grant Presidential Library, the Ulysses S. Grant Association, Grant Cottage and other Grant facilities around the country are wonderful resources.*

Made in the USA
Middletown, DE
03 July 2025